ORGANIZATIONAL CHANGE

Other titles from The Macmillan Press

Organizational Change

The Managerial Dilemma

Edmund Brooks

M

First published 1980 by
THE MACMILLAN PRESS LTD
London and Basingstoke
Associated companies in Delhi Dublin
Hong Kong Johannesburg Lagos Melbourne
New York Singapore and Tokyo

Printed in Hong Kong

British Library Cataloguing in Publication Data

Brooks, Edmund
  Organizational change.
  1. Organizational change
  I. Title
  658.4'06   HD58.8

  ISBN 0-333-26691-9
  ISBN 0-333-26692-7   Pbk

This book is dedicated

to Gail

who changed certain elements of my life

Contents

Preface

The book begins, in Chapter 1, with a study of the pressures and demands made by the economic and business environment upon organisations and the responses of management to the problems directly affecting organisational systems of operation. The chapter identifies the major stumbling-blocks in organisational (work) relations which frustrate and undermine the collaboration needed by specialist functions in large complex organisations in order to resolve operational problems directly affecting business performance.

Chapter 2 examines and appraises the different schools of management thought which have contributed to an understanding of the problems and issues facing managers concerned with improving the performance, efficiency and operating capability of organisations. The focus of this chapter is upon the co-ordination and control of operations – the need for developing and sustaining co-operation, the nature and character of organisational decision-making processes, the application and manipulation of bureaucratic rules by different interest groups, and the need for organisations to adapt their structure and functioning to meet the needs of a changing environment.

Chapter 3 provides a conceptual framework for understanding the structure and functioning of organisations. It highlights the principal policies and tasks of organisations such as product development, quality control, cost control, resource management, etc. The various possible technological methods and modes of operation are viewed in terms of their contribution to management's efforts to schedule and organise the work flow and to control administrative procedures and working practices. In that an organisation's structure attempts to define and prescribe work relations, an assessment is made of how the autonomy and power of specialist functions are affected by organisational hierarchies of authority, work specialisation, the institutionalisation of rules and regulations and by different degrees of centralisation and decentralisation of the decision-making process.

Attention is then focused upon the needs and interests of organisational members and upon the conflict with the goals of the organisation, which is highlighted by resistance to management-directed change. Recognition is given to the influence of work groups and the controls they exert upon various work systems.

Chapter 4 examines and puts to the test the beliefs and assumptions underlying management's efforts to reorganise and rationalise work systems and the tasks of organisational members. The findings of research on job enrichment, work motivation and autonomous work groups are looked at in terms of how far they may have contributed to improved job performance. The essential consideration is in establishing what the necessary and sufficient conditions for changing work patterns are, and the demands this imposes upon the manager and his style of management.

Chapter 5 identifies serious malfunctions in the structure of organisational operations and critically examines and questions whether management has sufficient control over individual and group actions to reorganise and rationalise work systems more productively. One of the principal aims of the chapter is to set out some of the necessary preconditions for planning and implementing changes in the structure and function of organisational systems of operation. Serious thought is given to the problems and constraints facing management in implementing organisational change.

Chapter 6 questions and challenges the value of traditional management training in organisations and introduces new viable alternative strategies of human-resource management as a necessary condition for achieving organisational change and development. The principal finding is that organisations cannot effectively release its managerial potential in solving business problems which frustrate overall performance objectives without changing the organisation's climate of working.

Chapter 7 seeks to pinpoint the causes and consequences of the factors which undermine managerial control over business operations. A critical assessment is made of how managers may best come to terms with the nature of power, authority and control of organisational members over changes directed at improving methods and modes of operation. The next step involves identifying appropriate management change interventions which remove some of the principal barriers to change.

Pressures for organisational change are invariably resisted in periods of economic uncertainty when the perceived outcomes of the changes to be made threaten to dislocate or disrupt systems of operation.

The final chapter seeks to establish how management can maintain effective control and influence over changes made necessary in a company's mode of operation. A strategy is devised for improving managerial accountability for operational control and for securing greater support and commitment to organisational-change initiatives.

References and Further Reading lists are to be found after the appropriate chapters.

E.B.

Acknowledgements

Writing a book is a solitary experience. It could not have been achieved, however, without the advice, support and wisdom of others. I should like to acknowledge some of the people I worked with professionally in organisations. Cliff Woods, Peter Gill and Brian Wallace were former colleagues of mine whose experience and knowledge of organisational change and development was invaluable. I owe a special debt to Jack Lang for providing me with the opportunity to undertake several projects and field work investigations, and to Phil Gibbons whose forward thinking and innovative efforts to improve business operations gave me the impetus for developing my ideas about organisational change.

The editors of *Industrial and Commercial Training* and *European and Industrial Training* have kindly permitted me to include material from my articles published in their journals.

Several of my friends have listened patiently to and read several passages of the book. I would like to thank Cleve and Vicky Baker, Derek Moul and Maurice Rosewell for their interest and encouragement. Richard Loundes and Dr Paisey were kind enough to review drafts of certain chapters.

A final but special mention must be made of Gail Hart-Porter for the time and effort she put in, not only reading and editing the chapters, but in helping me to clarify my ideas and forcing me to think through some of the problems and issues I faced in writing this book.

Introduction

Modern industrial society has witnessed the breath-taking pace of technological change from the time of the development of the combustion engine. Yet the application of advanced technology entails considerable risk in capital investment which in the cases of Rolls-Royce and *Concorde* has proved to be financially disastrous. Certain enterprises are surviving only because of government aid. Industries such as newsprint, steel-making and textiles have been unable to modernise systems of operation and consequently have found themselves in serious decline.

The resistance of unions to technological change and the use of industrial sanctions in the car industry, for example, has dramatically affected the competitiveness of British car firms. With the growth of union power, and the increasing dependence of large organisations on sophisticated technical controls such as computers, there is always the threat of industrial action being taken which seriously undermines the predictability of normal business operations. Economic stability and industrial order are essential for managers to regulate and control systems of work.

Organisations are increasingly experiencing a lack of control over their work environment in the face of economic and social change. There is a very real crisis of confidence among management today, in its ability to cope and adapt to the pace of change in modern industrial society. There is, for example, an inability in almost all organisations to accept and know how best to come to terms with the idea of worker directors. There is grave concern and a fear of the fundamental clash of interests and the consequences for the viability of commercial companies. The challenge to managerial control is the key factor in explaining such a crisis of confidence. The failure of managerial performance controls which are served by computerised information-retrieval systems and various management techniques of objective-setting and work measurement to identify the efficiency of business operations undermines the already shaky foundations, or rather notions, of managerial authority.

Management is uncertain whether to combat or yield to pressures for change. There is increasing uncertainty as to how best to adapt the organisation's structure and functioning to meet the needs of a changing environment, without undermining its own power and authority. This is the dilemma that managers find themselves in. Managers will be unable to evolve radically new methods and modes of tackling the problems which beset them until the conflicts of interest and the struggle for power and authority are resolved within organisations. This book will address itself to these problems and issues.

New managerial strategies of work regulation and control are needed. There is, however, a basic lack of managerial skill in diagnosing and implementing the necessary changes in an organisation's structure and mode of operation. At the same time, organisational structures are insufficiently adaptive to change, due to inflexible procedures and boundaries between specialist functions, which consequently frustrate the close collaboration and joint problem-solving which is needed in order to overcome outmoded methods of business operation. This book questions and challenges the constraints of traditionally outmoded organisational procedures and managerial practices.

The challenge laid down before management is that of creating a new, more productive and innovative climate of working. There is a strong body of opinion based on the literature published to date which believes that more profitable companies happen to be de-centralised, have a participative system of management and adopt sophisticated control and information systems. The problem is, however, in explaining why such firms are more effective than other comparable organisations. The answer lies in being able to understand and explain how they are operationally more successful. This book is written to that end.

1
The Problems of Managing Organisational Change

The Rising Costs of Operation

A business organisation resides in a pressing economic environment. Rising world prices in raw materials and production fuels have of necessity raised production and manufacturing costs. The competition for international products and material resources of a domestic and industrial nature has inevitably led to rises in import prices. Faced with increasing production costs, tighter cost controls have been felt necessary in order to ensure the survival, let alone the profitability, of a company. Since 1945 local industrial plant bargaining has grown and pressures have been exerted by unions and shop stewards in attempts to raise wage earnings. Shortages in skilled and semi-skilled labour have forced management to raise wage levels and overtime payments. Inter-firm comparisons by unions have served to put pressure on management to equalise wage differentials. With rising import and domestic prices, wage levels have been pushed up to maintain people's living standards at levels comparable with the general cost of living. With rising prices and increasing costs, industry has of necessity been forced to raise its efficiency and productivity in order to bear ever-increasing labour and material costs. In an attempt to improve organisational performance and effectiveness, management has been called upon to deal with these problems and to overcome the internal obstacles to adaptation and change.

The need for cost-effectiveness

One means organisations have of exerting cost control has been to de-man and rationalise its service support systems to mainstream operations. Nowadays managers and departments are much more stringently cost-accountable. A measure of a manager's performance is his ability to reduce costs and thereby improve productive levels of efficiency. However, market product demand has grown in both sophistication and diversification, and this has led to a need for more technological advances – which have proved costly in terms of product development. Industry has been forced to realise that if it is to capture larger markets and to compete effectively in foreign and domestic markets, it has to grow in size as well as financing the vast output of technological refinements and improvements in the research, design and development of products. Economies of large-scale production have thus helped the multinational companies who have been able to finance and invest in technological advancement in spite of enormously high costs of product development. With the growth in the size of companies in terms of complexity and diversification, so specialist functions have developed in response to technological advancement and the need for enlarged productive capacity of companies, typified by functions such as Engineering, Research and Development, Production Planning and Control. Marketing has at the same time grown in importance in order to ensure wider market penetration and sales revenue. Financial control has become more and more essential because of a company's need to stabilise and keep down costs. Financial accounting has consequently assumed a more critical and significant role in organisational decisions on matters related to investment and expenditure.

The impact of expenditure restraints

Inevitably, with the growth of specialist functions, a diversity of interests and concerns grow up. For instance, production departments in a manufacturing enterprise are predominantly concerned with maximising output, while engineering maintenance aims primarily for a cost-effective service to mainstream operations. Although these interests do not seem to be directly in conflict, increasing edicts by top management to cut operating and maintenance costs have brought tension and discord between the two camps. If forced to minimise its cost, engineering maintenance may attempt to maintain the existing level of maintenance to production departments with a reduced staff level. However, this can create problems for production managers who need engineering services and support systems to be readily available whenever output is jeopardised by mechanical or technological failures. Because of limitations on resources, production losses may arise and thus undermine the production levels required from mainstream operations. Production losses may also mean that marketing may lose sales because the productive capability of the manufacturing system is not able to cope and adapt effectively to breakdowns in its system of operations.

Competition for scarce resources

An enforced rationing of services from support systems inevitably produces competition and conflicting claims over resources and priorities among production managers. Whenever sectional interests are threatened, managers and departments seek to ensure that they are in a position to block moves which threaten their control and influence over technical, financial, material and human resources. Because production departments are pressed to reduce their operating costs by cutting overtime working and manning levels, they may well be pressured by sales departments to raise production levels in order to meet the delivery dates agreed with customers. Production departments are reluctant to meet unrealistic or tight deadlines. At the same time, efforts to meet these deadlines by restoring overtime working brings the power and influence of shop stewards and unions to the forefront. Realising management's predicament of wanting to cut costs but maintain production levels and meet its commitments with clients, unions and their representatives can often force management's hand. For example, management's request for weekend overtime working may be refused unless all staff operatives are given the opportunity to do it. Attempts to recruit short-term contract labour to fill the breach tends to be staunchly resisted by unions. Demarcation is another issue which prevents management from using its labour force more efficiently.

Divisions between operational and service functions

In a period of restraint on capital expenditure efforts to improve the productive efficiency of operations are severely curtailed. At such time, service support systems are restrained by production managers from instigating and carrying out improvements in plant design and production methods because of the need to keep operating costs down as much as possible. Line-managers demand proof of cost-effectiveness before installing any modifications in the operational system. Pressures for continuous production deters the introduction of technological change. This is a major factor affecting the contribution which service support functions are able to make, particularly in regard to any significant modernisation of plant operation which allows for performance improvement in production levels. Production departments operate on a short-time perspective. They are required to meet weekly production targets and ensure schedules are geared to meet them. Support systems, on the other hand, are involved in the design and development of new modes of operation which involve much longer time perspectives because their work involves major overhauls and changes in the system of operation. These factors are continuous sources of friction and strife between operating departments and service support functions which are built into the system of operation.

The management of organisational boundaries

Sited at critical control points around a manufacturing company are positions held by people who operate at the interface between the activities of the organisation and outside groups. The purchasing officer operates at the interface between the manufacturing unit and the supplier organisations. The sales representative operates at the interface between the marketing department and the outside customer. The industrial relations negotiator operates at a less well-defined interface between the production unit and different unions. Rationally, these 'boundary' managers operating between the organisations and outside agencies have clearly defined objectives which are associated with the ultimate success of the company's operations. Socially and emotionally however, their subconscious objectives may be sympathetic to the needs of the people on the other side of the interface. What should be emphasised here is that most of the strife and conflict which appears in organisations as being 'destructive' springs from emotionally constructive motives.

Dependence of the 'internal executive'

The purchasing officer, in his role as 'boundary' manager, holds a very powerful position. Upon the success of his departmental efforts depends the success of other significant people (internal executives) in the organisation. Material cost changes associated with his activities affect cost control and budgeting of operating departments. Variations in the supply of material resources significantly affect the organisation. Material cost changes associated with his activities affect cost control and budgeting of operating departments. Variations in the supply of material resources significantly affect the ability of the production planning and control department to run a smooth operation. Failures in supplies cause frustration and labour problems as well as cost variances in the manufacturing unit; and in the minds of those executives responsible for these operations the fault (not just the responsibility) lies with the purchasing man. Thus because of the executives' dependence upon the activities (directly or indirectly) of the purchasing agent, strife is built into the system, since the slightest variation of reliability in systems of operation which affects the job of the dependent person gives rise to tension and dispute of one kind or another.

Organisational status and barriers

In addition, the purchasing agent is often seen as a barrier to the outside world by people who feel they need to communicate with outside bodies. The production manager feels he is barred from telephoning the vendor directly on an issue which he wishes to have some say on. The quality control and technical manager sometimes feels frustrated at not being able to build up a personal relationship with a supplier's representative because of the position of the purchasing agent. Then, the purchasing agent is often seen by other executives as having a privileged position. His presence at board level meetings with supplier executives seems to give him status higher than that which other executives would normally give him.

These, then, represent a few of the simple bases upon which friction can and does arise between executives of a manufacturing unit on the one side and the purchasing agent as an 'external boundary manager' on the other. It should be emphasised that these barriers may well be unreal and exist only in the minds of the internal executives through their interpretations of the motives of the purchasing officer.

Reactions of the 'boundary manager'

Inevitably, therefore, the purchasing agent may subconsciously develop a feeling of 'not belonging' to the manufacturing group and a feeling that he is being pushed to the fringes of the organisation because of the nature of his function. In these circumstances the purchasing agent seeks to satisfy his social needs with people outside the organisation – most of whom (e.g. commercial representatives) are only too delighted to assist in this respect. It is certainly basic to the success of a representative to establish good personal relations with the purchasing officer, and therefore the more the relationship is developed, the more adverse reaction it causes from the 'internal' executives, and the more the purchasing agent seeks external satisfaction. Thus, when operational failings occur, such as bad deliveries which upset production, there is often a very poor social basis for effective communication and co-operation, and strife results.

Rational and emotional objectives

In such circumstances of strife, it appears that the common objectives of the parties involved are frequently lost sight of. When the production manager, for example, is unable to realise his objectives, because of unrealiability of material resources from outside suppliers, he may try to lay the blame with the purchasing officer. On the other hand, the purchasing agent may defend the supplier because of his social relationships. He will often go to great lengths to prevent a change of supplier to satisfy the internal manager, even when the rational facts of quality, delivery and cost suggest alternative supply arrangements.

Answers

There is no book of rules to help the manager solve problems of social conflict in every organisational situation. The manager must be constantly and continuously raising his awareness of the constraints within which he has to operate or constraints in the systems of operation which he can possibly affect. The social constraints that exist in any organisation are powerful and real and cannot be applied directly to the material-variance account or the profit-and-loss account, but that is where the effect shows up. This glance into some underlying causes of managerial behaviour in, for example, the purchasing area, highlights the problems facing practising managers concerned with improved performance through effective functional interrelations. These kinds of inter-functional concerns and differences are basically inherent in the complex and technologically interdependent nature of organisations. What is of concern to an organisation is its ability to cope with and adapt to these problems through joint problem-solving and greater co-operation and inter-dependence. However, severe obstacles to such aims are the autonomy of functions, their concern with organisational control and influence, status rivalry, and the furthering of career developments within functional boundaries.

The conflict of interest between functions

Faced with rising operating costs, industry has attempted to reduce such costs by running down its labour force and maximising productive capacity (labour, plant and machinery). Invariably support systems such as technology and engineering are hit hardest as far as having to fulfil their commitments with limited resources and in being pressured to cut down on their establishment. Sharply rising fuel prices since October 1973 have assumed greater importance than wage increases and labour costs because fuel consumption is the biggest single cause of escalating costs of production in process industries such as oils and chemicals. Thus a major cost saving can be realised from refining and conserving fuel resources more effectively. However, such improvements in fuel utilisation are only possible if technological and engineering services are extended in terms of support capability and capacity, and if these services are efficiently deployed.

However, support systems do not always find it easy to gain access to plant operations in order to promote cost-saving improvements. A frustration from the point of view of support systems is their inability to gain authorisation to tackle key problems such as plant overhaul. In the short run plant managers are very reluctant to forsake productive capacity for long-run improvements in plant capability in terms of output. This is basically because the production manager is held accountable for maximising output and minimising costs *week by week*. While support systems such as engineering maintenance are concerned to reduce operating costs, any extensive schemes of improvement in plant capability may disrupt output levels, operating costs and work schedules of mainstream operations. Even when plant operations personnel recognise the need for major plant design changes in order to raise levels of plant capacity, tighter cost controls and frequency of cost review of operating resources (labour, plant and machinery) constrain initiative and plans for rationalisation and technological modernisation of operating plant.

The avoidance of operational problems

In large organisations there are several administrative levels in the organisational hierarchy. Inevitably orders and information pass up and down through several levels. Managers consequently become many steps removed from influencing the key decision-makers who are exerting these tight cost controls and policies of rationalisation of the productive process and service support systems. Tighter cost controls and frequency of cost-control information wanted from above allow little autonomy and discretion over resource utilisation (human, material and financial). Inevitably increasing account-ability and responsibility for tighter cost control can lead to distortions in upward communications and the withholding of unfavourable cost information whenever directives and feedback have to pass up and down through several levels of the organisational hierarchy.

Managers accountable for either production operating costs or support system costs are clearly anxious to keep a tight reign over the management of resources (human, material and financial). However, supervisors often suppress operational malfunctions and problems which may put them in a bad light and jeopardise their career. Therefore, managers tend very often to make decisions and manage their operations without all available information. Problems do not get looked at. One of the major drawbacks is that as these problems grow, grievances and discontent build up. One day a manager may find himself assailed by irate and furious workers. The manager, in his surprise and discomfiture, is faced with handling a heavily charged meeting and having to cope with and respond to long-standing grievances of which he has no previous knowledge. However, these communication breakdowns very rarely come to the notice of higher levels of management. It is not surprising, therefore, to find that the problem persists. Loyalty to the department and fear of disclosure creates a situation of problem avoidance in that the basic problem issues are left undisclosed and unresolved.

The following piece of dialogue typifies some of the undisclosed issues and problems which fail to be tackled within departments, let alone looked at in joint co-ordination meetings between different functions:

Is the priority the optimum stock level?
No!
It's surely production cost minimisation.
Why?
I think it should be optimum stock level.
What's the net profit figure up to June?
We haven't met our targets.
Do we take investment growth as gospel?
How will costs be affected by changes in production schedules?

A major organisational problem is one of inter-functional divisions and internal politics. The career development and prospects of company personnel rests in maintaining and furthering departmental/functional claims and interests, at the expense of others if need be.

Maintaining political balances and power

In that functions are reasonably independent of one another there is a need to preserve political balances and powers which are not destructive to any one or more function. How often have higher management meetings been characterised by open confrontation between departments on operating problems and joint problem-solving? They tend to be defensive information exchanges which serve to highlight the constraints and handicaps suffered by each function in not possessing adequate service support and operating personnel. There is a marked avoidance of problem issues which upset the delicate political balance. The autonomy of departments is in large part a deterrent to any senior functional manager to attempt a trouble-shooting role. Instead, there is an over-involvement with those problems which can be resolved, and key issues are blocked or subverted and remain undisclosed and denied open debate and resolution.

At lower management levels one may find a greater willingness and initiative to deal with these problems – i.e. open up issues – largely because the interface problems produce real operational difficulties at the shop-floor level. Some of these issues involve integrating line and staff work, tackling demarcation issues and other problematic areas of dispute where the responsibility, the authority and the accountability for performance standards are not clearly delineated to the satisfaction of various parties. However, lower management can exert little influence to overcome these problems. Unable to cope and adapt to changes enforced by higher management, it is not surprising to see lower levels of management fending off and resisting performance improvements in the light of such constraints. For fear of sanctions and jeopardising their careers, people do not readily confront issues, do not take up problems, and do not risk being open about their concerns and thus trusting in their relations with others. Individuals search assiduously for positions of greater power and influence where they can exert the power and authority to take action and make decisions. Inevitably we have people jockeying for position, seeking recognition and favour from whatever higher source of management they can cultivate. In competing for recognition and advancement people tend to conform rigidly to the norms of the system in which they operate. They question less, confront less, avoid emotive issues, risk little and sidestep or brush aside difficulties of a functional or hierarchical nature. Thus a tentative conclusion can be drawn: proposals for change and innovation within a sub-system or between sub-systems will encounter opposition and resistance from those who wish to preserve the status-quo.

The Problems of Changing Organisational Relations

From an exploration and assessment of how organisational relations are conducted, it can now be understood why ineffectual change initiatives by management, low levels of commitment to change and high levels of resistance to anticipated changes in organisational systems of operation arise. The following observations illustrate some of the behavioural responses in organisational relations that make the management of change problematic. For example, a manager may ask probing and direct questions on performance deficiencies but give long, elusive and tentative answers to questions directed at him. The questioning of his staff could reflect anxious concern that his performance demands were being subverted, resisted or not strictly adhered to. His own answers to questions may be a reflection of his uncertainty and doubt about his staff's efforts, or they may be due to an absence of direction and control from higher management.

A member of one department might intervene relatively frequently in other departments' trouble-spots but might be rather withdrawn and inactive in his own department when difficulties arise and meetings are called to examine problem areas. It could be that the individual is fearful of stirring a hornet's nest in his own department. There is probably a greater reluctance for self-criticism in that department, whereas there is more co-operation and support for change initiatives in the other department. While change proposals may be seen as vital for the success of the department, they may well be seen as threatening to the status quo in his own department. Some people emerge strongly and vociferously in defence and support of their own views and proposals, reflected by attempts to outdo others, but are invariably reticent on matters of joint problem resolution. Sometimes they are withholding information or evidence which could be damaging to them in situations where the examination of alternative change plans are being considered. It may be that the functional heads are quite naturally seeking to protect and advance their departmental claims for improved resources by outlining and underlining the constraints under which they have to operate. This calls into question the support capability and efficiency of other functions. The absence of joint interventions and problem discussion may reflect the separate and distinct problems and concerns of each function – or, rather, the inability of functions to work together towards the needs of the organisation (e.g. sales, profitability, market growth, cost-effectiveness, product quality, company development) and to put aside their own individual objectives and interests. The absence of interdependence among the functions can be a consequence of the separation by function, products, locality or hierarchy. The absence of joint problem-solving may serve to cover up departmental rivalries and vested interests by suppressing conflict and preventing problem resolution. Problem-solving would raise fundamental issues and differences which would need attending to.

Managers who are responsible for directing and controlling operations are not always able to confront and tackle service support personnel on performance variations and setbacks regularly. This may be due to the manager's lack of authority on a particular issue or because of his lack of forcefulness and drive. The authority and responsibility of the manager in his position or office may be undermined by service support departments persuing conflicting performance objectives. Pressures are often exerted from above for a manager to clamp down on his staff and to investigate declining performance standards more vigorously. Yet the manager may be anxious not to hear criticism of his efforts in tackling operational problems which may throw unfavourable light on his own ability and competence to cope.

A manager who tacitly agrees with over-all policy may interpret this policy in a sufficiently ambiguous way so that it becomes evident that he does not support it in reality. This may be due to personal reservations about the validity of the policy, and the tacit agreement may be an instinctive response in defence of his position and standing with his superior. It could be that the manager concerned feels he has to defend himself or the function which he represents from attack.

On the other hand, he might be trying to save face. He may feel he has to be seen to be consistent in his support of over-all policy for reasons of credibility and professional/organisational standing as in labour–management negotiations. What are apparently constructive managerial actions can be construed as ulterior acts, serving to raise the suspicion and mistrust of a work-force towards its supervisor. It could be that the manager's motives are viewed as suspect. He may be seen as manipulating people for his own ends, or acting as the agent of higher management, unwillingly imposing the latter's demands on contentious matters which involve changing people's roles, responsibilities and powers of authority.

A System of Management in Organisations

Let us look more closely at some of the critical problems facing a large multinational corporation endeavouring to improve its performance capability and efficiency. The relationship between main-stream operations and service support functions is central in the sense that improvements in the productive capability of the system are reliant on their support and collaboration because of their close interdependence. The intention is to illustrate how the system of management adopted at the interface between production and engineering maintenance in a large oil and chemical products company constrained initiatives directed towards improving systems of operation. In a manufacturing organisation the aim is to balance planned production requirements in operations departments with efficient engineering maintenance practice and resource deployment in support of these operating objectives. In that plant performance is dependent upon effective service support and efficient resource management, both operations and maintenance are concerned to ensure a reliability and quality of service provision and resource deployment in order for planned production requirements to be met at economic cost. In anticipating and reviewing future product and service support demands both parties are attempting to shape and influence engineering maintenance policy, procedures and working practices. The purpose of this is to establish the quality and level of resource provision to different plants because it affects production requirements and engineering efficiency (such as cost-effectiveness). Demands are imposed on both functions to operate within certain control parameters (e.g. production yields and engineering costs) in order to meet production programmes and operating budgets. Pressures are therefore put on both parties to achieve high levels of performance control and operational management. A key issue is whether there is common understanding, agreement and interpretation of the desirable (optimum) level of service provision from engineering maintenance which is consistent with over-all organisational objectives and performance standards.

The Management of Organisational Relations

An examination of working relations between the two primary functions (operations and service support functions) serves to illustrate some of the dysfunctional elements of organisational relations and the problems associated with the management of boundaries and interfaces between autonomous but interdependent functions each with their own goals, values, priorities, etc. In highlighting some of the problems and difficulties at such interfaces it is intended to assess the consequences of dysfunctional relations and working practices and their impact on organisation efficiency and performance. From such an examination it will be possible to explore and evaluate some of the performance-improvement possibilities within organisations.

With all working relations certain demands are made and expectations are built up about the level and quality of service provision necessary to achieve operating reliability and efficiency. Operations impose pressure on engineering maintenance to meet production programmes and to avoid production losses. For their part, engineering maintenance departments question, challenge and resist unrealistic demands and the political ploys they consider operations departments sometimes use to demand and press for greater availability of labour and equipment. It is not altogether unexpected to find that operational demands for additional resources will be challenged and resisted by service support functions. A rather more fundamental issue is that the interpretation and translation of the role and function of a service department is disputed by operational departments. Major differences and disagreements which exist on operational practices, procedures and on performance efficiency or capability of service support erode and undermine working relations and operational performance.

Inter-departmental conflict

Now, inter-departmental divisions, and the reasons for them, are investigated because of the ways in which these can detract from the over-all performance of the organisation. The following situation illustrates how working relationships break down and reduce the efficiency of service support functions and thereby directly impact on the performance capability of mainstream operation in an oil and chemical products company.

Factors undermining service support

Service support agencies who are required to work with limited resources at their disposal are never able to respond to all the pressures and demands made on them. Where the reliability of equipment is suspect, then the machinery for planning and processing work orders will be undermined by operational breakdowns which disrupt work schedules, job lists, priorities and resource provision. When a backlog of work builds up, service support functions are unable to respond to all work requests as efficiently as they might like to because of limitations on their resources. Because of work being delayed, or left unattended to, increasing pressure is put by operating departments on service units. As a consequence of the frustrated demand for services needed to deal with outstanding operational problems, higher and higher priorities are attached to work orders by operating departments, and this does not readily assist service support efforts to distinguish between different priorities and the real urgency associated with resource demands. Because of the pressures exerted by operations to bring equipment back into service in order to avert production losses, engineering maintenance departments often have to work in haste, sometimes incorrectly diagnosing the underlying problem. Not unnaturally, premature failures arise, leading to increasing breakdowns of equipment and plant – which rapidly undermines the performance capability of operations and the over-all standards of engineering maintenance. There is considerable pressure on both sides to avoid blame or criticism in such circumstances, which can produce conflicting claims and counter-claims as to the nature and cause of operational problems and production losses.

Pressures and constraints imposed by higher authority to minimise costs and to cut back on manning and resource provision restrain concerted efforts to tackle and resolve production problems. Preventive action cannot be undertaken adequately because of the number of emergencies and major breakdowns. The problem is compounded by the fact that it is difficult for operations personnel to anticipate where and how failures will occur, or for service functions to respond quickly enough because of the technical sophistication and complexity of the plant and its production processes. There are additional problems of redirecting and mounting an intensive maintenance operation at short notice. Because of these constraints management is required to change its plans, schedules and deployment of labour. As a consequence there are many large-scale problems of resource co-ordination and control.

Figure 1.1 illustrates how these factors may undermine productive efficiency in organisations in terms of how resource-support problems are tackled. Both service support functions and operations tend to close ranks and consume energy in defending their own position over problems which could not be anticipated, and are therefore unplanned. When performance difficulties are highlighted in weekly programme meetings it is difficult for both sides to reach agreement on what is the best course of action to take. By engaging in mutual blame, criticism and scapegoating of the other side, conflict and dispute reign. Problems therefore become deflected on to the other party, or the basic problems of resource utilisation and efficiency are skirted around in discussions. What is required is that both parties look more closely at the causes of operational failures in the system, which are critical in terms of production losses, and at what failures can be anticipated and action planned so that resource-utilisation problems can be resolved more effectively.

Differing performance criteria

A factor which causes significant dispute is the different performance criteria adopted by the principal parties in evaluating the resource contribution of support functions to operational performance. The gearing of engineering maintenance performance standards to the time taken to perform a job of repair, may adversely affect the reliability of plant and operating equipment when, in order to maintain and uphold performance efficiency levels the particular piece of equipment sent in for repair is hurriedly overhauled, and is consequently insufficiently attended to, particularly if it has been held up in the work-shop and operations are pressing for its release so that it can go back into service.

Equipment which has been returned in such circumstances can prematurely break down and lead to unavoidable production losses when insufficient time is available to rectify the fault. Service support functions have been challenged by operations over such matters because of what has been considered to be unavoidable production losses. This has led to operations pressing for maximum throughput over and above planned production requirements as a means of cushioning themselves from such production losses. This strategy puts pressure on service support capability and can lead to an inefficient use of resources (as well as increasing costs). This can add

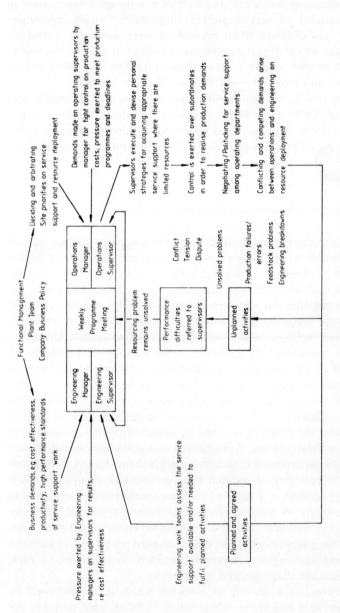

FIGURE 1.1 *The operation of managerial control systems*

an unnecessary burden on the level of maintenance expenditure in organisations. A service support department which experiences blame and criticism when pressed to meet seemingly unrealistic demands which stretch its resources to the limit will be reluctant to discuss its own scheme of operations or have its own shortcomings exposed and mode of operation placed under scrutiny.

If the function of engineering maintenance is thus essentially 'fire-fighting', i.e. it reacts and responds to operational failures, then it cannot act in a planned and controlled fashion in organising and deploying its human and material resources towards *preventing* any need for maintenance.

Barriers to collaboration and problem-solving

Efforts to engage in constructive problem-solving with operations departments will be an anxiety-provoking experience when mistakes and errors of judgement are highlighted. Critical problems and issues are not readily forthcoming because of the spotlight which can be put on the organisation and performance capability of service support functions, involving the co-ordination and control of autonomous specialist functions which are managed independently. Unable to rectify operational difficulties at grass-roots level, problems are pushed up the hierarchy, and the decision-making process becomes more and more centralised and unilaterally imposed. The autonomy leads to fragmented working among service support functions which is very difficult to overcome because of the political balance between them and the different interests of authority figures, concerned to preserve the status quo. A reaction to such a deadlock situation is for different departments to demand sharply defined areas of responsibility to be clearly delineated between one task or operation and another because of a failure to obtain agreement on joint areas of responsibility in matters of co-ordination and control of service support to mainstream operations. However, in a fluid and constantly changing work situation managers need people to take initiative and responsibility for responding quickly to problems by early identification, diagnosis and rectification.

However, in a climate of working which is characterised by defensiveness and blame when action is taken once mistakes are made, the necessary co-operation between operations departments and service support groups is likely to be impaired by the adoption of such tactics. In these situations boundaries harden between departments, and instead of clarifying and defining areas of responsibility among functions it can blur such responsibilities. Each interested party on a particular assignment attempts to avoid problems being attributed to it so as to preserve its own image and personal standing with the superiors to whom they are accountable. Some of these barriers to interfunctional collaboration and problem-solving are illustrated in Figure 1.2.

The introduction of change

The normal procedure by which change initiatives are implemented is for management to set out certain desired performance objectives and outline the operating plans which have been designed to realise them. Control systems are applied so that performance levels can be monitored regularly, thereby enabling management to decide what corrective action needs to be taken if performance levels (i.e. production targets) are not being met. A fundamental function of management is to co-ordinate and integrate the performance objectives of different service support and operating departments. Figure 1.3 illustrates some of the forces and influences which effectively preclude joint collaboration and commitment to closer working and more productive relations.

A diagramatic form is presented of the nature of organisational structures: the network of functional reporting relations in terms of the jobs people fulfil, and the authority which they exercise over others; the position they hold in the hierarchy which enables them to carry out their responsibilities; the role and function of departments; the managerial or supervisory practices and procedures commonly adopted to get jobs done and to overcome operating difficulties; the commonality and differences of operational service support demands and expectations and how these are played out in the work situation by management and supervision at different hierarchical and functional interfaces. This serves to identify some of the maladaptive workings of the organisation and the stumbling-blocks to an improved system of management.

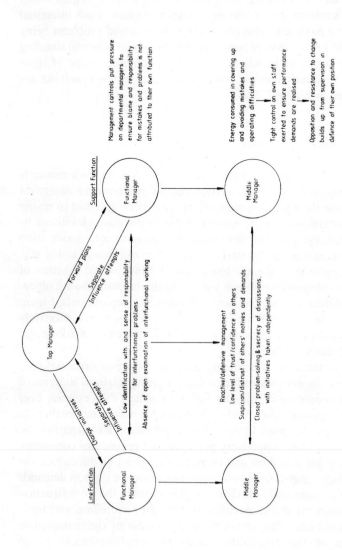

FIGURE 1.2 *Barriers to interfunctional collaboration and problem-solving*

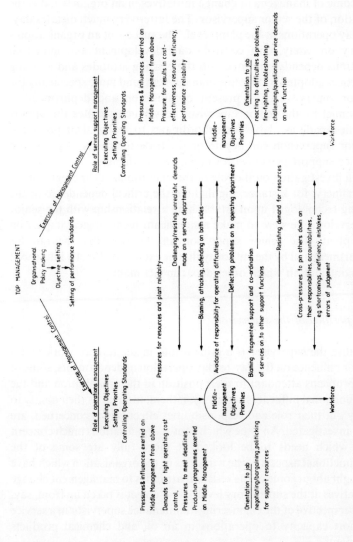

FIGURE 1.3   *The management of interfaces – a conflict model*

Resistance to change

A critical point in the management system regarding the nature and outcome of management change initiatives in an organisation is the position of the senior supervisor. The latter very much dictates day-to-day operations at the plant level. The success of an organisation's policy on safety, cost control, staff development and industrial relations depends very much on the existing attitudes and working practices adopted by first line management, and more specifically the senior supervisor. The present organisation and deployment of personnel by the senior supervisor very much dictates the opportunities made available for subordinates to realise their potential. Senior supervision can negate or frustrate the needs of plant and service support personnel for carrying out changes.

An investigation on the role of the operational technologist on an oil refinery, for instance, highlighted the critical dependence of the young technologist upon establishing a relationship with the senior supervisor if he were to make a significant technological impact on the plant. The senior supervisor, in the way that he ran his department and by the authority that he exercised, directly influenced the contribution which other departments made.

The position of the supervisor

Because the supervisor is a critical link in the flow of work and a major influence on the day-to-day operation of departments, some of the problems attendant to their position in the organisation and the dysfunctional influences acting upon them, in so far as their ability to carry out their role and responsibilities effectively is concerned, are now investigated. An issue which causes organisations much concern and which needs to be looked at more fully are some of the dysfunctional aspects of the workings of the organisation which have brought about some of the resistant attitudes to management change initiatives at the supervisory level. This subject is taken up from, say, the perspective of the engineering maintenance supervisor in a service support capacity to operations in an oil and chemical products company.

The job of the supervisor is essentially one of instigating and carrying out the maintenance of technical operations among production units. This involves a long chain of activities including investigating production failures, plant operability, equipment histories, writing out job instructions, work planning, cost control, work scheduling, requisitioning materials and numerous communications associated with getting the work done on time at certain specified standards of engineering and plant operation. Much of the maintenance work undertaken on the technical system of production departments cannot always be mechanised, standardised, or preplanned. The work flow tends to be variable and uneven. The consequence is that the organisation does not readily have control over the volume or make-up of its work load at any given time. In addition, the demands of the work are frequently of an emergency nature and non-deferable and this demands a constant readiness which places a heavy burden of responsibility upon the engineering function and the supervisor in particular, who has to act on the problems involved while, at the same time, maintaining safe and reliable technical operations among production units.

The emergency nature of the work invites a certain exploitation of uncertainty and ambiguity by production departments, some of whom may not hesitate to make unreasonable demands upon organisational facilities and scarce resources on the grounds of 'emergency'. For example, supervisors in engineering maintenance often consider themselves to be pressured by production departments by what they describe as 'political ploys' adopted by operation managers who claim that production losses could have been avoided had engineering maintenance been able to respond effectively to equipment failures on their units. Not unnaturally, supervisors become resentful at the blame attributed to them when they find or suspect that the initial failure was due to maloperation.

Engineering maintenance functions are anxious to make mainstream operations aware of the need for greater attention to the smooth efficient running of equipment and adherence to formally prescribed operational practices and procedures which help them and operations maintain production units in continuous operation and in reliable order. Fewer breakdowns of machinery and equipment on production units enable engineering to deploy the limited labour and material resources at their disposal more efficiently and thereby provide a more extensive support service at improved standards of engineering maintenance. The pressures and demands made on supervisors in the maintenance function are added to by the need to co-ordinate, progress and generally supervise anciliary engineering work, which tends to divert maintenance supervisors from their primary task.

Management by crisis

The non-deferable nature and character of the work and the relative inability of maintenance departments to anticipate some of the demands for its services often lead engineering managers and supervisors to adopt a management-by-crisis instead of a management-by-objectives approach in running their organisation. In an effort to deal with the numerous number of work demands the supervisor tends to take short cuts and changes his plans in order to meet unforeseen equipment failures and unit breakdowns. In dealing with immediate production problems the supervisor sacrifices some of the time required to plan, organise, co-ordinate and control the limited resources made available to him in fulfilling the range of maintenance tasks befalling him and his department. In an attempt to respond to the pressures and demands of their task(s) the supervisor undertakes as many work orders as he can, and completes the jobs as quickly as possible because of the volume of work which is outstanding. The net effect is that he tries to fulfil too many work orders too quickly without adequate time and resources made available to him so that essential maintenance tasks are not always carried out properly. Equipment failure on production units is then attributed to engineering maintenance units.

Operations management's criticisms of inefficiency, bad planning and lack of organisation embarass and discomfort higher management. Because of premature failure on equipment put back into operation, additional work is generated. This puts more work demands on maintenance supervision and creates even greater incentives to take short cuts in order to complete the outstanding work orders as speedily as possible. The number of production failures tends, however, to increase in such circumstances.

The supervisor thus becomes trapped in this vicious spiral of escalating work demands which cannot be fulfilled adequately because of constraints in the system such as unanticipated work demands, resource limitations and unrealistic deadlines on work completions. At the same time inflexible policies and procedures on resource deployment and wage payments restrain a supervisor's ability to overcome shortfalls in availability of manpower and to fulfil high levels of resource demand.

A problem for the supervisor in ensuring that work demands are met is avoiding industrial action being taken by the labour force on matters related to work-sharing, manning levels, pay and working conditions. Supervisors rely very much on successfully negotiated industrial-relations policies and agreements made with unions which foster support and collaboration from the work-force in terms of flexibility of working and efficient utilisation of labour, in order to achieve desired levels and standards of work performance.

Because of inefficient working practices and procedures, or neglect of them by certain tradesmen, the quality of work is not always satisfactory. Supervisors therefore blame some of the production failures and higher costs of maintenance upon bad workmanship and attribute the low quality of craftsmanship to their inability to discipline effectively those persons responsible, through the power of dismissal or by authorising changes in working arrangements and practices. Higher management is not often willing to dismiss employees or reprimand poorly motivated or inefficient employees for fear of provoking retaliatory action from shop stewards and trade unionists which would threaten to disrupt production. Without management's support in efforts to discipline staff whose perform-ance is not adequate, the supervisor's authority is severely under-mined in the execution of his job, at least in so far as exerting control over the work-force is concerned.

The supervisor considers himself to be powerless to arrest falling levels of productivity without sufficient influence and say in labour relations and real control over the labour force. Because of wide-spread occurrences of bad workmanship, which supervisors are not able to deal with, the quality and reliability of service support falls away and more frequent cases of operational breakdowns occur, increasing the demand for engineering maintenance. Caught up in this vicious circle the supervisor is vulnerable to blame and criticism for the level and quality of work put out. There is quite naturally a reluctance on his part to take responsibility for operational dif-ficulties and to avoid accountability for problems associated with systems of operation – which the supervisor considers to be outside his control.

In addition to these factors, the supervisor has to contend with maintaining old production plants with machinery and equipment which are not very reliable and which require regular attention and close supervision. Because of the particular technological nature and character of different production units, the supervisor develops certain tried and tested ways of coping with the complexity and multitude of resource demands made by each one. Not unnaturally the supervisor will seek to defend his position and vindicate the actions he takes. Exposed to criticism and blame it is not altogether unexpected to find the supervisor rigidly and defiantly trying to preserve his own methods and modes of operation which he considers enables him to cope effectively with the demands and pressures in his job.

To cope with the pressure for ensuring desirable results, and the demands for meeting deadlines and maintaining effective cost control, the supervisor builds a protective wall around himself in order to fend off criticism and defend himself against any failures or shortcomings in engineering support capability and efficiency. An example of this is the resistance operations face when it presses for malfunctioning equipment to be brought back on line earlier than engineering maintenance consider to be practical. Alternatively, unauthorised methods of working are sanctioned by supervision to deal with inflexible procedures and operating constraints. First and foremost, the supervisor concerns himself with defending and maintaining his own interests, working in secrecy or complicitly with his men, while denying responsibility for declining standards of performance and cost-effectiveness, so as to preserve his insecure position and uncertain standing.

A study in the management of change

There now follows an account of a high-level management meeting on an oil refinery which was convened to decide on what action needs to be taken in response to a top-management decree. This account is presented so as to illustrate some of the principle reasons for low levels of commitment to change and why high levels of resistance in an organisation's system of operation occurs. This study also reveals, significantly, the inability of senior management to cope and adapt to the need for change when faced with having to implement operational changes over which they have had little or no control and influence.

Operational technologists in process industries are key figures in the instigation of new methods and modes of operation for purposes of improving the reliability and efficiency of systems of operation. The operational technologist reported to operations management in the organisational structure, though there was a technology department in the system which was also responsible for such activities. Operational technologists were more fundamentally concerned with monitoring, investigating and correcting deviations from existing levels of known plant performance on a day-to-day basis, whereas field technologists were concerned with studying and appraising plant capability so as to arrive at ways and means of extending it.

A major study had been conducted to decide whether the technological expertise currently provided by operating technologists was fully utilised or not. Contrary to much of the advice of the report, the head of the organisation decided to transfer the operational technologist back into the technology department. The head of operations strongly opposed this move but was powerless to do anything about it. He called a meeting of his senior managers to discuss what impact this decision would have on operations. In their opinion the transfer would not improve the level and quality of technological resource support. However, the decision was reluctantly and disapprovingly accepted by the senior managers in operations. It soom became evident to them that the transfer would impose limitations on their present system of operation. There would, for instance, be an additional work-load and loss of technical expertise in monitoring deviations from desired levels of plant performance and in identifying the different operating costs incurred. Operations did not therefore believe that the production levels required of them would be fulfilled with the loss of the operational technologist.

The transfer was bitterly resented by the field technologists who had hoped for a move into operations sometime in the future, because of the responsibilities and powers they would have in the job which would enable them to achieve a more visible and immediate impact on plant operations through instigating changes in the working practices and procedures of operatives and supervisors entrusted with operating equipment and manning the plant. The immediate consequence of the transfer decision was that the role and the function of the operational technologist were no longer controlled by the production units. The primary concern of the operation managers was the loss of their expertise and support in monitoring and acting on deviations from desired levels of plant performance and costs of operation. An overriding issue of importance to the organisation was the need for operations and technology to establish in over-all terms what were the needs of operations to meet the planned production programmes and what was the appropriate technological resource support to meet desired levels of performance efficiency. However, because the issue was seen in terms of winning and losing power and control over a key resource, there was no discussion on this matter.

The managers in operations failed to come to terms with the reasons for the changes. Although a rational for such a change had been prepared, there was no desire to examine, let alone accept, it. While various proposals for change had been looked at prior to the decision, the managers of both operations and technology had no say in the matter, which added to their rejection of the reasons for change which were circulated by top management. An air of resignation and fatalism reigned over the meeting. The frustrations of the managers were evident in their disenchantment with the decision-making process adopted. There was a marked lack of conviction in consultation as a process of managing change as a result. With the transfer of the operational technologist the head of operations still had to resolve the outstanding problems facing operations as a consequence of the decision. In a working environment which fosters the avoidance or denial of problems and rewards people for the ability to work within constraints rather than to challenge them, the managers in operations were reluctant to examine or discuss the need for change and the impact of the decision on how systems of operations would be affected. At the same time, the problems presented to operations by the transfer of the operational technologists created a very immediate need to look less at defining over-all operating requirements in relation to current and future manufacturing needs but rather more at filling in the holes left by the decision to place the operating technologist in field technology.

Because of the opposition and resentment towards the transfer, there was little motivation to analyse the work activities involved in operations in order to establish what the job demands were for the purpose of sustaining the present level and standard of operational performance. This would have helped in seeing what emerged in terms of specific tasks inadequately covered with the prospective reorganisation of technological resource support. What initiatives *were* proposed were to solve immediate practical problems with as little structural change as possible. The important decisions which were faced, those arising over the problems which were envisaged by the change, appeared to unsettle the senior managers when they had to approach their staff about it. They appeared not to be confident in approaching the staff with the unresolved problems. There was, rather, a greater desire to deal with these problems independently, rather than involve their staff in resolving them. The practical implications of the resultant changes needed to be appreciated and agreed to if there was to be any real sense of responsibility and desire to improve present working arrangements for the better. Instead, excuses and obstacles preventing and detracting from the changes envisaged in the roles and responsibilities of managers and supervisors alike were raised. In taking what was an unpallatable action and without seeing or recognising the need for change, the managers in operation did not achieve the 'change-over' from one system of operation to another effectively.

Although the decision regarding the transfer necessitated that greater managerial responsibility for cost control and identifying deviations from specified levels of plant performance (i.e. desired levels of production) fell on the shoulder of supervision, in reality this did not occur. In some instances the former operational technologist did it, which meant that the technological expertise which was potentially available was not fully utilised. In other instances it fell between one or more supervisors, and in the end no one supervisor claimed responsibility or fulfilled his responsibilities for operational costs and production control adequately.

The above case study aptly illustrates and reinforces some of the fundamental reasons we have identified for the failure of organisations and the managements who run them. The underlying problem is to identify the malfunctions in an organisation's structure and functioning. The challenge to management is to investigate and explore what changes are needed in the organisation's system of operation in order to improve business performance. However, a very important consideration and potential stumbling-block to management initiatives is the response of personnel to a changing work environment. Figure 1.4 highlights some of the problematic features and necessary considerations for a manager.

In a changing and uncertain external environment there are social,

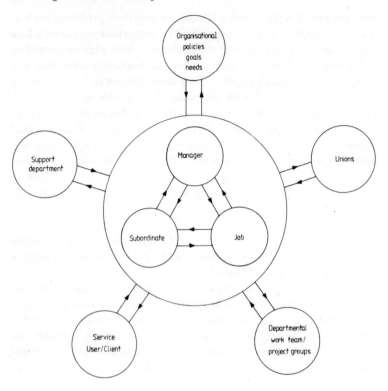

FIGURE 1.4　*Organisational environment*

economic and political pressures and demands placed upon managers who run large organisations. Changes which are not only
enforced upon companies but which cannot be readily predicted lead
to uncertainty and indecision. The resultant lack of clear unambiguous corporate policies and decisions serves to promote even further
uncertainty and indecision among all staff. Set against this background are a host of competing and conflicting demands and
expectations about the role and function of service support functions
vis-à-vis mainstream operations – which often leads to unproductive
working relations. At the same time, because of internal constraints
in terms of the rules and procedures imposed on managers and their
staff in performing their task(s), there are often deep-seated frus-

trations and unfulfilled demands pent up inside people. One of the consequences is variable task commitment and unpredictable performances from managers and staff alike.

By identifying the sources of these problems we can more readily understand the reasons underlying the ineffectualness of management change initiatives and the resistance to organisational change of those people involved. Once we have done that we can begin to examine how stumbling-blocks in the system of operation frustrate change and innovation and how they may be tackled. The analysis presented here points to the fact that there are a variety of potential sources of conflict and dispute which need to be carefully considered before organisations decide on an appropriate course of action.

In summary, the purpose of this examination and analysis of organisational behaviour has been to provide an explanation of the underlying causes and consequences of the managerial problems associated with improving the performance efficiency and operating capability of organisations. A major concern was with identifying the changes which would be necessary in the system of operation and in the capability of management to cope and adapt to them.

The remainder of the book is devoted to dealing with the problems posed in this chapter which are directly involved with organisational change; and this is done by looking at the ways and means managers have of overcoming these problems.

The next chapter will examine and appraise the different schools of thought which have contributed to an understanding of managerial problems. The intention is to lay down clear guidelines to organisations of the different forms and kinds of management systems which will enable them to improve their operating capability and performance efficiency.

2
Theories and Approaches to Managing Organisations

This chapter begins with a critical appraisal and evaluation of the contribution to organisational managerial change of the major schools of thought on the subject. It serves to provide an understanding of how organisations are structured and how they function and what initiatives management can take to improve the operating capability and performance efficiency of an organisation which needs to be receptive and responsive to changes in its environment.

Scientific Management

The scientific-management school of thought attempted to find the most efficient means of executing the organisation's task by paying particular attention to the internal regulation (administration) of the organisation's system of operation. Writers such as Fayol (1949), Mooney (1947) and Urwick (1947) claimed that high performance came from a staffing structure which was hierarchical in nature, emphasising a chain of command, clear lines of authority (through which communication passed downwards), delegation of tasks and responsibilities, and role specialisation. Management was seen as the supreme co-ordinating authority, charged with the responsibility of executing the organisation's task. At the top of the organisation a central body is seen as responsible for deciding on a corporate strategy which expresses the over-all goals of the organisation. An all-embracing policy is then formulated in order to articulate how the strategy ought to be adopted and an economic policy drawn up which would define how the strategy could be realised. Certain key performance objectives are then devised as a measure of the success or otherwise of the policies and plans formulated by top management.

The task of an organisation is broken down so that managers of various departments can exercise their authority over certain key functions. These departments are engaged in specific activities, performed by persons made responsible for certain specialist tasks because of their knowledge and expertise. The manager's task is to define his organisation's goals (plan) to build a structure which will lead to the achievement of these goals (organise), to establish and maintain the functioning of his subordinates from above. His position gives him the authority to co-ordinate and control several specialist activities and work groups and individual contributions to the task of that particular manager. The manager is accountable for the resource utilisation and efficiency of his staff measured in terms of product output, product quality and cost-effectiveness. His organisational performance is judged in terms of such performance measures or standards which are either set or agreed with his immediate boss. By placing people in positions of authority and responsibility over the activities of different work groups and production units within a hierarchical organisation, a chain of command is erected which provides a formal reporting relationship between a superior and his subordinate, and which allows for a regular review of certain work developments for which the subordinate is responsible, enabling him to account for certain duties discharged by him and at the same time to record and measure the progress and performance he has attained.

The purpose of a staffing structure is to define and prescribe those individual and work-group roles which people are expected to enact by behaving and acting in a particular manner – necessited by the demands of their job influenced by the organisation's view of how that person should carry out his duties and obligations. The purpose of a hierarchical structure is to ensure that, by providing a unity of direction to people's efforts, the organisation's goals will consequently be realised. As the formal leader, the manager's task is to delegate down a well-defined chain of command to those subordinates whose own positions and roles are clearly stated in order to illuminate prescribed areas of activity which contribute to the overall task of the organisation.

To manage, says Fayol (1949), is to forecast and plan, to organise and to command, to co-ordinate and control. Forecasting and planning involve an appraisal and assessment of needs and resources. This involves identifying and agreeing priorities, and distributing scarce resources accordingly. Such activities may involve the re-deployment of staff and reorganisation of tasks in response to perceived or expected changes in production plans. Organisation involves managers determining the most efficient use of plant, personnel and finance. This could involve a restructuring of services and modes of operation given a recognition of unsatisfactory levels or standards of performance. Managers will be required to devise methods of formulating a chain of command in order to ensure that its plans are executed.

Given that even comparatively low-level personnel are required to act on their own initiative, the command function is difficult to apply effectively. Management's co-ordination of diverse areas of activity implies recognition of interdependent areas of work common to all. Co-ordination mechanisms, such as steering groups or project groups, can be developed to permit and foster a co-ordinated effort to deal with changing organisational needs and problems. The possi-bility of co-ordination is sometimes problematic. The competing and conflicting aims and priorities of different departments may lead to an apparent lack of co-ordination of effort. Managerial control is equated with establishing quality controls (checks) related to areas of activities concerning the effectiveness of working relationships established between management and the work-force. This, however, is a difficult function to perform.

Theoretically a manager has the authority which allows him to exert the required control over his subordinates' actions which enables him to influence directly the level and quality of individual job performance. In fact the authority conferred upon a manager and vested in his position or office within the organisational hierarchy does not always enable him to exert satisfactorily the authority he might wish because he is constrained by his inability to control the reward system. Ensuring that people behave in a certain desired way is dependent on the ability to control the perceived or actual rewards of those persons concerned. The effectiveness of managers in motivating their staff is dependent upon the degree to which the rewards given are congruent with those that are expected by subordinates. In particular managers and supervisors are not in a position to increase or defer rewards because of their inability to decide on these reward factors which their subordinates view as sources of job satisfaction and motivation (such as salary increases, promotion, fringe benefits, holiday entitlements, etc.).

The influence of supervision is limited on two major counts. First, the supervisor does not possess the means necessary to control the need satisfaction of his staff. Second, his authority is undermined by his inability to stop an individual's pay or dismiss him for negligence or incompetence on the job. Such matters are taken out of his hands and are invariably dealt with by management–union representatives. At the same time, management is reluctant to impose sanctions or dismiss employees based on a supervisor's claims, for fear of provoking industrial action among the work-force instigated by militant shop stewards which might disrupt the work flow and system of operation.

Because of the inability of a supervisor or manager to reward or punish his staff effectively, the authority conferred on him does not provide the desired predictability and control he would wish over his subordinates' actions for purposes of effectively regulating and maintaining desired levels of performance for the part of the operational sub-system he is accountable for. Organisational control is undermined when individuals and work groups exercise personal initiative and discretion which is in contravention of company policies and formally agreed practices. Supervisors sometimes allow certain malpractices to go on which enable people to earn more money than the particular payment system allows as a means of obtaining co-operation and ensuring trouble-free work relations by minimising any possible agitation and unrest among the work-force. Supervisors may waive or ignore certain unauthorised working practices and procedures adopted by their staff when there are constraints upon the efficient performance of their job, such as production deadlines, resource limitations, demarcation and in-flexible administrative arrangements. A network of informal re-lations and work practices which are founded upon mutual interests can be built up between the supervisor and the work-force. For example, safe working practices are not always enforced by super-visors because of the restraints they sometimes impose on production levels – which can affect the success or otherwise of a supervisor realising his performance targets; nor are they necessarily adhered to by the work-force because they may restrict the level of take-home pay if workers are subject to bonus or incentive schemes. In such instances it might be said that the actions of the supervisor were in contravention of organisational policy but relatively effective in maintaining standards of performance at desired levels of output.

How, in such cases, does one assign a qualitative value to leadership? What constitute good leadership? How can effectiveness be measured in a managerial capacity? What is required of a manager to ensure that policies and plans are implemented responsibly? The *human-relations movement* arose in the 1930s in response to these previously unanswered questions.

Human Relations

The human-relations school of thought focuses on the effects that the members of an organisation have on all aspects of its operation. They are the organisation, the human resources which influence and control the utilisation of other productive resources in the organisation's system of operations. The social scientist sees the organisation primarily as a system of interacting and interdependent human beings (interest groups) who shape and determine how the organisation's task is defined and executed in relation to the organisation's goals. Individual members of an organisation are known to bring to the organisation a set of attitudes, beliefs and goals which condition and decide their pattern of behaviour and ultimately influence and shape their response to the work situation on matters of work-sharing, work levels, responsibility to the job, lateness, absenteeism, etc.

The Hawthorne investigations of Elton Mayo (1933) were the first significant piece of evidence to show that work performance depends to a large extent on acceptable social relationships being established between levels of management, supervision and the work-force. Recognition must be given to informal norms, values, attitudes to work, and sanctions of work groups.

The 'principle of supportive relationships' requires management to recognise the importance of 'work groups', and indeed to operate through them:

> Management will make full use of the potential capacities of its human resources only when each person in an organisation is a member of one or more effectively functioning work groups that have a high degree of group loyalty, effective skills of interaction and high-performance goals (Likert, 1961).

Communication does not just flow downwards from superiors to subordinates; it flows up, down and across – and in order to cope with the communication problems raised by increasing openness in individual and group relationships, managers will need to acquire a more highly developed 'interpersonal competence' (Argyris, 1962). One of the major tasks of management, says Mayo (1949), 'must be that of organising team-work, that is to say of developing and sustaining co-operation'; and management succeeds or fails to the extent that it is accepted by members of the organisation as having authority over them and possessing leadership qualities.

At a time of increasing change and uncertainty, such a theory of organisation seems to be more closely attuned to reality; flexibility and adaptability are more likely to be achieved by organisations which recognise that every member has individual and social needs which have to be considered when work patterns change, and which can indeed contribute to the emerging new pattern. Trist and Bamforth (1951) clearly show the adverse effect of imposing mechanised mass-production techniques of retrieving coal on a traditionally organised work-force, by the impact it has on levels of output, absenteeism, lateness and morale.

In Gouldner's (1955) study of a gypsum factory the previous manager had indulged in loose, almost indulgent practices in regard to rule observance and other working practices and procedures. There was no orientation towards cutting costs and improving productivity. The enforcement of more stringent rules and codes of conduct removed the privileges and rewards people had secured under the old system. The studies of Gouldner (1955) and Guest (1962) highlight the dysfunctional nature and character of an autocratic system of management in creating tensions and divisions between managers and the work-force – which are reflected in the high production costs, poor quality of output and labour grievances which ensued. In Guest's study of a motor-car factory experiencing these problems, the unsuccessful manager attempted to increase productivity by close punitive supervision, but his successor decided to use more personal contacts with his subordinates and bring them into the decision-making process, and this improved performance levels significantly. Patchen (1969) found that supervisors who obtained rewards for their subordinates, such as pay rises, promotions and changes in work schedules, or successfully defended them on disciplinary charges, were instrumental in high performance norms among work groups. Bowers and Seashore (1966), in a study of forty life-insurance company agencies, found that the effective supervisor not only provided support but also stressed the achievement of work-group goals and facilitated interaction among group members.

People redefine their work situation to accord with their interests and needs. If they are threatened or undermined by any management change initiatives, then opposition and resistance build up and actual or potential conflict situations arise which make the question of control and authority a key issue in whether the task of an organisation is achieved and how successfully the organisation is managed. For instance, individuals or work groups whose job is critical in ensuring continuous production have the power to halt production or disrupt it if any management action is disputed.

Attitudes to power and authority are central in the explanation of organisational behaviour. Warren (1968) found that people conformed more readily to the threat of punishment (coercive power) if there were direct surveillance, and similarly in the case of reward power (French and Raven, 1960), where people outwardly conformed in order to gain acceptance either in terms of job security or career enhancement. However, outward compliance did not mean that there was any internalisation of organisational norms of behaviour and performance. In fact, Etzioni (1961, 1964) makes the point that opposition can become even more determined and behaviour even more subversive, or alternatively apathetic and indifferent to organisationally desired performance norms.

Since both coercive power and reward power lack effectiveness in creating attitudinal conformity, they must rely on some form of overt control such as rules or surveillance. Rushing (1966) indicates that as organisations grow in size, direct surveillance is more problematic and tends to be replaced by organisational rules. Individuals conformed more readily when they agreed with the position and objectives of the organisation at large, including its leadership, and thus the manager's powers of action were considered legitimate. Yet situations arise where work groups conform to norms in opposition to management's goals.

An important feature of organisational life is the expressed sense of powerlessness and lack of identity among the work-force in relation to centralised decision-making bodies and committee structures. However, lower participants in organisations do achieve a measure of control and influence, not by using the hierarchical structure of the organisation, but rather by circumventing, sabotaging and manipulating it. Mechanic (1962) found that the most effective way for lower participants to achieve power was to hold and control access to persons, information and material or physical resources. To the extent that this was accomplished, lower participants made high-ranking participants dependent upon them. Thus dependence, together with the manipulation of the dependency relationship, was the key to the power of lower participants. Hinings *et al.* (1974) explained this power dependence in terms of the difficulty of substituting people who made themselves indispensable.

An example from a petrochemical company can be cited to illustrate this. A senior engineering maintenance manager reported on the failure of a performance measurement scheme to provide accurate and reliable information for planning work loads and resource requirements because of the opposition of supervisors to using it. Their power was largely due to the dependence of engineers on supervisors. This dependence resulted from the engineer's short tenure and his lack of direct influence upon the men under the charge of the supervisors. While the supervisor notionally took on responsibility for updating and measuring performance levels and planning future work requirements, they did not actually comply. Information was withheld or fudged in order to give an impression of proper monitoring of work performance. Management consequently had difficulty in obtaining the information needed to identify performance-improvement possibilities.

Power differentials are restored by the lower-rank workers withholding information from higher authority and contravening formal organisational policies and objectives. Procedural neglect and deficiencies are covered up. Smokescreens are erected to confuse the real nature of problems and difficulties found in adopting new schemes of operation.

Thus the separation and divorce between higher and lower levels of the organisation is a major factor in explaining the divisions between management and the work-force and the resistance which is put forward to management change initiatives.

Argyris (1973) contends that there is an inherent conflict between the individual and the organisation. A healthy personality reflects a desire for interesting and challenging work, a fair measure of discretion and independence of judgement and action. Argyris compares this with the needs of the formal organisation for specialisation, a chain of command, unity of direction and so on. He finds that there is conflict between the two sets of needs (Argyris, 1964). The impact of the formal organisation is to place individuals in work situations where:

   (i) they are provided minimal control over their workaday world;
  (ii) they are expected to be passive, dependent and subordinate;
 (iii) they are expected to have frequent use of a few skin-surface shallow abilities; and
  (iv) they are expected to produce under conditions leading to psychological failure.

Argyris (1958, 1960) suggests that employee reaction to the formal organisation is to devise informal activities such as absenteeism, turnover, apathy and indifference as defence mechanisms in order to be independent and creative. A further reaction from management is to view these activities as 'outputs of irresponsible people rather than as unintended consequences of the very strategy [it uses] to organise and control human effort'. Thus more controls are imposed, which stimulates still more defensive reactions from employees, until eventually individuals may become so apathetic and indifferent, or so hostile and aggressive, and in either case so alienated, that their mental health can be seriously affected. On the other hand, the organisation will become so rigid and inefficient that it will deteriorate (Argyris, 1973).

The human-relations school of thought makes the case, which is supported by evidence on performance efficiency, labour turnover and absenteeism, that management can motivate the individual and responsibly involve him in decisions affecting the process of work, and in doing so make him feel responsible and accountable for his actions (Bowers, 1964; Coch and French, 1948; Mann, 1957; Morse and Reimer, 1956; Seashore and Bowers, 1963). Commitment must be obtained from people. Management cannot any longer assume it. At the same time, management must earn the trust and confidence of its employees for it to secure the loyalty, support and backing for its policies and plans. These conditions can be secured if there is appropriate participation, communication, consultation, democratic leadership, and if people are allowed an element of discretion within their jobs.

Likert (1967) observes that 'if an organisation is to function well it needs to have objectives which represent a satisfactory integration of the needs and desires of all the major interest groups and members involved'. He points out that no situation is stable and unchanging; and as the desires and needs change, so should the objectives of the organisation. In fact, he claims that:

> in every healthy organisation there is consequently an unending process of examining and modifying individual goals and organis-ational objectives as well as consideration of the methods for achieving them. With the re-setting of objectives must come the restructuring of roles and responsibilities of individuals and departments that creates the conditions required for individuals to be motivated enough to achieve them.

Bureaucracy

The 'bureaucratic' school of thought seeks to remove the power which could arise from vested interests among individuals or groups. According to Max Weber (1948), an organisation must have a distinctive set of rules governing the behaviour of its members, and in a bureaucracy control is more effectively exerted when it is applied by experts. Authority should be vested in a managerial role or position in the organisational hierarchy rather than in the person. This is considered to be both a more rational and legitimate basis for deriving stability and order in systems of operation, so as to enhance the predicability of performance outcomes and in enabling the organisation to achieve its goals in terms of the formally laid down practices and procedures which define the activities which personnel should be engaged in.

The impersonal set of rules and procedures of an administrative system restricts the arbitrary exercise of authority by people in positions of power in the organisational hierarchy, because the superior is no less bound to adhere to formally established rules and regulations than his subordinates are. These considerations imply that the formalisation of roles and responsibilities restricts the scope and discretion of centralised authority.

The more effectively formal rules and standard operating pro-cedures guide decisions and actions, the less need there is for directives from a central authority to effect such guidance. Accordingly, formalisation and standardisation promote decentralisation, not centralisation, and therefore permit greater flexibility in systems of operation at lower levels in the management system.

Unambiguous performance standards give rise to an authority structure that permits less rigid task performance in organisations. The reasoning underlying this is that standardisation, by making performance more reliable, provides objective grounds for delegating decisions, because it reduces the risks entailed by possibly poor managerial decisions, and these lesser risks furnish a rational basis for top management's delegation of decisions to subordinate managers.

One way of dealing with exceptional cases not adequately covered by existing sets of rules and procedures is to supply additional rules specifying under *what* conditions *which* standards are to be applied. This enhances individual task performance and enables those with specialist knowledge of various key operations to act on that knowledge and to decide what is the best course of action to take in a particular situation. This avoids the possibility of a rigid application of inappropriate standards which detract from desired standards and levels of performance. Such impersonal mechanisms of control lessen the risk of delegation, while still giving top management some ultimate controlling power (Blau, 1970).

It is often considered preferable by management to be guided by rules and regulations governing working practices and procedures so as to restrict the element of uncertainty in people's jobs which surrounds changing needs and problems in an organisation. Any ensuing conflict or ambiguity arising through the changing demands of their tasks can be resolved more easily if there are formally laid down rules and procedures which specify a means of regulating and predicting performance efficiency.

The merits of a bureaucracy are seen in its technical efficiency, which is derived from conformity to formal rules and procedures. If, in carrying out their tasks, individuals are provided with clear guidelines and an underlying rationale in terms of the administrative procedures needed for carrying out essential tasks, it serves to eliminate the querying and the questioning and the possible misunderstanding and misinterpretation of rules and regulations. Bureaucratic systems of operation are designed to enhance the precision and speed of decision-making, the impartiality of decisions and rulings, expert control, continuity of operations, unambiguity, uniformity of thinking, and consistency of action. Its intention is to remove non-rational considerations such as hostility, anxiety, conflict and dispute. The bureaucrat's official life is planned for him in terms of a graded career structure through the organisational devices of promotion by seniority, pensions, incremental salaries, etc., all of which are designed to provide incentives for disciplined action and conformity to official rules and procedures.

However, these very devices which increase the probability of conformity may lead to too much concern with strict adherence to regulations which induce timidity, conservatism and resistance to management change initiatives for purposes of improving the efficiency of the administrative process. Bureaucratic systems of administration which foster this kind of behaviour can become maladaptive, particularly when the structure and functioning of the organisation needs to be flexible and responsive to environmental changes and people's exact authority and responsibility. In this formalised system of operation individuals can defend themselves against any possible adverse criticism or blame arising from taking an untried and uncertain course of action which superiors may dispute or take exception to. Adopting tried and tested, officially sanctioned ways of working eliminates possible errors of judgement and minimises fear of failure which springs from taking risks and dealing with previously unknown factors or considerations. However, strict adherence to a set of rules and formal procedures imposes constraints on the way that new problems and changing needs can be tackled, and this may prove to be ineffective in dealing with previously unknown forces and influences acting on the system of operations in the organisation, thus undermining performance efficiency.

Bureaucratic systems of authority which emphasise a simple hierarchical application of a fixed set of rules and routine procedures would be unable to accommodate the changing nature of problems and needs facing an organisation. Such organisations become ineffective in responding to external pressures and influences and lack the innovativeness needed to grow and develop.

Blau and Scott (1963) define bureaucracy as 'the amount of effort devoted to maintaining the organisation in operation rather than to directly achieving its objectives' – it is the administrative machinery, not the rule-encumbered inefficiency it is often viewed as. In that bureaucratic procedures and practices encourage consistency and uniformity of action, it provides management with influence (Merton, 1957). If the rules constrain or hamper individual task initiatives, then inefficiency may arise in the system, and the formal bureaucratic system may defeat its purpose of maintaining the organisation in operation when the means (rules) become ends in themselves.

An effective bureaucratic system of operation demands reliability of response and strict adherence to regulations. However, as the human-relations school of thought amply illustrates, informal leadership, divergent group norms and unofficial sanctions which are not congruent with the organisation's goals and values will seriously undermine the bureaucratic system of administration because of the absence of compliance and conformity to laid-down rules and procedures. Exerting more managerial control through bureaucratic processes of administration does not necessarily enable people to deal with diverse and disparate sectional interests, or to eliminate and offset the sources of conflict and dispute between different interest groups, because of their differing definitions of organisational policies, priorities and performance objectives. Because of career development needs which can usually only be realised within specialist functions, an individual's interests and loyalties centre around his department's needs and problems rather than upon the organisation's over-all aims and objectives.

In conditions of uncertainty a way in which operating units have been known to deal with managerial and hierarchical controls and irreconcilable inter-unit performance objectives has been by manipulation of rules as a means of protecting their own claims and interests and in gaining independence from direct and arbitrary interference from those higher up. As rules cannot regulate everything and cannot eliminate all arbitrariness, areas of uncertainty emerge which constitute the focal points around which collective conflicts become acute and where instances of direct dominance and subordination re-emerge. In such cases the group which can control the unregulated area (by its strategic position either in the structure or in the work flow) can control the unregulated area and derive considerable political advantage – which is naturally used in order to improve its bargaining position and ensure a greater share of the organisational rewards and privileges from the powers it has (Mouselis, 1967).

The function which is most critical to the organisation and upon whom others are dependent is the most powerful and able to impose its own controls and performance objectives. In a manufacturing enterprise the product is directed towards the customer. The company is reliant on the ability of the marketing department to create and sustain the demand for its product(s). Sales departments are therefore more able to control and influence company policy on matters such as product delivery dates, quality, and product demand and cost. Sales departments are then able to impose various constraints or conditions on the other functions and to influence strongly their method and mode of operation and any changes they consider necessary in the light of perceived changes in market conditions and consumer demand.

One of the powers of sales departments which may impose conditions on the production department is price-setting and output adjustments to meet changes in market opportunity and competition. Sales campaigning and advertising may also alter the nature of the product and the service provided to the consumer. As the link between the customer and producer, the sales department absorbs most of the uncertainty about the diffuse and changing market or customer environment. Its role and position in the organisation provides the sales department with the power and authority to override the concerns and interests of other departments such as production, research and development (Perrow, 1971).

The power held by maintenance departments in manufacturing organisations also serves as an illustration of how production units can become dependent on service support functions to keep their operations going. The conflict and dispute which ensues is referred to by Crozier (1964) in his account of the struggles between production and maintenance departments in the French tobacco industry.

The division of authority in organisations does not readily define for different technical functions how organisational policies should be carried out and in whose domain decisions lie on matters of joint concern. For example, mainstream operating departments are responsible and accountable for making decisions on matters affecting the performance capacity and capability of their units. On the other hand, service support functions are responsible for acting on their own judgement and 'know-how' of what needs to be done to maintain or improve existing levels of unit performance. However, such divisions of responsibility and authority cannot be readily and clearly delineated.

Wherever there is conflict between the interests represented, dual lines of responsibility result in a lack of clarity about the powers of the respective parties involved. For instance, service support functions such as engineering maintenance and mainstream operating departments have overlapping responsibilities and authority for dealing with plant performance and capability which can cut across each other's initiatives or plans when either party threatens or undermines the other's priorities and performance objectives. An engineering department's efforts to provide a cost-effective service by alerting operating departments to malfunctions and to improved methods of plant maintenance may be counteracted by the operating department's claim that systems of production require more speedy breakdown maintenance and planned preventative maintenance to minimise losses in output. Breakdown maintenance stretches maintenance resources to the limit, and is uneconomic in terms of resource utilisation, thus restricting maintenance efficiency. On the other hand, a policy of preventative maintenance is both expensive and difficult to justify when a company is endeavouring to cut back on costs of operating by making savings in engineering costs. In periods of restraint on maintenance expenditure operating departments may be trying to avert production losses by pressing for equipment repairs to be overhauled more speedily than the engineering department feels able to perform confidently. Engineering will seek to avoid any possibility of 'premature' failures for which it would be held responsible. For purposes of self-protection and self-interest, both parties will seek to impose their own demands and expectations on the other, issuing commands and independently interpreting organisational policies and manipulating procedures in ways which advance their own claims.

A major factor is the absence of direct authority and control over the decisions and plans of other departments upon whom it is dependent for either securing support resources or work orders. Each is reluctant to be held accountable for performance deficiencies and shortcomings in work-flow integration and systems of operation where responsibilities are blurred or made confusing by changing circumstances (i.e. new tasks) and unforeseen contingencies (i.e. operating problems). For example, in the former case, when work demands originated by the system are not clearly identified as belonging to one or other function, then any action or initiative taken by one group may be challenged by another because it infringes upon its own sphere of activity. In the latter case, while one party may wish to forestall making a decision on a problem, the other party may wish the other to take prompter action so as to avert the problem which is of immediate concern to it.

The conflicting pressures of maintaining, for example, a central industrial-relations policy and of providing a fair degree of autonomy for operational units at successive levels in the organisational hierarchy produces an organisational structure that contains a good deal of uncertainty and conflict. Industrial-relations departments seek to regularise and maintain a certain set of rules and procedures for enabling operating departments to deal with labour grievances, and this reduces the element of uncertainty over what actions management can take without contradicting or undermining the orgaisation's position. Industrial-relations departments, for instance, will be reluctant to commit the organisation to a decision on an issue of dispute between a union member and an operating department when the latter is pressing for steps to be taken which are not laid down by agreements made with unions, or are likely to create serious breaches between the organisation and the unions. This creates a situation of indecision, and leaves the operating department uncertain as to what its powers are and what decisions, if any, it can take to deal with a labour dispute which is adversely affecting levels and quality of output.

The co-ordination and control of service support work undertaken by different specialist functions cannot be achieved by clearly differentiating specific areas of responsibility and accountability between them. This is because of unclear or complex differentiation of roles, responsibility, authority and accountability which cannot be handled by devising a simple set of rules and procedures which operational units implement, especially when so much depends on the changing nature and specific circumstances surrounding a particular operational problem. What happens is that each party seeks to have its own way in areas relevant to its interests but does not seek to assume sole responsibility. Because of industrial action and disputes, industrial-relations departments have devised and implemented policies and procedures which govern labour relations, and through this process they have directly affected the organisation of production. However, they do not assume direct responsibility and accountability for this work organisation. Thus the industrial-relations department avoids responsibility for carrying out the policies and decisions it has made, while dictating and thereby controlling systems of operation.

In nearly all situations authority is shared in the execution of the organisation's task. For example, industrial-relations and operations departments share responsibility for labour relations. When industrial action is taken by members of the work-force it is the operations departments who are held accountable for any problems which may arise because they are directly responsible, while industrial-relations departments are able to avoid accountability. This situation of dual authority and single accountability, as described above, prevails in other spheres of activity, such as between production departments and engineering maintenance, purchasing departments and all those to whom they supply material resources of one kind or another, and between production and product development departments in manufacturing enterprises. Since the changing problems and needs facing an organisation often involve ambiguity of functional roles and responsibilities, joint problem-solving and decision-making become important processes of conflict management.

The decision theory school has developed from the writings of Simon (1957), and Cyert and March (1963). According to Simon, all managerial action is decision-making, and the manager's job 'involves not only making decisions himself, but also seeing that the organisation or the part of it that he directs makes decisions effectively'. Managers have to make a decision without being able to scan all possible alternative courses of action. In Simon's terminology, he 'satisfices', in the sense that he is only able to choose one or other course of action because of the constraints he faces, such as a lack of resources or information required to deal with the problem under consideration.

All managers face some obstacle or constraint hindering or preventing satisfactory implementation of the organisation's task. A major concern of managers is to be able to decide on a course of action which will enable them to realise the performance objectives towards which they are striving. The principal task of the manager in such circumstances is to achieve a change of state in the organisation's system of operation – to overcome, circumvent or offset the obstacles or constraints under which he is working. The basic decisions that all managers are faced with involve setting goals, deciding upon the means to those ends, coping and adapting to external pressures and problems and resolving internal conflicts and disputes which detract from performance efficiency.

Decision issues involve two major dimensions: beliefs about cause-and-effect relationships, and preferences regarding possible outcomes (Thompson, 1967). In instances where one is clear on what outcomes are preferred but uncertain of what the cause-and-effect relationship is in achieving this desired state of affairs, personal judgement is called for in the decision-making process. Before an effective course of action can be considered the nature of the problem or constraint must be recognised and the cause of it understood as far as possible. This is very much dependent on the availability and reliability of the information to hand. Where the situation is reversed, and there is certainty regarding cause and effect but uncertainty regarding outcome preferences, there is a need to secure commitment and support for a common or consistent course of action which does not undermine the position of the people concerned or detract from over-all performance objectives and organisational goals. The organisation may, however, be constrained in its choice among alternative courses of action by, for instance, a shortage of resource materials in the production process.

Since all organisations are social units interacting with their wider environment, any involvement or consideration of the human element in either the cause or the effect of the problem or obstacle introduces an element of uncertainty. Complete knowledge is rare indeed and the desired outcome is problematic because the knowledge available is not always verifiable. Managers have to decide on courses of action without complete knowledge of the cause and effect of decisions they take, because some elements of the decision-making process are beyond the organisation's control, such as fluctuations and unpredictability in product demand and changes in government policy and legislation, as on industrial-relations matters. At the same time, managers cannot always be clear as to what strategy to adopt when their own organisation is in competition with another; and they do not always have control over their own organisation's marketing policies, nor do they necessarily know what will be the result of their actions.

Knowledge and understanding of cause-and-effect relationships are vitally affected by the belief system (i.e. the views and opinions people hold). The dominant view or opinion which is adopted tends to serve as the mechanism by which information coming into the system is interpreted on a cause-and-effect basis, leading to different kinds of decisions. The interpretation of information entering the decision-making process is crucially important, in that it affects the outcomes of the decisions that are made (Hall, 1972). The adoption of a different belief system could lead to entirely different decisions based on the same information. Because of competing resource demands and conflicting interests, priorities and performance criteria of different departments in an organisation, each tends to see its own objectives as the prime objective, and the greater part of managerial decision-making needs to be focused on dealing with the problem of managing this 'coalition' of interests.

Desired outcomes from the decision-making process are also affected by the fact that when human beings are involved in the process of working towards the realisation of certain desired ends such as performance improvement, people quite often experience certain conflicting desires. For instance, individuals want more authority in order to implement certain decisions but wish to avoid responsibility or accountability if their actions prove unwarranted because of the absence of sufficient control or self-determination of desired outcomes.

Added to these constraints upon the decision process are the limits of individual rationality. Decisions are made on the basis of 'bounded rationality' (Simon, 1957). There is a limit to the ability of managers to handle complex multivariate factors without adequate inform-ation and yet still make correct decisions. No decision can properly anticipate all unforeseen contingencies. At the same time, the successful initiation and implementation of changes in one sub-system will inevitably have an impact on another – which in the long run may not be in the best interests of either department.

We shall assess and evaluate in succeeding chapters how the conflict and dispute which may arise from the actual decision-making process and the consequences of decisions made may be dealt with in as rational a way as possible. In working towards greater rationality in the decision-making process, managers need to consider all the key influences acting upon them in constraining or serving as obstacles to an improved system of operation such as problems arising from the diversity of interests in an organisation (Cyert and March, 1963).

Systems Theory

The basic principles of systems thinking are that any phenomena are part of a system, are a system in themselves, and contain other systems called sub-systems. In organisational terms a research and development department within a commercial enterprise would be incorporated within a system of manufacturing operation and located in a particular sub-system which would be connected to the production and marketing departments because of its interdependence with them.

An organisation can be studied and analysed in several dimensions using a systems approach. The analytical features of a system involve:

(i) the boundaries of the system (both internally and externally);

(ii) its sub-systems;

(iii) relationships between the system and its sub-systems;

(iv) the relative importance of each sub-system;

(v) the order and dependencies which exist among sub-systems;

(vi) how a system or sub-system provides feedback;

(vii) how systems or sub-systems interact; and

(viii) the nature of the linkages between systems or sub-systems.

Taking the organisation as a socio-technical system gives two important dimensions. First, there is the process of translating the resource input into a product output by examining the activities of individuals and sub-groups within the system. For example, various groups of people work together in some defined role relationship which is closely associated with the operation and maintenance of technical systems of operation. The technical procedures and controls of the department or unit concerned vitally affect or condition the social interaction and affiliation of the persons responsible for operating the procedures and controls in existence. There is another consideration in viewing an organisation as a socio-technical system, i.e. there is a process of feeding back the product or information output back into the system as a further input of a different sub-system. For instance, in a product assembly unit of an engineering firm there are various stages through which the final end-product must go before it is properly assembled. Because of various technical requirements and processes of operation information on the character and reliability of the technical process needs to be fed back by product managers to engineering maintenance, i.e. the machinery and equipment involved, in order to help that department determine the nature and scale of its own operations in terms of the work output required of it in terms of servicing and scheduling maintenance operations of production plants.

By examining certain interrelated systems and how they cohere or fragment we may identify how systems' functioning is determined by individual and group actions and how the operation of one system which becomes the input for another system enhances or undermines the organisation's functioning and over-all levels of performance in terms of product output, product quality, service efficiency, cost-effectiveness, manpower utilisation, etc. The primary emphasis in general systems theory is the interdependence of the parts of the system, the actual relationships between the parts and an examination of the structure of the system.

For instance, additional resources granted to one of the sub-systems must decrease the efficiency (by decreasing the resources) of the other sub-systems. Similarly, as the sub-systems are interlocked, any change in one sub-system must give rise to a chain reaction of adjustments in the other sub-systems. For example, if one system such as engineering maintenance in a manufacturing organisation is prevented from providing a normally efficient break-down service to mainstream operational units because of industrial grievances and disputes over manning levels and pay rates among the work-force, then product output can be seriously affected when production failures are not attended to promptly. Until management is able to resolve its differences with the work-force or union representatives, the maintenance system will be operating at below capacity, and this will reverberate throughout the system. Orders will be lost if production does not meet the demand, and sales departments will be exhorting operating departments to raise their levels of output. In their turn operations will be pressing the maintenance department for more availability of limited resource support. Competition for these resources among operating departments will inevitably mean that one department's gain will result in the loss of those same resources by another department. These examples illustrate that if order and integration between the parts of the organisation's system of operation is being threatened or undermined by interaction within an unstable or turbulent external environment, the interrelationships between sub-systems will also be adversely affected. These sub-systems will now be looked at in more detail.

The production sub-system

The production sub-system is concerned with processing the input of raw materials, labour and capital into some desired product output through the mode of production or technological process adopted. The organisation needs to specify the nature of its objectives for this process to take place. A major task of the production system is to programme and organise the method and mode of operation, to schedule and monitor the mix of inputs, and to review levels of resource utilisation and product flow. The degree of fit between them is an important point of comparison between organisations in terms of the cost-effectiveness of resource inputs and output levels. There are two complicating variables that affect the way the production system works.

First, the structural arrangements required to organise the production process normally take the form of an appropriate division of labour based on specialist skills. However, such structures also create positions of power and are used for administrative control. Key personnel may exercise greater decision-making power than others, irrespective of their hierarchical position of authority and formal status in the organisation. One of the consequences of this is that key personnel are able to control the channels of information. So the department or appropriate structure is both production-supportive and power-creative. Clearly these two dimensions will be interlinked. A project co-ordinator may be heavily engaged in co-ordinating and planning task work without the same authority and control over his colleagues in a task force as the departmental manager to whom they may be solely accountable.

The second complicating variable is in the definition and interpretation of organisational roles associated with the task that is assigned to a given individual. The demands made of a person are subject to the degree of specificity or lattitude in his task and the expectations of others in the organisation as to how he should carry out his role. Should there be changes in the various components of the sub-system just described, then there is likely to be a change in the expectations of the role, from either the person involved or from others associated with him. There is the possibility of role ambiguity or conflict becoming apparent which may require resolution. For example, a manager who faces new demands on him which he wishes to resist may be experiencing role stress as a consequence of having his own position questioned and challenged by another department.

The boundary sub-system

Essentially, this is concerned with two areas. The first is with supporting the production process by securing necessary inputs from outside and by marketing the output. This is a major area of activity in industrial organisations, involving such departments as purchasing, marketing and advertising. An essential element is the past experience and present expectations of management and staff, and this introduces a personal and pre-existing definition of the role of the boundary sub-system within the organisation which may well affect the method of operation of the purchasing, marketing and advertising departments. By means of 'hard selling', for example, a manager may consciously project a new, innovative market image. At the same time, a new purchasing manager, for example, with ideas about securing supplies of resource materials more cheaply may well have his plans modified by the pressures and influences of production managers concerned with quality and reliability.

The second main type of boundary exchange concerns the obtaining of support and approval for product development within the organisation and the launching of the end-product on the market. In the case of the product being developed by a project manager the success or otherwise of the market launch may well depend on the manipulation of consumer opinion and the creation of a favourable image of the organisation. To do this, the marketing department has to establish with its prospective customers an identity different from that of its competitors which gives its products an edge over others in terms of cost, quality and/or delivery. Advertising is one powerful means of attracting attention to a new product, or in endeavouring to distinguish one's product from those of other manufacturers.

The maintenance sub-system

This works to keep the organisation in a healthy and effectively functioning condition. There are two types of maintenance activity which can be clearly identified. First, the setting up of rules and formal procedures for organisational activities creates the necessary predictability in human interactions that prevents as far as possible organisational breakdown. Second, it creates an appropriate system of rewards, material or psychological, in order to retain the motivation of members to work productively. The main function of personnel departments, for example, is to ensure that the personnel within the organisation are both able and willing to fulfil the means for production by administering policies and procedures which overcome or tackle labour-relations problems on matters such as pay and conditions of service which, if unresolved, could lead to a loss of production because of possible sanctions imposed by the work-force such as a policy of 'work to rule', 'go slow', or 'non-co-operation'.

The adaptive sub-system

This serves the purpose of alerting the organisation of any changes which are necessary in its current structure and functioning in order to enable it to respond appropriately to environmental pressures and demands. Industrial organisations devote much of their resources to market research, product development and in investigating ways and means of improving service support to production departments in order to counteract falling profits and contracting markets. Feedback is essential for management to have sufficient knowledge about the performance capability of, say, a service support function in order for it to be able to make a realistic and accurate assessment of the problematic situation and in order to decide what corrective action needs to be taken. Adaptive flexibility can be built into the organisation by setting up units which would be concerned with projects or tasks of an investigatory nature involving problem identification and resolution. There would be two main tasks: first, an attempt to forecast future changes in the organisation's environment and matching these with development plans; second, an analysis and presentation to management of existing findings suggesting what would be the consequences of implementing such findings. This is a

process of planned adaptation of the organisation to the environment. Steering groups tend to operate in this capacity and likewise
special task forces. There must also be a mechanism to deal with
unexpected problems that have occurred, indicating immediate
necessity for change. These might best be provided by staff consul-
tations or team approaches of one kind or another.

Fundamental to all adaptive processes is adequacy of feedback to
the relevant decision-maker, so that channels of communication
carrying appropriate flows of information can be sufficiently
rationalised for this task. Organisations that are arranged hierarchi-
cally frequently face difficulties here – by creating blockages in
feedback systems.

The managerial sub-system

This involves management activities in three particular areas. As
organisations are principally hierarchical in their structure, someone
has to resolve conflicts that arise between different levels by use of
sanctions and authority. In this instance the manager is an arbitrator.
The various systems have their own demands which they fight over.
The manager must obtain a balance between the demands for
maximum production as against the maintenance of a working
structure, while simultaneously adapting systems of operation to new
demands and controlling the intensity of boundary activity, for
example inter-group conflict and competition for resources. The
manager is in this sense a co-ordinator and controller. The manager
must concern himself with the long-term survival of the organisation
by increasing its potential and optimising its use of productive
potential both in terms of physical and human resources. The
manager in this sense is a long-range planner.

Open-systems theory is a useful tool of analysis because it emphasises
the interlinking of all parts of the system. For example, a decision to
set up a team working on a special project in a department
immediately has an effect on what task is pursued and how that task is
tackled. The team comprises a structure utilising members' specialised abilities in a new way, but it also reallocates the focus of power
and authority in a team-consultative context.

The role of the manager is changed and he faces some potential areas of conflict which must be resolved. The team redesigns the input of resources, and perhaps its production programme, which may well affect levels and quality of output reflected in the performance of individuals and the group alike. Their image or standing may be favourably or unfavourably received depending on how successfully it relates to other teams or departments. In so far as members of the team receive greater work satisfaction, they become more committed members of the work-force, and in so far as they operate as a team they initiate particular loyalties and attachments to their group.

As an initiator of a change situation, the team is involved in adapting the organisation to a new situation. Using a team structure, the members may well develop new communication channels so that feedback is adequate for decisions to be taken, and their decision-making procedures may then be based upon this wider dispersion of information and wider diffusion of authority. The project group or product development team involved in designing or modifying a new method of production may well be called on to operate such managerial activities in order to sort out its conflicts, co-ordinate its activities and plan for new technical developments. So in this one change within the production sub-system interlinked changes are made within that sub-system, and also in activities concerned with boundary management, maintenance of the system, adaptation (involving feedback and communication systems) and the management of the business.

A Contingency Theory of Organisations

Studies by writers like Burns and Stalker (1966), Woodward (1965), Thompson (1967), Lawrence and Lorsch (1967) have emphasised that different organisational structures and systems of management are required to cope effectively with different business environment conditions. At the same time, an organisation is a social system, and management must take into consideration two important variables – the 'environmental variables' and the 'needs' of individuals and groups who are drawn into the system.

These studies have emphasised that there is no one best way for organisations to be structured and organised. The best system of operation reflects the nature of the work to be done and the needs of the people involved. Enterprises with highly predictable tasks perform better with highly formalised procedures and rules laid down centrally by higher authority. With highly uncertain tasks that require more extensive problem-solving, on the other hand, organisations that are less formalised and emphasise autonomy (self-control and self-determination) and member participation in decision-making are more effective.

Managers must design and develop organisations so that the system of operations (structure and functioning) fits the nature of the task(s) to be done and the needs of the people involved. This is illustrated and supported by the findings of Morse and Lorsch (1970) in a study of two research laboratories with unpredictable research and development tasks, and two container plants involving the manufacture of standardised items with automated high-speed production lines. One plant and one laboratory had significantly higher levels of performance efficiency. The study showed that the more successful units had a better 'fit' between structure and organisational climate than the less successful units. The higher-performing laboratory was perceived by the scientists working there to have minimal and flexible rules, a long-term approach to performance reviews and reporting, minimal control on their behaviour and high influence in the instigation and design of the task(s) they were involved with. In contrast, the less effective laboratory was more restrictive on individual actions and initiatives, more rule-orientated, and more formally structured roles and responsibilities were given to people, with more decisions made at the top.

At the shop-floor level of the high-performing manufacturing plant there were comprehensive rules, procedures and control systems and short-range reporting on production levels and short-term performance-review sessions. There was relatively low rank-and-file influence with a 'directive' type of supervisor in charge. Influence tended to be concentrated at higher levels, where the decisions were made. Conversely, in the less effective container plant managerial practices and operational procedures were less controlling and formally structured with a more participative kind of supervision of the work-force. In the higher-performing research laboratory and container plant employees expressed more feelings of competence than did their counterparts in the less effective organisations. The researchers concluded that the more effective fit betwen task, structure and climate of working resulted in more feelings of competence and, finally, in task achievement.

Where there are different tasks and methods of operation involved (technology of production), a different system of management may also be required. On routine, standardised, mass assembly production tasks there is often a need for a more formal system of operation, more procedure, more guidance and control so as to eliminate any element of uncertainty involved in large-scale production and in order to extend the range and application of procedures which can be applied for dealing with known or predicted operational problems.

Units of production involving more individual and highly varied means of production, where failures in equipment or modes of operation are more difficult to anticipate and the frequency of them is high, there is a greater desire for, say, more control and influence in ironing out the problems which arise in an individual's sphere of activity (Flectcher, 1969).

Contingency theory

A number of forces in the organisation's environment change over time, including client needs, employee predispositions and attitudes to work, technology, product development opportunities and competition in the market-place.

Contingency theory implies that if an organisation's environment is undergoing major change, it is likely to require alterations in its structures, tasks and behaviour if it is to remain responsive and adaptive to that environment.

A number of empirical studies show that many effective organisations in stable environments or with stable technologies are characterised by a high degree of formality in rules and procedures, with roles and responsibilities clearly differentiated among departments and between functions, but concentrating authority at the top. However these same studies show that effective organisations in rapidly changing environments are characterised by less reliance on formal rules, and more reliance on interdependence of unit operations and shared responsibilities for coping and adapting to organisational changes. There is a greater emphasis on joint planning and problem-solving, with greater responsibility and authority placed upon individuals at lower levels in the organisation for deciding what initiatives to take. More widely dispersed centres of influence necessitate that management is open to new ideas and approaches to operational matters and is able to accommodate and resolve differences which are manifest in the conflicting and competing practices and procedures adopted by specialist units, as noted above in production departments as opposed to research and development departments. (See Burns and Stalker, 1966; Dill, 1962 and 1958; Emery and Trist, 1965; Starbuck, 1965; Thompson, 1967; Lawrence and Lorsch, 1967.)

For example, if the nature of the needs and problems facing an organisation is in the process of change, then fixed rules and procedures become quickly outdated. Since change often involves unknown or unforeseen influences and outcomes, joint colaborative problem-solving becomes a more appropriate process than the formal application of procedures by central authority (management) which are based on outmoded customs and practice.

Differentiation

In a comparative study of organisations in different environments, Lawrence and Lorsch (1967), Kandwalla (1973), and Negandhi and Reimann (1973) found that the more diverse and complex the organisation's environment, the greater the internal differentiation needed among operation units if the organisation as a whole was to meet environmental demands. Differentiation refers to the division of labour or specialisation of knowledge. This differentiation is necessary so that different work groups can develop orientations which are appropriate for the issue posed by the different parts of the organisation's environment.

In the manufacturing enterprise there are a number of specialist functions (activities) undertaken so as to enable the organisation to realise its goals and over-all purpose. The research and development department is looking to technological innovation and advancement in its knowledge of product characteristics and properties because of changing product specifications and the increasing demands made by consumers for improved quality and economy of product or service. The purchasing department seeks to ensure that changing material specifications and resource availability (equipment, etc.) can be secured as speedily and economically as possible. The marketing department, for example, is involved with expanding product demand, and the sales department is concerned with negotiating the price and delivery of the product in the face of either changing market conditions and consumer tastes or competition from other organisations.

On the other hand, the personnel department is concerned to promote and foster trouble-free relations between management and the work-force. Agreements are negotiated with unions on matters related to the terms and conditions of employment of industrial staff. They are regularly reviewed and re-assessed whenever changes either in production plans and work programmes or in the technological process call for different arrangements of work distribution and payment.

Each department has a clearly differentiated task from the other and develops its own policies, procedures and practices which it considers necessary in fulfilling its own task, expressed in terms of certain specific performance objectives.

Production departments work towards attaining a certain desired level of output by striving to sustain a smooth uninterrupted flow of work and system of operation, which can be planned in advance and executed in a highly deterministic way. Production units tend therefore to be tightly controlled and reflect a high degree of formality and structure in the sense that individual roles and responsibilities are clearly and precisely defined. Centralised planning and programming of work schedules assist production systems to be as efficient as possible. Service support functions such as engineering maintenance departments in manufacturing can also be more efficient if they can centrally plan and co-ordinate the deployment of their resources.

However, although both production and maintenance systems are essentially concerned to maintain the predictability and stability of their own operations, they both have to cope and adapt to unforeseen contingencies. Enforced changes in production plans and unit operations, or unanticipated equipment failures, disrupt work schedules and undermine productive efficiency and resource utilisation.

A conflict of interest ensues when the production system and service support functions cannot realise their own objectives except at the expense of the other. If a production department cannot attain certain desired levels of output, except by increasing its resource support to meet shortfalls in productive capacity or performance efficiency, this stretches the scarce resources available from the service support function, putting pressure on it to raise overtime working or waive certain operating rules and procedures, which either reduces the cost-effectiveness of the service or undermines the level and standard of maintenance performance.

Conversely, if the maintenance of a production system is insufficiently flexible or responsive to production problems, then operating units will not be able to realise their production schedules and work programmes.

The people working in purchasing and marketing are concerned with coping and adapting not only to the demands of the internal system of operation but also to the external environment. The latter imposes constraints on the reliability and quality of resource materials fed into the production system and the marketability of the end-product because of fluctuations and changes in market demand.

Changes in the quality of a resource material or in a supplier because of rising prices, and the need to keep production costs down, may significantly alter the reliability and availability of supplies because of certain decisions taken by the purchasing department. The impact of such initiatives may adversely affect the ability of the production, planning and control department to run a smooth continuous system of operation. At the same time, failures in supply involve higher costs of production and reduce levels of output.

The marketing function also effects the operation of the production system in that it will seek to maximise sales and to provide each potential customer with the best possible terms and conditions which he might otherwise secure from a competitor. By making changes in pricing policy or in product specifications sales departments can cause friction with production departments. Conflict arises between production and sales departments in that production managers want to limit the range of products in order to increase the volume of output, and thereby reduce unit costs. Having to alter or modify systems of operation to comply with changes in product specifications involves the production system having to revise its work schedules and plans to accommodate new systems of operation and changes in working practices and procedures. There are often difficulties associated with this in terms of industrial-relations problems which spring from resistances to changes in manning levels, job specifications and modes of operation.

The members of the various sub-systems in a manufacturing enterprise are clearly differentiated in terms of personal goals, with sales personnel concerned with customer problems and the market-place; production, personnel and maintenance departments with cost reduction and efficiency; and research and development personnel with scientific matters, process improvement and modification of the technology.

Here the differentiation between departments in terms of the specialist task(s) each is required to perform can be seen. These differences are directly related to the kind of work environment that the various departments must deal with in their activities. Because of the complex demands made on different departments each develops its own distinctive system of operation – which contains elements of potential conflict.

The function of the management system is to integrate and unify the over-all system of operation by, for example, co-ordinating and controlling the interdependence between sub-systems and by carefully planning the changes required in operations in response to the demands of the organisational environment.

Integration

Successful organisations have been found to attain greater integration among diverse operating units than less successful organisations. Research evidence suggests that the greater the differentiation between work groups in terms of the specialist skills and expertise required, the greater the decentralisation of authority needed so that people can carry out their specialist roles and responsibilities. (See Dill, 1962; Thompson, 1967; Perrow, 1967; Lorsch and Allen, 1973.) However, the greater the interdependence required among work groups and operating units, the lower the level of autonomy that is possible on shared tasks. The more complex the interdependence, due to the differentiation of functions, the more pressing is the need for integration. Integration can be achieved more easily when interdepartmental decision-making is effective and conflict can be resolved. Several factors can be identified as contributing to an organisation's ability to resolve conflict and achieve integration in the face of high internal differentiation. These include the following: organisational norms which stress problem-solving and openness; the use of integrating devices to facilitate conflict resolution (such as interdepartmental teams, task forces, integrating roles); and persons known as 'integrators' who are seen as possessing high levels of influence and competence in the organisation, and whose task is to co-ordinate and control activities (projects) involving two or more specialist functions (Lawrence and Lorsch, 1967).

In analysing and evaluating how well the organisation is structured and functioning in order to meet environmental needs, the character and nature of the system in operation and the demands of the organisational environment should be examined and appraised. For example, if the organisation's environment is in the process of rapid and turbulent change, the organisation's structure should be able to facilitate rapid decision-making and response and should minimise the number of levels in the hierarchy through which information must pass before decisions are made. Similarly, the capacity to resolve conflicts and solve problems becomes especially important, and a heavy reliance on rules and procedures is inappropriate. If the organisation's task is complex and its environment is highly diverse, it indicates a need for functional differentiation within the system, and uniform procedures and rules cease to be universally applicable for the numerous specialist units coping and adapting to different organisational needs and problems.

There are certain specific activities (tasks) undertaken by different specialist functions in an organisation which must satisfy client needs. In examining and appraising the system of operation which is designed to fulfil these needs the question as to whether the different operating units of the system (such as production and maintenance) should develop different attributes, orientations and goals needs to be asked. For example, in one organisation I had worked in, an analysis of its operations indicated that if the system were to meet the needs of a growing number of new customers, with varying product specifications, it had to bring about major changes in production design and technology and develop new production programmes and methods. However, it was found that the central-planning/customer-services group had developed goal and time orientations that were so similar to those of the production units that they were only focusing on immediate needs and trouble-shooting activities. As a result the central-planning function was not dealing with the larger and longer-term needs of the organisation.

Major changes in product design called for extensive investigations into the development of new systems of operation which no one operating unit could plan and implement by itself but which a central production planning team could focus on and help develop. Because it had a longer-term goal and a strong orientation to change, it could help the organisation improve its system of operation. Hence a need for greater differentiation existed.

Similarly in other parts of the system, the needs of a changing customer population required more and better engineering services on an individual basis. However, it was discovered that product servicing personnel were spending much of their time performing administrative chores, such as checking on delivery dates and inventories on existing orders from customers. As a result they were not providing the specialised services that were needed. In this case the engineering servicing group's goals and attitudes were so similar to that of central administrative services that the system was clearly ineffective in dealing with individual customer problems. A need clearly existed for greater differentiation between customer-service departments and central administration. The need for integration is indicated by the extent to which meeting environmental demands requires interdependence between different parts of the organisation. A diagnosis of the need for integration can be made by identifying which groups must collaborate in order for the system to meet environmental demands effectively.

Where one is meeting the needs of a changing market and customer population, there is a need for major product innovations or changes in the methods or mode of operation in order to fulfil new product specifications on matters such as cost, reliability and servicing. In these cases integration between production, planning and design engineers becomes especially important in terms of all parties closely examining and appraising how improvements in levels of production and cost-effectiveness can be attained at the same time as improved product quality.

If differentiation between functions needs to be maintained, and perhaps sometimes increased, it is important that the organisational members develop the interpersonal and conflict-resolving skills needed to function effectively within a differentiated system of operation. It is essential that top management understands why differentiation is needed, and accepts the need as legitimate. Otherwise, subsequent efforts to develop norms which support differentiation within the system are likely to fail. This is especially important for two reasons. First, and most important, greater differentiation will increase the potential level of interdepartmental conflict within the system (Lawrence and Lorsch, 1967; Walton et al,

1966). Unless top management is aware of this possibility and understands its own task, which is to unify and integrate different systems of operation, it may not respond constructively to the emergence of interdepartmental conflict. Second, many organisations actively exhort staff to believe that task orientations should not differ within the system and that service support functions (units) should share the immediate goals and orientation of production personnel. It is especially critical that top management legitimate and support the need for different groups to have different task orientations because of the complex and specialist demands made on each one by the task environment in which they operate.

If a high degree of integration is required among several operating units in different parts of the system, then a formal integrating system of management may be needed (Child, 1977). Several types can be used: interdepartmental task forces; and integrating and co-ordinating roles and groups. Which of these mechanisms is appropriate depends on the importance and complexity of the interdependence and the degree to which differentiation is required. For example, if a need for integration exists between production units and service support functions, then the use of a task force or co-ordinating committee may be useful and efficient as a vehicle for setting priorities on service support resource allocation and resolving conflicts between them and as a channel through which personnel can communicate their needs to senior management.

If a stronger need for integration exists, a co-ordination role can be assigned to a person for purposes of bringing about major changes in service support directed towards improving mainstream operations. His task would be to facilitate the planning and integration of the diverse efforts of several different departments and individuals. In the role of co-ordinator and programme controller he is able to identify conflicts and help those concerned work together so that production needs can be met.

Summary

To summarise, management is concerned to put into operation the organisation's task – its primary function is related to performance.

Chester Barnard (1938) saw the need for different responses to different situations as part of the management process in carrying out 'the specialised work of maintaining the organisation in operation'.

It is the responsibility of management to make of the organisation what Donald Schon (1973) calls a 'self-transforming system', adaptive and responsive to the changing environment in which it needs to exist and survive.

What the five major schools of thought provide is an indication of the principal functions of management:

   (i) *Scientific Management* – planning, organising, commanding, co-ordinating and controlling.
  (ii) *Human Relations* – developing and sustaining co-operation.
 (iii) *Decision-making* – improving decision-making processes.
 (iv) *Bureaucracy* – depersonalising the application of rules.
  (v) *Contingency* – responding and adapting to changing environmental conditions.

The succeeding chapters will endeavour to examine more closely how these principal management functions are being maladaptively applied and how they might be applied more appropriately in the formulation, instigation and implementation of organisational change initiatives.

The next chapter will provide a conceptual and theoretical framework for establishing how an organisation is structured and functions so as to assist in identifying and providing an underlying explanation of the major factors to be considered by management in introducing organisational change and the chief constraints involved. So far, the contribution of the different schools of thought on management has been described, and this goes some way to explaining:

   (i) The outstanding problems and concerns facing management in organisations.
  (ii) Why the organisation's system of operation must fit in with the diverse and complex task of the organisation and the needs of its members.
 (iii) What demands are made upon managers, by changes in the organisation's environment, in adapting and developing a new improved system of operation.

The next task is to establish how these major considerations can be incorporated in the management of organisational change. The next chapter serves to establish what the process of managerial change in the organisation's structure and functioning involves and how that process can be analysed.

References

Argyris, C. (1958) *Personality and Organization* (New York, Harper & Row).

Argyris, C. (1960) *Understanding Organizational Behavior* (Homewood, Ill., Dorsey Press).

Argyris, C. (1962) *Interpersonal Competence and Organizational Effectiveness* (London, Tavistock).

Argyris, C. (1964) *Integrating the Individual and the Organization* (New York, Wiley).

Argyris, C. (1973) 'Personality and Organization Theory Revisited', *Administrative Science Quarterly*, vol. 18, no. 2, June.

Barnard, C. I. (1938) *The Functions of the Executive* (Harvard University Press).

Blau, P. M. (1976) 'Decentralization in Bureaucracies', in *Power in Organization*, ed. M. N. Zald (Vanderbilt University Press).

Blau, P. M. and Scott, W. R. (1963) *Formal Organization: A Comparative Approach* (London, Routledge & Kegan Paul).

Bowers, D. G. (1964) 'Organizational Control in an Insurance Company', *Sociometry*, vol. 27, no. 2, pp. 230–44.

Bowers, D. G. and Seashore, S. E. (1966) 'Predicting Organizational Effectiveness with a Four Factor Theory', *Administrative Science Quarterly*, vol. 11, no. 2.

Brech, E. F. L. (1975) *Principles and Practice of Management* (London, Longman).

Burns, T. and Stalker, G. M. (1966) *The Management of Innovation*, 2nd ed. (London, Tavistock).

Child, J. (1977) *Organization – A Guide to Problems and Practice* (New York, Harper & Row).

Coch, L. and French, J. P. R. (1948) 'Overcoming Resistance to Change', *Human Relations*, vol. 1, no. 4, pp. 512–32.

Crozier, M. (1964) *The Bureaucratic Phenomenom* (London, Tavistock).

Cyert, R. and March, J. (1963) *A Behavioral Theory of the Firm* (Englewood Cliffs, N.J., Prentice-Hall).

Dill, W. (1962) 'The Impact of Environment on Organizational Development', in *Concepts and Issues in Administrative Behavior*, ed. S. Mailick and E. H. Van Ness (Englewood Cliffs, N.J., Prentice-Hall).

Emery, R. E., and Trist, E. L. (1965) 'The Casual Texture of Organizational Environments', *Human Relations*, vol. 18, February.

Etzioni, A. (1961) *A Comparative Analysis of Complex Organizations* (New York, The Free Press).

Etzioni, A. (1964) *Modern Organizations* (Englewood Cliffs, N.J., Prentice-Hall), see ch. 6 'Organizational Control and Leadership', pp. 58–64.

Fayol, H. (1949) *General and Industrial Management*, trans. Constance Storrs (London: Pitman).

Fletcher, C. (1969) 'Men in the Middle', *Sociological Review*, vol. 17, pp. 341–54.

French, J. R. P. and Raven, B. (1960) 'The Bases of Social Power', in *Group Dynamics*, ed. D. Cartwright and A. Zander (Evanston, Ill.: Row, Peterson) pp. 607–23.

Gouldner, R. (1955) *Patterns of Industrial Democracy* (London, Routledge & Kegan Paul).

Guest, R. (1962) *Organizational Change* (Homewood, Ill., Dorsey Press).

Hall, R. H. (1972) *Organizations: Structure and Process* (Englewood Cliffs, N.J., Prentice-Hall).

Hinings, C. R. Hickson, D. J. Pennings, J. M. and Scheneck, R. E. (1974) 'Structural Conditions of Intraorganizational Power', *Administrative Science Quarterly*, vol. 19, no. 1, March, pp. 22–44.

Khandwalla, P. N. (1973) 'Variable and Effective Organizational Designs of Firms', *Academy of Management Journal*, vol. 16, no. 3, pp. 481–95.

Lawrence, P. R. and Lorsch, B. W. (1967) *Differentiation and Integration.* (Harvard Graduate School of Business and Administration).

Lawrence, P. R. and Lorsch, B. W. (1969) *Developing Organizations: Diagnosis and Action* (Reading, Mass., Addison–Wesley).

Likert, R. (1961) *New Patterns of Management* (New York, McGraw-Hill).

Likert, R. (1967) *The Human Organization* (New York, McGraw-Hill).

Lorsch, B. W. and Allen, S. A. (1973) *Managing Diversity and Interdependence: an organisational study of multi-divisional firms* (Harvard University Graduate School of Business Administration Division of Research).

Mann, F. C. (1957) 'Studying and Creating Change: a Means to Understanding Social Organization', in *Research in Human Relations* (Madison, Wisconsin, Industrial Relations Research Association).

Mayo, E. (1933) *The Human Problems of an Industrial Civilisation* (New York, Macmillan).

Mayo, E. (1949) *The Social Problems of an Industrial Civilisation* (New York, Macmillan).

Mechanic, D. (1962) 'Sources of Power of Lower Participants in Complex Organizations', *Administrative Science Quarterly*, vol. 7, no. 3, December, pp. 349–64.

Merton, R. R. (1957) 'Bureaucratic Personality and Structure', *Social Forces*, vol. 18, pp. 560–8.

Mooney, J. D. (1947) *The Principles of Organization* (New York, Harper & Row).

Morse, J. J. and Lorsch, J. W. (1970) 'Beyond Theory', *Harvard Business Review*, May–June.

Morse, N. and Reimer, E. (1956) 'The Experimental Change of a Major Organizational Variable', *Journal of Abnormal and Social Psychology*, vol. 52, pp. 120–9.

Mouselis, N. P. (1967) *Organization and Bureaucracy: an Analysis of Modern Theories* (London, Routledge & Kegan Paul).

Negandhi, A. R. and Reimann, B. C. (1973) 'Correlates of Decentralization: Closed and Open System Perspectives', *Academy of Management Journal*, vol. 16, no. 4, pp. 570–81.

Patchen, M. (1970) *Participation Achievement and Involvement in the Job* (Englewood Cliffs, N.J., Prentice-Hall).

Perrow, C. (1967) 'A Framework for the Comparative Analysis of Complex Organizations', *American Sociological Review*, vol. 32, April.

Perrow, C. (1970) 'Departmental Power and Perspective in Industrial Forms', in *Power in Organisation*, ed. M. N. Zald (Vanderbilt University Press).

Rushing, W. A. (1966) 'Organizational Rules and Surveillance:

Propositions in Comparative Organizational Analysis', *Administrative Science Quarterly*, vol. 10, no. 4, March, pp. 423–44.

Schon, D. A. (1973) *Beyond The Stable State* (New York, Norton Library Series, Norton).

Seashore, S. E. and Bowers, D. G. (1963) *Changing the Structure and Functioning of an Organization* (Ann Arbor, Michigan, Institute for Social Research).

Simon, H. A. (1957) *Administrative Behaviour*, 2nd ed. (New York, The Free Press).

Thompson, J. D. (1967) *Organizations in Action* (New York, McGraw-Hill).

Trist, E. L. and Bamforth, K. W. (1951) 'Some Social and Psychological Consequences of the Longwall Method of Goal-getting', *Human Relations*, vol. 4, no. 1, February, pp. 3–38.

Urwick, L. F. (1947) *The Element of Administration*, 2nd ed. (London, Pitman).

Warren, D. I. (1968) 'Power, Visibility and Conformity', *American Sociological Review*, vol. 33, no. 6, December, pp. 951–70.

Weber, M. (1948) 'From Max Weber: Essays in Sociology', ed. H. A. Gerth and C. W. Mills (Routledge & Kegan Paul) chap. 8.

Woodward, J. (1965) *Industrial Organization* (London, Oxford University Press).

Starbuck, W. H. (1965) 'Organizational Growth and Development', in *Handbook of Organizations*, ed. J. G. March (Chicago: Rand McNally) pp. 451–533.

Walton, R. E., Dutton, J. M., and Fitch, H. G. A. (1966) 'A Study of Conflict in the Process, Structure, and Attitudes of Lateral Relationships', in *Some Theories of Organizations*, ed. A. H. Ruberstein and C. J. Haberstroh (Homewood, Ill., Irwin).

3
An Organisational Framework for Managing Change

The product or service provided by an organisation can be described as its task. The nature and form which it's product operations takes, however, is dictated and influenced by the way individuals and departments contribute to the task or purpose of that organisation.

Considerable managerial effort and 'know-how' is involved in ensuring that the diverse activities of different individuals and interest groups are effectively drawn together in a co-ordinated and controlled manner. The responsibility for structuring and organising the system of operation falls upon management and is reliant on its ability to harness the skills and knowledge of people who are engaged in the process of converting material resources into product outputs.

The efficiency of this conversion process and the technology involved is an indication of how well the organisation's structure is designed to fulfil the system in operation, and how effectively people are working within it so as to enable the organisation to achieve its various goals. The attainment or otherwise of these goals establishes how well an organisation is performing.

However, the attainment of these goals is critically dependent on the predictability of the environment external to the organisation and the success with which management can control or influence the environment internal to the organisation.

If external bodies (institutions outside the organisation) decide to suspend their inputs of raw materials, labour, cash, etc., perhaps because of a credit squeeze imposed by governments on bank borrowings, or because of strike action initiated by a union, the organisation cannot function effectively. On the other hand, fluctuations in product demand necessitate that constant surveillance and corrective action is taken by management on matters relating to product pricing, quality and quantity.

Taking steps of this nature affects the conversion of inputs into outputs in that alternative methods and modes of operation may be necessary to cope with externally induced pressures and influences. Management may also of necessity be called upon to structure and organise operations very differently. Management's control over its environment is essential, and without that it can justifiably be claimed that an organisation is unable to achieve its stated goals, and ultimately will not survive.

In a wholly rational world an organisation's energies could be solely directed towards its objectives, but all organisations, irrespective of their complexity, life-span or typology are in continuous interaction with a changing environment. There are also the many different needs, goals, values and sentiments of their work-forces, and the ambitions and vested interests of its managers, which organisations must come to terms with.

A fundamental aspect of the organisation's task is to achieve its goals, which can often be expressed in terms of product/service performance within the circumstances or constraints within which it operates and which prevent their instant realisation. External constraints and internal obstacles hinder or frustrate management in its implementation of the organisation's task.

In an attempt to achieve certain organisational performance objectives a change of state in the organisation's structure and functioning may be required. In order to realise this change of state management needs to overcome or circumvent the obstacles and constraints which the organisation's system of operation imposes.

This briefly outlines the nature and scope of organisational change and what it demands from the managers who are entrusted with initiating and seeing it through.

Before beginning to understand the management function in planning, organising, co-ordinating and controlling organisational change, and how management change initiatives involve altering working relations, the complexities and intricacies of this subject will now be examined in more detail. Figure 3.1 focuses on the major determinants of organisational change.

Another way of illustrating the key elements involved in the task of organisational change management and how it might be studied is to view the change process as one of providing inputs of managerial

FIGURE 3.1   *Elements of organisational change*

skills and expertise directed at carrying out certain essential task(s) necessary for achieving a state of change in the organisation's structure and functioning for purposes of enhancing organisational performance (outputs).

Figure 3.2 shows five major areas which management must be aware of, and responsive to, if it is to make an effective contribution to organisational performance. The model provides a conceptual framework which focuses on the key variables influencing the success or otherwise of management change initiatives.

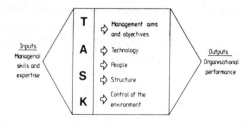

FIGURE 3.2

For purposes of illustration, a production controller in a manufacturing enterprise must plan and execute a set of performance objectives. He needs to monitor and review the resource capability and capacity of the technical system of operation to meet these objectives, and to identify potential problems associated with the co-ordination and control of resource schedules and production programmes. The information needed can only be obtained by developing a close working relationship with other members of the organisation who are involved in a range of activities supporting production control. At the same time, a production controller requires a certain degree of authority in the organisational hierarchy so as to be able to influence the level of production and to ensure that fluctuations in levels of output are corrected and that agreed standards of operation are adhered to. The production controller must above all understand the complexity of the organisational environment in which he works and the constraints within which he operates. Should a high level of technical failure occur in the production system, the production controller, with careful diagnosis and examination of the problem, can establish how to rectify the situation and restore previous levels of output.

Such an individual bases his actions upon the information he has acquired over a period of time, and recognises what is considered to be an effective or appropriate course of action. If there is insufficient understanding of the production system by the work-force, and aspects of technical operations are neglected (i.e. misuse and damage of equipment), low levels of productive efficiency may result. Similarly, inadequate information and understanding regarding the acceptability of management change initiatives may effectively frustrate the production controller's efforts to correct operational malfunctions in the production system.

Erroneous models of organisational functioning based on incomplete or mistaken notions about the number and nature of critical variables, together with a lack of understanding of the complexities or interactions among them, can lead to adverse consequences for the organisation in terms of its performance objectives. For example, if the production controller finds that levels of output are falling, he may urge that the production supervisor take certain essential steps to deal with high rates of equipment failure. However, the supervisor may be greatly hindered in his ability to maintain high standards of performance, on account of the opposition and resistance of his subordinates, to improve operational practices and procedures, either in terms of working to rule or imposing an embargo on new methods and modes of operation.

Organisational Task

Organisations, particularly multinational corporations, large commercial enterprises and government bodies, fairly often diversify their task, i.e. product or service, beyond a point which can be easily comprehended in terms of the organisation's structure and functioning. First, an outline will be given of the range of tasks which are involved in the stages by which material resources secured from outside the organisation are converted or transformed into products which are marketed and sold within a manufacturing enterprise.

The primary function of a commercial/manufacturing organisation is to make and sell products or provide services at an economic cost and at a price which guarantees the company sufficient profit on its investment, taking into consideration the costs of production and the level of market demand. Varying amounts of resource materials, i.e. equipment, machinery and plant, are bought by the purchasing department and a work-force is specifically engaged in transforming the raw material by means of a manufacturing process into the desired end-product. In an effort to realise market demand a sales force is deployed for the purpose of enhancing the sales of the product.

Should sales decline, whether because of changing product specification or increased competition from other organisations, it is the function of the research and development department to establish what improvements can be made in either the nature or character of the product in order to recover lost sales. Changes may then be necessary in the manufacturing (production) process so that the product conforms more closely with consumer demand.

Should consumer tastes change or the company recognises new market opportunities which are not being met by its competitors, then that organisation may well decide to look to developing a new product which is either more profitable to manufacture or is competitive in relation to other products sold on the market. In this situation the research and development department will work closely together in designing and planning the production of a new product. The production department will also be involved in assessing and evaluating with the other departments how the new product can be produced commercially on a large scale. Various other functions such as engineering and technical departments will be required to service and maintain the equipment and machinery adopted by the production department in the manufacture of the product. Various quality controls and checks will be built into the system so as to ensure that the particular method and mode of operation called for is functioning appropriately.

Figure 3.3 serves as an aid to the explanation of the scope and nature of the organisation's task. It illustrates the interrelationship between resource materials and production and how the process of product development, manufacture and diversification is arrived at.

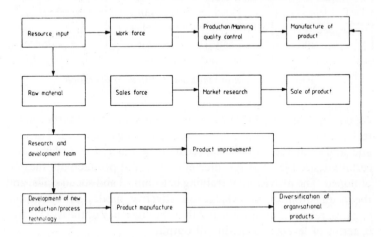

FIGURE 3.3 *The resource/product flow of an organisation*

As an analytical device the concept of organisational task is instructive in the determination of why an organisation exists and which component parts of the system are truly significant in terms of the organisation's output (product/service).

Organisational Technology

What management needs to establish is how the task(s) of the organisation can be achieved and what the major determinants of a successful system of operation are, both in terms of administration and production, in order that the organisation can realise its goals.

In the simplified outline shown in Figure 3.4 there are three primary elements associated with task performance. One is the actual production system involving the process of converting resource materials into product output. The key issue at stake in determining productive efficiency is the resource utilisation of materials (labour,

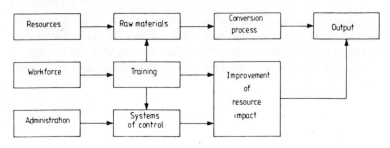

FIGURE 3.4   *An organisational system of operation*

capital and machinery). The role of the work-force is to carry out the technical operations required by the technology involved. The skill and ability of the work-force needs to be realised in order that a certain desired level of resource efficiency and productivity may be obtained. The provision of training in technical and social skills, and the acquisition of knowledge on effective modes of operation, enhance resource utilisation and thus the efficiency of the work-force in terms of levels and quality of output.

The administrative function entails the execution of various operating plans devised for purposes of achieving the organisation's over-all objectives. The principal function of management is to co-ordinate and control the system of operation and to execute and review the production plan in relation to matters of resource allocation and efficiency.

The training of management and supervision is essential in that new and better methods of securing productive and human efficiency and co-operative effort need to be adopted.

With the growing size, mechanisation and specialisation of organisations, it is important to realise that in a technologically based society almost all industry probably requires a higher level of mental ability to co-operate effectively under complicated centrally run progress-control systems than it does to be responsible for simple and routine progress control on the shop floor or within an administrative department. These systems save the supervisor and manager time and effort but make greater demands on his understanding and on his powers of administrating and executing impersonal controls and automatic processes at work.

The technology of an organisation comprises those activities which are intended to achieve its stated task(s). If we accept that all organisations are required to be responsive to their internal and external environment, then organisational technology can be expressed as the practices and procedures which an organisation adopts in order to achieve the smooth conversion of its inputs into product outputs. Organisational technology can be defined as the characteristic way that it acts upon the work-flow.

The technology adopted by each part of the organisation may, and often will, be necessarily different depending upon the particular task of the sub-system. In a manufacturing organisation the technology on the shop floor will reflect the application of skills related to the use and development of machinery. In the administrative offices of the same organisation, however, the technology may reflect not only the skills of cost accounting and financial management but those of personnel management, policy-making and economic decision-making bodies in different parts of the system.

A primary element of the management function is to plan, organise and execute the task of the organisation within certain agreed aims and performance objectives. Responsibility is entrusted to individuals and staff groups for carrying out the work required by adopting a particular method and mode of operation.

The performance efficiency of an organisation is critically dependent on the relationship between the factors involved in determining the task and technology adopted by an organisation. These factors are outlined in Figure 3.5.

The task of the organisation is to meet the needs of its client or customer, and management must therefore be responsive to the changing requirements in matters such as product specification, pricing, delivery dates, product quality, etc.

However, the organisation may be somewhat constrained in its ability to fulfil its task because of the fluctuating nature of product demand. At the same time, resource availability may be unreliable, and this creates major problems in ensuring that delivery dates can be met and product demand not frustrated. If the quality of the resource material used in the production process is variable, this will require the assistance of specialist service support staff in monitoring and evaluating product quality and correcting deviations from product specification.

If product demand has changed because of new customer requirements, the production system may not be able to respond effectively

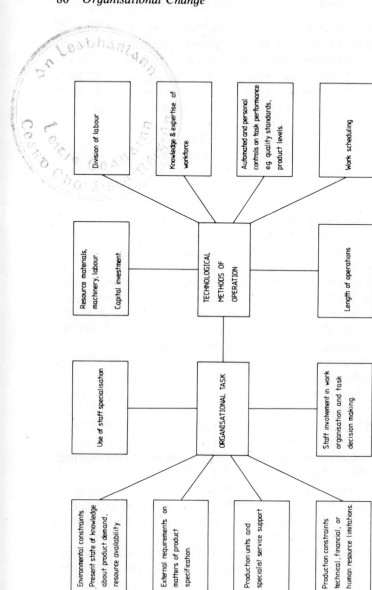

FIGURE 3.5   *Task and technology adopted by an organisation*

in the short term because of technical, financial and human-resource limitations and constraints in production capacity. Changing product specifications may well necessitate new methods or modes of operation performed by the work-force. These new methods require different skills from those which the work-force currently possess. However, because of the specialisation of work in organisations, this may create difficulties as people tend to be narrowly skilled. Introducing improvements in the operating capability of existing plant, machinery and equipment so as to raise levels of output and lower costs of production may not be achieved easily because of inadequate financial resources and/ or because of resistance to change by the work-force, who may feel that their jobs are threatened by introducing more automated methods of production.

In fulfilling product demand production units must liaise closely with service support units, which are required to carry out certain essential tasks such as plant maintenance, so as to maintain desired levels of output and performance capability and reliability. However, resource limitations may impose constraints on the ability of production units to raise levels of output because of equipment failure, and production losses suffered on account of inadequate preventative maintenance.

The task of the manager is to try and overcome these problems by carefully planning and organising the resources available and by raising the skills and expertise of his staff. Involvement of staff is necessary in deciding on how best the work team can circumvent operational problems and fulfil its share of responsibilities in organising and executing its part of the organisation's task.

At the same time, performance efficiency is very much dictated by the methods and modes of operation adopted by a production unit. The manager has to review and assess what mix of resources, i.e. materials, machinery, labour and supervision, is required to achieve a certain level of output at a particular cost of production. The manager's decision will be important in determining the level of capital investment required in improving plant capacity or capability.

Various individuals will be grouped together and made responsible for carrying out a sequence of operations requiring different skills and knowledge from each person. Operating programmes will be planned and work schedules devised so as to enable the work group to realise production plans. At the same time, the method and mode of operation needs to be as flexible as possible to allow for disruptions in work schedules. A major reorganisation of the work programme may be necessary because of technical failures in the system of operation which necessitates reviewing and revising the work load imposed on plant, machinery and people. Fluctuating product demand or unreliability of resource materials interrupts production and undermines the planning and organisation of work schedules. Changes in work programmes require staff to be redeployed and consequently affects the cohesion and unity of different work groups.

An essential requirement therefore of the management system is to record levels of performance efficiency in terms of product quality, cost-effectiveness and desired levels of output by means of automated or manual controls.

By such means the manager can review and appraise the present system of operation and the factors which contribute to deviations from desired levels of performance. In considering alternative methods of dealing with the problems associated with not obtaining continuous and trouble-free operations, the technological methods of operation must be carefully looked at and well understood. Having examined the essential character of the technical system in operation, the manager must decide on how best to fulfil the organisation's task for which he is responsible by taking certain corrective steps in modifying the method or mode of operation being adopted in the organisation by the work-force.

The decisions and actions of management in this respect may or may not enhance the profitability and viability of the organisation, measured in terms of performance improvement and efficiency. This is dependent on how responsive the organisation is to changes in the external market environment, and how adaptive the internal environment is to the task(s) befalling it.

If we assume an organisation to be a problem-facing and problem-solving system of interdependent activities, then management's task is to execute the appropriate methods and means of achieving the adaptation and change of the organisation's system of operation, i.e. its structure and functioning. Administrative procedures and working practices need to be responsive to changes in the organisation's task and environment. Managerial skill and expertise is required for anticipating operational problems and dealing with those environmental forces which threaten to disrupt the system of operation employed by the organisation.

Decisions are required by the organisation on the quantity, quality and economy of output in order to meet changing business demands. Decisions have to be taken on what resources are needed to fulfil uncertain estimates of product demand and on how to structure and perhaps reorganise work schedules and operating programmes of production units and specialist service support functions.

The need for management to act on the work-flow, and thereby respond to problems allied to task performance, leads us to the notion of managerial decision-making and the machinery for decision-making in organisations. Appropriate methods and techniques of managerial control are required over resources (human, physical and financial) for an appropriate course of action which enables the organisation to achieve its goals.

Interruptions in the work-flow or failures in the production system alert a manager to the fact that something which is perhaps either unintended or unanticipated is detracting from over-all levels of performance efficiency.

One of the major preoccupations of a manager or supervisor is with finding causes for delays or hold-ups in the work-flow, responding to breakdowns in the technical system and in having to deal with work which has not been accepted by normal quality-control checks.

The first step is for the manager to identify the problem area and then to gather information and ideas in order to determine clearly what the problem is. An important element of defining the problem is pinpointing the cause of the problem from the various links observed in the chain of events leading up to the malfunction in the system of operation.

The next major step is to assess and evaluate what course of action is required in relation to the organisation's performance objectives. Alternative courses of action need to be examined and measured in terms of certain essential performance criteria. The final decision as to what action needs to be taken to sustain or improve levels of performance should take into account the uncertainty and the likely probability of the desired outcome.

An important consideration in the application and use of technology is the organisation of the production process (work-flow) and the ability of management to put into effect the various administrative, procedural and operational control systems at their disposal.

Machine automation, by displacing routine jobs, alters both the composition of responsibilities and the amount of information exchange which can be planned in advance, and thereby limits the value of written rules and procedures. Those who plan for, set up and operate more automatic equipment are highly independent, and these activities are less likely to be well documented.

Increases in either task variability or plant automation necessitate more extensive two-way communication between individuals involved in the work process. This is because it either reduces the length of any single production run or because any breakdown in the automated process requires immediate problem-solving. Impersonal controls such as performance reports and formal rules and operational procedures are rendered inadequate in these circumstances. Instead, the organisation must design smaller administrative units to facilitate face-to-face interaction problem-solving and joint decision-making (Tracy and Azumi, 1976). In large organisations unit effectiveness increases with increased delegation in terms of efficient performance, initiation of work improvements, scheduling and coordinating operations and achieving work reliability (Mahoney *et al.*, 1972).

The supervisor who is not tightly controlled administratively can absorb operational and technological uncertainty about operational efficiency and possible interruptions to the flow of work and act as a buffer for the work group from outside pressures and demands (March and Simon, 1958; Thompson, 1967). The resultant insulation fosters group solidarity and enhances autonomy and participation (Hrebiniak, 1974).

Khandwalla (1974), in examining the differences between high-profit and low-profit companies, suggests that strongly mass-output-orientated technologies (large-batch, assembly-line and continuous process) would be more productive if they considered vertical integration, decentralisation of top-level decisions and the adoption of a sophisticated control and information system, as opposed to crude and punitive performance measures.

Moch and Morse (1977) found that innovations are adopted more frequently in large, specialised, functionally differentiated hospitals which decentralise powers of decision-making to lower levels. However, in large organisations lower-level personnel are in a better position to facilitate the adoption of innovations which suit their needs and interests while resisting those which do not (Wilson, 1966; Zaltman *et al.*, 1973).

Research on organisational control systems and measures of performance indicate that standardised and centralised bureaucratic control procedures can adversely affect organisational effectiveness (Child, 1974–5; Dunbar, 1977; Negandhi and Prasad, 1971; Turcotte, 1974). Child reported that firms which had higher sales growth used fewer highly formalised procedures, particularly for justifying new projects. Rosner (1968), in a hospital study, found that as standardised control procedures came more to the fore, so fewer new drugs were tested. Product innovation was deterred by the control system and the need to avoid detection in making any test errors.

Reimann and Neghandi (1975), in a study of thirty manufacturing organisations in India found that more effective organisations, measured in terms of an average of profits and sales for the preceding five years, adopted formalised procedures to control decentralised decision-making with respect to human and material resources. The least effective firms chose a similar strategy of control; however, they mainly emphasised those procedures involving the control of material resources and tended to neglect their human resources in the sense of formalising manpower planning, employee selection, performance appraisal and training.

The more effective firms also revealed a greater ability to hire, utilise and retain high-level manpower, sustain morale and job satisfaction, and achieve good interpersonal and interdepartmental relations adopting formalised procedures to control decentralisation of decision-making processes. Having identified the essential facts of managerial control of business operations, an inappropriate control system is now looked at, to what changes are needed in the control structure of an organisation. In a petro-chemical company, because of the large volume of business and the complex technology of a process plant, responsibility for sales, production and plant maintenance was given to specialist departments, who exercised tight control over departmental performance by devising an extensive set of working procedures and rules, requesting daily written reports on production levels, maintenance costs and sales. Deviations from desired performance levels were promptly jumped on and separate management initiatives were taken by the heads of each department in order to correct operational deficiences in their own sectors. Little information about current problems was shared and delegated responsibilities were poorly defined; and the jurisdiction of subordinates overlapped.

In passing on the highly variable demands of the market for

chemicals the marketing department often failed to check the feasibility of the commitments they had made with the production department. Changes in production schedules were sometimes impossible to fulfil. Large amounts of plant maintenance were held back in attempts to meet new product demands at short notice. Sale commitments, however, were still not fully met. Production failures and problems of starting up and shutting down plant processes meant that senior supervisors were more often than not running from one crisis to another, temporarily resolving each new problem as best they could.

At the same time, higher management continually adopted a close surveillance of unit cost performance, material wastage and lost production time. Subordinates bitterly resented acceding to unreasonable demands and accepting responsibility for providing performance reports which might incriminate them.

An attempt was made to exercise greater control over the organisation's environment and the unpredictability of product demand. Work groups were regrouped so as to meet the needs of individual plants and units of production. Specialist services were undertaken by staff whose responsibility was to design and implement new technological processes which minimised plant failures and prevented variability of the product in terms of quality and quantity.

These steps reduced the variability of the production system and increased the response capacity of each production unit and the maintenance forces attached to it in handling the multiple changes in operating schedules which arose. Quite clearly serious consideration has to be given to the organisational control structure and to the training, selection, appraisal and planning of manpower needs in ensuring that the operational control system is working effectively.

One of the features of the reorganisation of work and specialist services was an investigation of the technological function and the role of specialists. Strong criticism emerged of the type of work load and who was best fitted to do it. Serious concern was also expressed about promotional steps being blocked. Misunderstandings occurred about who should deal with technical problems at the plant level. This was partly due to the mismatch and imbalance between people's skills and experiences. Questions were asked about how the company was planning to motivate people who might be stuck in jobs for a long time and on a maximum salary level. Criticism was made of the annual staff-assessment exercise and of the undue emphasis on managerial training and the absence of on-the-job training. The feeling was that certain managers could see themselves moving on to other jobs and would be more concerned to make a name quickly rather than worry about the long-term consequences of their actions because of uncertainties about career development.

Organisational Structure

The structure of an organisation can be viewed in terms of a hierarchy of people in jobs of various technical descriptions who have been made responsible for enacting a part of the organisation's task and authorised by the position or office they hold. In this hierarchical position, individuals and work groups are expected to fulfill a particular role or function. People are required to behave and act according to the particular demands of their job and are influenced by the organisation's view of how they should carry out their duties and obligations.

The structure of an organisation is not, however, the charts and job descriptions and work-flow diagrams usually employed to describe those roles and the relationships between them. The structure of an organisation is the pattern of actual behaviours as it is created and recreated by the members of that organisation.

Changing an organisation's structure implies changing the pattern of recurring behaviour. A feature of management is the holding of performance-review meetings, in order to tackle outstanding service support problems to mainstream operations. This involves the co-ordination and control of various interrelated tasks. When this becomes a continuing management practice, a norm among managers and an expectation on the part of subordinates, it will then be part of the role structure of the organisation and it will mark a change in the structure and functioning of the system in operation put in by management (Kahn, 1974).

At any one time people can and invariably do extend and redefine their jobs (tasks) so that the formally prescribed roles, responsibilities and authorities of an individual may be at variance with the expectations of relevant others of the particular position or office he holds. This is largely a question of people acting out and exercising certain powers and initiatives that they possess in situations over others in different parts of the organisation. For example, service support functions may challenge and resist acting on a work order submitted by an operating department because the latter is unable to resolve competing and conflicting resource demands from those service support units. At the same time, service support functions may decide to exercise personal initiative in co-ordinating and controlling other support work because it facilitates the speed and progressing of their jobs. However, such initiatives may well undermine or frustrate the plans and work schedules of other departments. The reason may be that there is an absence in the organisational hierarchy of an appropriate level of authority conferred on a manager for co-ordinating and controlling projects involving different specialist departments. Wherever such problems arise, it is always difficult to pin down distinct areas of responsibilities and levels of accountability. However, unless this is achieved there will always be some avoidance of responsibility for operational problems, and separate initiatives will be taken in order to advance or protect the different interests and goals of each department.

These problems of organisational structure create conflict and competition and make it difficult for individuals, groups and departments to work together harmoniously. The formal rules and procedures which management imposes by laying down desired working practices and procedures may not help or advance an individual's efforts to respond to changing task demands and unforeseen problems. This is because of his inability to work within formal organisational structures where there are competing and conflicting needs and goals among people occupying different roles and responsibilities.

The outcome of any efforts of management to bring about improvements in performance efficiency is very much dependent on how flexible or rigid the organisation's structure is, and whether it enables people to act on change initiatives by exercising the appropraite level of discretion needed to deal with the changing demands made upon them in their task.

The specificity and complexity of the organisation's task demands a complex division of labour and the allocation of tasks among functions and specialists within it. Although an individual task may be routine, a large measure of co-ordination is required. The occupational specialisms found in engineering maintenance departments, for instance, mean that various different trades and skilled workers are required, which calls for a large measure of co-ordination of effort, in spite of the fact that the actual work may be routine. Therefore, developments in methods and modes of operation in order to improve performance capability and reliability of operations involve complex programme changes. Efforts to adapt the system of operation so as to enable the organisation to be more responsive to changing business needs is constrained by concentrating authority at the top of the organisation, because changes in work programmes require specialist knowledge and skill from people lower down the management hierarchy. People with the technical expertise required for implementing changes in the planning and designing of systems of operation need to be involved. (See Aiken and Hage, 1968; Hage and Aiken, 1970; Thompson, 1965.) The impact of specialists in the decision-making process is through them having some power in the hierarchy. If they are without these decision-making powers, their contributions are minimised and the rate of innovation and programme change decreases. Organisations with a large number of specialist functions and several layers of authority in the managerial hierarchy are associated with higher rates of programme change than smaller tightly controlled enterprises (Aiken and Hage, 1967). Joint programmes of work require interdependent relations among different specialist functions and occupational groups. The planning and execution of programme changes can involve a great deal of conflicting and often competing ideas and proposals which need to be constructively managed and resolved. Collaboration is required among the departments involved at a level which enables the organisation to achieve a unity of purpose and collectivity of effort. The need for integration is required by the conflicting demands of the working environment and the complexities of the different tasks and modes of operation adopted by specialist functions.

The management of change programmes requires quite significantly different orientations of departments being taken into consideration, such as the particular goals of the departments, and the different practices and procedures adopted. Departments therefore vary not only in the specific tasks they perform but also in the underlying behaviour and outlook of their members.

An important aspect of the organisation's structure is the type and extent of formalisation with regard to the rules and procedures designed to handle contingencies faced by the organisation. In highly formalised, standardised and specialised situations, the occupant of a particular role or function may well have his behaviour highly specified with few options that he need consider in carrying out his job. This would not be compatible, however, with a non-routine and non-uniform task situation involving different specialist groups working in conditions of change and uncertainty. The rate of programme change decreases with the increase in the formalisation of rules and procedures. A formal system of operation is therefore not as flexible or as adaptive as it might otherwise be in coping with unforeseen developments or contingencies. In organisations that establish highly specific routines for the members to follow there is likely to be little time, support or reward for involvement in new ideas and programmes of innovation which enhance performance efficiency.

Impersonal rules and formally prescribed procedures with which individuals are asked to comply delimit an individual's sense of responsibility and initiative in his job. In periods of changing business needs an organisation may be unable to respond adaptively enough because its ways of working are too rigid and inflexible. Since the rules prescribe the kinds of decisions to be made, those in decision-making positions tend to create more rules when situations arise for which there are no precedents. Rules become security for the employees. The personnel in the system may become increasingly less able to operate on the basis of their own initiative, and in fact may want the amount of freedom they can exercise reduced. On the other hand, the questioning and challenging of a problematic situation by a subordinate may be viewed as undermining the authority of a superior, which may effectively frustrate the organisation's need to apply the subordinate's specialised ability or skill which is required to solve a particular operational problem. Alienation from the job and the organisation is found among professionals where authority in organisations is centralised and the members possess little opportunity to participate in decision-making (Aiken and Hage, 1966).

The behaviour of individuals, if inappropriately guided by the organisation by either too much or too little specification, can have negative performance outcomes for an organisation. If the demands made upon an individual by the formal requirements of his job are incompatible with those people with whom he has to work (who consequently persuade him to act differently), he will experience conflicting demands made upon him, which can be described as *role conflict*. In some cases the organisational demands themselves may be in conflict, such as when a supervisor requests someone to acquire material which is unavailable through normal channels and at the same time prohibits violations of normal channels (Kahn *et al.*, 1964).

When a person is asked to perform a series of tasks that are incompatible with one another, he can be said to experience 'role overload', in the sense that it is impossible for him to complete all his assigned tasks at one time. The 'overload' can be viewed in terms of a conflict of priorities where the individual must decide which pressures to comply with and which to fend off. If it is impossible to deny any of these pressures, the individual will be unable to exert effective influence or control on the events for which he is responsible. Where there is a lack of clearly laid-down guidelines and terms of reference in a job, the incumbent may not know what he is to do and the uncertainty he is faced with can be described as *role ambiguity*.

The degree of formalisation of the expectations about how a particular role should be played is an important component of how the role is played and how the individual reacts to his situation in the organisation. From the standpoint of improving the performance of individuals within the organisation, increasing their morale and improving the over-all performance of the organisation, the often changing demands of the job must be considered in terms of how clearly definable can and should roles and responsibilities be and to what degree can and do personal and interpersonal relations obstruct or alternatively contribute to the realisation of company and individual performance needs. Sufficient flexibility in the organisation's rules and procedures is required to enable the personnel in it to realise their goals. The more complex and uncertain the task is, and the more specialist the knowledge of individuals, then the more necessary it is that individuals are capable of exercising initiative and discretion and are able to act on the work-flow to forestall or correct a fault in the system of operation. Powers of decision-making must lie in the hands of those persons who alone can exercise proper judgement on what action to take. In instances where the assignment demands close collaboration of specialist functions then decisions need to be arrived at with the commitment of those involved in order to ensure that work plans will be carried out responsibly.

If individuals and work groups can agree to work within certain performance standards, then it may be more productive to relax or modify an existing set of rules and procedures which are not as appropriate or applicable as they might be, either because of operational constraints or because of the need for the system of operation to be adaptive to continuously changing demands and unforeseen developments.

Although it has been argued that less rigidly defined roles and responsibilities encourage the adaptability and responsiveness of organisations to uncertainty in a constantly changing environment and provide more favourable conditions for innovation and change, there are several problems associated with a more flexible system of operation.

In devolving responsibility and authority to lower levels of the hierarchy, and among different specialist functions, there is likely to be a struggle for power and influence between different sectional interests. Competing and conflicting expectations and demands will arise about programme changes and the role and contribution of each function because of the different objectives, time perspectives, rules and procedures and methods of operation independently adopted. At the level of the individual, anxiety will be hightened by assuming accountability for work of a complex nature, requiring interdependence and support from other specialist functions in conditions of uncertainty when the individual is not always able to control and influence the actions of others and predict the likely outcome of whatever decisions and courses of action he takes. Unless the conflict and anxiety is arrested and channelled productively, efforts will be made to enforce programmed changes by asking for a restoration of rules and procedures, centralisation of decision-making and by insisting on the rights of office and by restoring the power and position of those in higher management. Flexibility of working is lost and boundaries will harden between functions, restricting the change initiatives being put forward which require close collaboration from other specialist functions. The integration and co-ordination of work operating programmes is disrupted when separate initiatives are taken without consideration of how it affects other units or sub-system modes of operation. Conflict will be settled arbitrarily and solutions imposed from above which may not satisfy any one party. Resistances will build up against externally imposed initiatives which threaten to undermine or supplant any part of that department's currently operating practices and procedures which it desires to preserve.

One of the prerequisite conditions for success in any significant organisational programme change is for the causes and consequences of these phenomena to be carefully understood and considered in the introduction and implementation of new methods and means of operation.

People within Organisations

An important feature of organisations is the development of social groupings which establish and maintain certain recognisable practices and procedures which may or may not adversely affect performance efficiency. Some industrial work groups are known to have firm attitudes to what is an acceptable and desirable level of output from its members. The regulation and control of work is very much influenced by such groupings on the shop floor which are sometimes based on seemingly irrational factors such as sentiment and friendship, and which conform to certain traditional values out of which the work groups develop thier own norms or expectations of what constitutes a 'proper' level of output. What this means in effect is that they impose control on a work group's behaviour which effectively undermines management's powers of enforcement of differing standards and desired levels of performance (Homans, 1959). It is not unknown for work groups to 'walk-out' on a job in protest over the alleged treatment or disciplining of a colleague by management. Earnings are sometimes forgone to protect a certain colleague's job when such actions limit the performance efficiency and productivity of a work team, either because of overmanning or inefficiency.

Resistance to change does not necessarily imply that people are opposed to working any harder or that they are hostile to the company. The social relations which people enter into at work tend not to be a result of deliberate planning in order to protect themselves from exploitation and promotion of their own interests but rather the result of common attitudes, interests and values. The imposition of sanctions and restrictions by work groups on output, in the form of 'go-slows', 'work to rules', or by adopting a policy of 'non-co-operation', may be explained in terms of a rational and realistic appraisal of their situation by workers.

There may be the fear of a decline and fall in earnings due to a loss of personal control over certain working practices and procedures which may be taken over by mechanical or administrative controls incorporated within the production system. This may well lead to manipulation of the payment system in order to ensure that earnings are preserved by counteracting the loss of certain informally held powers of initiative and discretion (Lupton, 1963; Roy, 1952 and 1954).

There may be a conflict of interest which, say, arises when technical innovation calls for changes in working arrangements which break down previously established social ties (Trist and Bamforth, 1951; Rice, 1958). The opposition of work groups and individuals to changes in their role and responsibilities may evoke anxiety and concern about the threat and loss of privileges and status as in earnings differentials between one work-force (craft) and another (Sayles, 1958).

Although management may well be aware of the informal practices and codes of conduct among different groups, it is important for managers to understand the basis for some of the underlying causes and consequences of work-group ties and loyalties based on shared norms and values. Careful judgement and discretion is needed in deciding what management change initiatives to introduce, because they may threaten to alter or modify existing working relations involving well-established customs and practices. Consideration needs to be given to existing social relations at work between people, because any changes which disrupt previous relations may well be strongly resisted.

In order to explain the behaviour of people it is necessary to look at the controls over individuals' behaviour – namely, technological, administrative, economic, quasi-legal and organisational controls within the system of operation (Crozier, 1964; Glegg, 1975; Georgio, 1973; Lawler, 1976; Rice, 1963; Woodward, 1970). The behaviour of individuals and work groups will normally be affected by the type of controls they are subjected to. The type of control will determine role expectations, and controls will differ from unit to unit. Therefore, the behaviour of workers in relation to output is seen as a *resultant* of the interplay of human forces, with the various controls exercised by the task, technology, structure and environment of that organisation. The interrelationship between them helps explain the actions of people in organisations and why attempts at collective control are made by members of the work-force over levels of output and earnings.

Relations between individuals which are generated by the production process can encourage the sharing of certain dominant values and norms about pay and working conditions which are contrary to management's own goals. Those managements who wish to introduce changes in working practices and procedures may be resisted or opposed by a work-force who believes that the changes envisaged do not appear to be in their best interests.

If management wishes to change people's job, in terms of the task they have to perform, the productive process they have to operate, or the responsibilities which they have held, then management must be prepared to bargain and negotiate on wage rates and on the deployment of labour affected by changes either in technical or administrative systems of operation.

Change involves uncertainty for people and arouses feelings of insecurity which they see as a threat to them, and consequently individuals and work groups try to prevent or resist it. Groups will have adopted work patterns which have become accepted, and which nobody may want changed. It is these customs and practices, and probably not the job, that change threatens.

On the other hand, change must be accomplished alongside current systems of operation within an organisation or system of work relationships. Paradoxically, the manager's job is to accomplish both stability and change. In order to maximise both the productivity of the technological process under consideration and maintain high motivation among subordinates, which facilitates productive efforts, he must endeavour to minimise the frequency with which the patterns of work-flow and co-ordination are disturbed. Disruptive changes in the work-flow which undermine the predictability and maintenance of a smooth, continuous and trouble-free system of operation are the major sources of low morale, debilitating stress and destructive emotional reactions (Beynon, 1973; Katz and Kahn, 1966). When the changes enforced are incompatible with the personality of the person concerned, they evoke emotional reactions which change the pattern of contact and interaction between people. Tension and anxiety may cause people to make mistakes or omit certain procedures, and this can adversely affect the work-flow sequence – which can reverberate throughout the system, creating further conflict and stress.

An important element of the manager's task is the detection of disturbances or problems in the system of human relationships which affect or alter the work-flow unit in his domain. At the same time, the manager continuously faces numerous technical problems directly related to the work-flow and the system of operation which invariably undermine his efforts in fulfilling his performance objectives. Certain major changes in the system of operation may therefore be required. For instance, changes may be necessary in methods and modes of operation in order to be able to raise levels of output so that market demand may be realised. Higher costs of production may require that the system of operation is modified so that performance efficiency can be improved for purposes of keeping unit costs down. The problems facing managers in introducing changes in methods and modes of operation require them to deal with conflicting and uneasy relations with their staff, whose patterns of work and associated skills may have had to be revised or fundamentally altered.

Change may well involve operational research, organisation and methods study and the use of new procedures and techniques, which can give people the impression that they may not be able to adapt and respond effectively to the enormity of change and that they are not essential once the new practices and procedures have been introduced. Certainly, the threat of redundancy can have a part to play in any resistance to change. The computerisation of many administrative clerical functions has enabled much speedier information-processing and greater facility of handling complex information. However, the rate at which information can be received and passed on tends eventually to heighten anxiety and insecurity concerning the validity of the more numerous decisions and actions that can be taken when the information is perhaps suspect or challengeable.

Most changes tend to disturb interpersonal relations as far as the influence and control element is concerned in working relations. The growth of the purchasing function, for example, as a control and information system as regards the price, quality and delivery of a product to a customer, can take away from a production manager the initiation and control over dealings with suppliers and in price negotiations with customers. With the control and influence that the purchasing agent now has over production schedules and costs of operation he can afford to be far less complaint and obliging to production managers than he might otherwise have been. He also threatens their authority by suggesting at times that they might use cheaper, lower-quality material.

Change may threaten a man's opportunity to initiate and control events. For instance, before computerisation a supervisor directed the staff who worked with him; after computerisation there is less opportunity and need for him to issue orders and initiate courses of action. The change may also mean that the supervisor who used to directly issue work instructions now has to wait passively for a higher authority to take the initiative.

On routine jobs, or on jobs where employees are used to being independent of others, direct orders from management occur infrequently. When change occurs, they become subject to all sorts of pressures from supervisors, engineers and superiors. Suddenly they find that someone is checking up on them and barraging them with far more orders than is usual. This sharp increase in control may well be resisted and resented because it is seen to reduce feelings of autonomy and independence. The use of time studies in accounting departments has often had this effect. Similarly, production managers often resist change when it is initiated by service support functions to mainstream operations because it threatens to undermine current operations and raise uncertainty of outcomes. Among service support functions there will also be resistance to change, from the cost accountant because the change is too expensive, or the personnel manager because it would disrupt a tricky union relationship. Here again the motives of the persons viewing the effects of change on their positions may create a resistance to change.

Engineers, for example, often resist suggestions by purchasing agents to utilise new materials which have come to the purchasing agents' attention through salesmen. Engineers feel that they should have exclusive authority to specify the material used, and that they should tell the purchasing agent what sorts of material should be used – not vice versa. So when purchasing agents try to influence the engineers, they are reversing the influence process (Sayles and Strauss, 1966).

In order to achieve support and co-operation for a particular course of action which effectively alters existing interpersonal relations, working practices and procedures, the manager above all has to consider how the persons concerned by the changed plans will respond.

Figure 3.6 summarises the principal elements in the management of business operations just described.

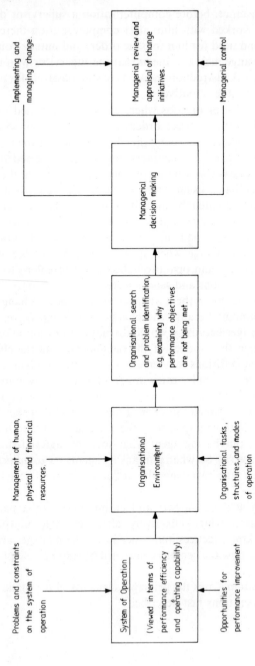

FIGURE 3.6   *A process for managing organisational systems of operation*

Identifying Organisational Change Needs

The model shown in Figure 3.6 serves initially to direct a manager's attention to the desired levels of performance efficiency and the current capability of the system in operation within organisations. Because of the changing problems and needs facing an organisation attempting to realise its performance objectives, an examination and evaluation needs to be made of the contributing factors associated with the particular nature and character of the organisation's task, technology, structure, management and human-resources systems. In its attempts to examine why performance objectives are not being met management must endeavour to search out the causes of failure in the system of operation which lies within the organisation's control and influence.

The following key groups of questions raise some of the problematic issues which management may need to face in order to overcome the forces and influences restraining or adversely affecting the organisation's performance efficiency:

(i) What is and/or is not being produced efficiently, at what standard of performance, for what reasons? What have been the causes and consequences, with what results?

(ii) Has there been the necessary co-ordination and control of systems in operation? Do individual work groups have clear-cut terms of reference and has the necessary liaison and co-operation been secured between separate but interdependent functions?

(iii) What is the level of absenteeism and labour turnover in the organisation? Does morale affect the level and quality of output? Is management able to secure the right level of responsibility and commitment from staff to work towards performance improvement?

(iv) How effective are managerial control systems in enabling the organisation to realise its performance objectives?

Process of managerial decision-making

Once management has identified the major stumbling-blocks to the organisation's goals, it needs, from alternative courses of action, to resolve certain outstanding problems. The decision-making body may need to consider what needs to be changed in the method and mode of operation: for what purpose, by whom, at what cost, and with what desired result? Changes may be needed in the management of the human-resources system and/or in the organisation's policies and procedures. Industrial unrest and grievances which lead to strike action by the work-force may serve to highlight that the company's industrial-relations policies and procedures need to be reviewed.

Implementation of change

Once a decision has been taken management needs to implement the plans and procedures devised for effecting a change in the organisation's structure and functioning. There are certain requisite managerial skills of communication, decision-making and problem-solving which need to be applied in a change situation.

Management requires feedback and information on the impact that their actions and decisions have had. By monitoring the progress of change initiatives and levels of performance attainment management can then establish how successfully the changes have been implemented. Management is then in a more informed position for purposes of reviewing and reappraising what changes are required in its plans, policies, administrative procedures and working practices, in order to realise the performance objectives set.

The functions of management

Having established what the organisation's task, technology, membership, structure and environment entail, it is now possible to establish more clearly how management can act on them.

While it is true that no two organisations are the same in the way that they function, because of the different tasks, structures, etc., to be found, one function which is common to all is that of management. The general managerial functions which can be established within the organisational framework developed in this chapter are as follows:

(i) Identifying the task domain – the needs of customer/client groups, and changes required in internal systems of operation.

(ii) Setting the necessary structure for ensuring that the organisation's performance goals are realised – by defining individual roles and responsibilities and by co-ordinating and integrating the specialist tasks of different functions and operating units.

(iii) Deciding on the necessary and appropriate technology for the performance and completion of the task.

(iv) Setting and reviewing managerial performance objectives.

(v) Reviewing and allocating scarce resources, i.e. men, money, materials.

(vi) Making decisions and taking courses of action on deviations from desired levels of performance.

(vii) Maintaining a balance between the competing and conflicting demands and interests of the membership (departments and personnel involved).

(viii) Evaluating decisions, task outcomes and levels of goal attainment.

The managerial functions outlined above provide a basis for enabling management to adapt and respond successfully to changes in its organisational environment.

A systematic approach to managerial change initiatives designed at making improvements in an organisation's system of operation may be achieved in the following manner:

(i) Setting organisational change goals.

(ii) Specifying performance objectives.

(iii) Designing and developing a plan for product manufacture.

(iv) Co-opting specialist expertise.

(v) Devising procedures for administering task operations.

(vi) Building a supportive climate for change.

(vii) Identifying changes needed in the system of operation, i.e. technical methods and modes of operation.

(viii) Examining and evaluating product resource requirements, including finance, and material resources.

(ix) Implementing change.

(x) Monitoring of performance after the changes in systems of operation have been made.

(xi) Identifying and rectifying problems of implementing change.

(xii) Evaluating the level of goal achievement.

Interdependence of Organisational Systems in Operation

In a complex organisation interrelated tasks, structures, technologies and systems of management have been developed. However, some of the functional relationships may not be closely integrated.

In the simplified outline (see Figure 3.7) of a complex organisation the component parts of the organisation can become remote from each other even though they are clearly interdependent. For example, perhaps because of the quality or unreliability of a particular piece of equipment adopted in the production process, breakdowns may be such that production losses are incurred. Requests by the operating department concerned for the purchase of what is a dearer but generally considered more reliable item of equipment may be baulked by administration because of the cost involved. While in certain cases lower levels of management could authorise certain amounts of expenditure, the staffing structure may be such that senior management may reserve the right to make the final decision on such matters in spite of the fact that the expenditure envisaged is within an agreed budget for those operational costs involving the renewal or replacement of equipment. Senior management may react to the expenditure request by demanding that lower levels of management establish, first, the reason for the breakdown of the equipment. Administration,

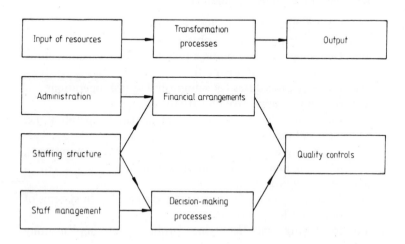

FIGURE 3.7   *Interdependence of organisational systems in operation*

on the other hand, may claim that the costs incurred are due to negligence and that the requisite operating procedures and rules could not have been followed properly.

What began as a simple decision to replace an existing piece of equipment with a new one produces underlying tensions in the work team involved in the production system experiencing failure. The manager of that group may be ordered to make an investigation so as to ensure that no shortcomings or errors of judgement can be accredited to him. Distrust and suspicion among subordinates about the nature of the investigation and fear of blame may well lead to real concerns and difficulties being hidden. Insufficient information is thus known of the true cause of production breakdowns in the system of operation, and quality control is seriously undermined. Certain working practices may be employed by different parties which are unknown to management and in contravention of formally pre-scribed administrative procedures, and this seriously undermines levels of cost-effectiveness.

The central question is: how can such problems associated with the organisational system of operation and the managerial control of them arise? As managers move to the top of the hierarchy (staffing structure), decisions lose coherence and rationality due to the increase in the number of systems, e.g. production-control systems, quality-control systems, cost-control systems and accounting sys-tems, and the manager's incapacity to deal with the complexities of all these controls without all the necessary information and understand-ing of human- and material-resource efficiency. This has a direct impact on the quality of staff management and managerial re-sourcefulness in that the manager's powers of decision-making are undermined and he may take incorrect initiatives which his work team cannot either act on, or cannot deal with any ensuing problems.

Also, the division of labour within the organisation causes its members to build biases towards their sub-goals which insulate them from the other systems that make up the organisation. Furthermore, there is the point that participation and the delegation of authority may be a necessity because of a lack of adequate control information on performance capability or communication sources. This results in uncertainty and confusion within departments and poor co-ordination across departments which are jointly responsible for a particular task or project. A further point is that influence within an organisation is determined largely by the organisation's communication system. It is possible that influence may be gained as a result of expert knowledge in relation to an organisational problem. Influence centres may therefore be separated from the decision-making centres within an organisation (Dunkerley, 1969).

The Management of Organisational Boundaries

The degree of adaptability of a company's scheme of operation is subject to the structure and functioning adopted within that organisation.

Organisation structures represent boundaries between functions with specific and overlapping tasks, responsibilities and authority to act. Because of the fact that various people define boundaries between functions differently, the actual exercise of responsibility and authority for deciding on service support and operational demands is not fixed or necessarily structurally determined. The eventual performance of an organisation in terms of what gets done, by whom and at what cost is determined by the management of boundaries.

The issue of responsibility and authority is particularly important in line/service support relations. The amount of influence an operating department has, or has not, over the decisions affecting the quality and level of service provision is directly related to the exercise of responsibility and authority by both parties. In some instances the line function successfully influences the desired level and quality of service provision by authorising certain steps to be taken. In other situations the service support function may resist attempts by an operations unit to dictate the level and quality of service support. In other cases one will find the responsibility and authority more evenly shared between different departments.

Although the level of responsibility and authority between departments needs to be as clearly defined as possible, changes in the demands of the business may be such that they need to be continuously reviewed and reassessed.

The following comments reflect the sort of situation where the level of responsibility/authority which ought to exist between departments is at variance with the wishes of those concerned with efficient operations:

'Whenever we are faced with a real problem other departments tend to be slow in responding.'
'Why don't priorities attached to jobs not reflect operational requirements?'
'It's difficult to get that function to recognise this problem.'
'Work is not co-ordinated properly.'
'We have little or no influence over decisions affecting the quality and reliability of the service support we get.'

Another aspect of felt responsibility and desired authority are the initiatives departments make to influence the practices and procedures of other departments. The success of any initiative is dependent on the amount of influence which can be exerted over decisions affecting one's contribution to another department's work. Departments which are called on to conduct certain investigations of operational capability and efficiency are not necessarily involved or influential to any significant degree in an evaluation and implementation of the findings. Potential improvements in service support provisions may therefore be missed.

Frustrated initiatives, resistance to change and disagreements between line and service support departments often signify the fact that people possess a high level of felt responsibility for a task and yet perceive an absence of authority, or rather control, over the decisions affecting their own efforts to provide a more efficient service support to mainstream operations.

Summary

This chapter has endeavoured to examine the component parts of an organisation's structure and functioning in an effort to recognise and appreciate the organisational forces and influences acting upon a manager in his task of coping and adapting to uncertainty in a changing work environment.

The adaptability of an organisation's structure and functioning to pressures and demands for change is essentially complex and difficult. In identifying some of the malfunctions in an organisation's mode of operation and systems of management the changes that are necessary if the organisation is to cope and adapt successfully to change have been signposted.

The following points at issue attempt to summarise the key organisational elements to the problem of managing organisational change:

(i) The various ways of allocating and distributing work and authority between different individuals, groups and functions.

(ii) The underlying nature and character of organisational conflict and co-operation inherent in the management of boundaries.

(iii) Human motivation, satisfaction and incentives (the impact of social relations upon systems of operation and the work-flow).

(iv) The dilemma inherent in organisations of individuals striving for freedom of action and self-determination – which then threatens an organisation's need for control and order.

(v) The network and systems of communication, information, rules and regulations which serve as orders and which constrain the personal initiative needed for individuals and work groups to respond to management change initiatives.

(vi) Technical and administrative changes called for in an organisation's mode of operation.

The next chapter makes an assessment of the very many different approaches and methods adopted by organisations for applying these management functions to these same problems. The purpose of Chapter 4 is to evaluate alternative systems of management critically and to consider new forms of organisational structure and functioning which are adaptive and responsive to environmental change.

References

Aiken, M. and Hage, J. (1966) 'Organizational Alienation: a Comparative Analysis', *American Sociological Review*, vol. 31, no. 4, August, pp. 497–507.

Aiken, M. and Hage, J. (1967) 'Programme Change and Organizational Properties: a Comparative Analysis', *American Journal of Sociology*, vol. 72, no. 5, pp. 503–19.

Aiken, M. and Hage, J. (1973) 'Organizational Interdependence and Intra-organizational Structure', *American Sociological Review*, vol. 33, no. 6, December, pp. 925–6.

Beynon, H. (1973) *Working for Fords* (Harmondsworth, Penguin).

Child, J. (1974–5) 'Managerial and Organisational Factors Associated with Company Performance', *Journal of Management Studies*, part 1, vol. 11 (1974), pp. 175–89; part 2, vol. 12 (1975), pp. 12–27.

Crozier, M. (1964) *The Bureaucratic Phenomena* (University of Chicago Press).

Dunbar, R. L. M. (1977) 'Control in Organisation', Discussion Paper, Berlin Institute of Management.

Dunkerley, D. (1969) *The Foreman – Aspects of Task and Structure* (London, Routledge & Kegan Paul).

Georgio, P. (1973) 'The Goal Paradigm and Notes Towards a Counter Paradigm', *Administrative Science Quarterly*, vol. 18, no. 3, pp. 291–310.

Glegg, S. (1975) *Power, Rule and Domination* (London, Routledge & Kegan Paul).

Hage, J. and Aiken, M. (1970) *Social Change in Complex Organizations* (New York, Random House).

Hall, R. H. (1972) *Organization: Structure and Process* (Englewood Cliffs, N.J., Prentice-Hall).

Homans, G. C. (1959) *The Human Group* (London, Routledge & Kegan Paul).

Hrebiniak, L. G. (1974) 'Job Technology, Supervision and Work Group Structure', *Administrative Science Quarterly*, vol. 19, no. 3, pp. 395–410.

Kahn, R. (1974) 'Organizations' Development: Some Problems and Proposals', *Journal of Applied Behavioral Science*, vol. 10, no. 4, pp. 485–502.

Kahn, R. L., Wolfe, D. M., Quinn, R. P., Snock, J. D. and Rosenthal, R. A. (1964) *Organizational Stress* (New York, Wiley).

Katz, D. and Kahn, R. L. (1966) *The Social Psychology of Organizations* (New York, Wiley).

Khandwalla, P. N. (1974) 'Mass Output Orientation of Operations Technology and Organizational Structure', *Administrative Science Quarterly*, vol. 19, no. 1, pp. 74–97.

Lawler, E. E. (1976) 'Control Systems in Organizations', in *Handbook of Industrial and Organizational Psychology*, ed. M. D.

Dunette (Chicago, Rand McNally) pp. 1247–1291.

Lupton, T. (1963) *On the Shop Floor* (Oxford, Pergamon Press).

Mahoney, T. A., Frost, P., Crandall, N. F. and Weigzel, W. (1972) 'The Conditioning Influence of Organizational Size Upon Managerial Practice', *Organizational Behavior and Human Performance*, vol. 8, no. 2, October, pp. 230–41.

March, J. G. and Simon, H. S. (1958) *Organizations* (New York, Wiley).

Moch, M. K. and Morse, E. V. (1977) 'Size, Centralization and Organizational Adaption of Innovations', *American Sociological Review*, vol. 42, October, pp. 716–25.

Negandhi, A. R. and Prasad, B. S. (1971) *Comparative Management* (New York, Appleton-Century-Crofts).

Reimann, B. C. and Negandhi, A. R. (1975) 'Strategies of Administrative Control and Organizational Effectiveness', *Human Relations*, vol. 28, no. 5, July.

Rice, A. K. (1958) *Productivity and Social Organisation: The Ahmedabad Experiment* (London, Tavistock).

Rice, A. K. (1963) *The Enterprise and its Environment* (London, Tavistock).

Rosner, M. W. (1968) 'Administrative Controls and Innovation', *Behavioral Science*, vol. 13, no. 1, pp. 36–43.

Roy, D. (1952) 'Quota Restriction and Gold Bricking in a Machine Shop', *American Journal of Sociology*, vol. 57, pp. 427–42.

Roy, D. (1954) 'Efficiency and the Fix: Informal Intergroup Relations in a Piecework Machine Shop', *American Journal of Sociology*, vol. 3, pp. 255–66.

Sayles, L. R. (1958) *Behavior of Industrial Work Groups* (New York, Wiley).

Sayles, L. R. and Strauss, G. (1966) *Human Behavior in Organizations* (Englewood Cliffs, N.J., Prentice-Hall).

Thompson, J. D. (1967) *Organizations in Action* (New York, McGraw-Hill).

Thompson, V. (1965) 'Bureaucracy and Innovation', *Administrative Science Quarterly*, vol. 10, pp. 1–20.

Tracy, P. and Azumi, K. (1976) 'Determinants of Administrative Control', *American Sociological Review*, vol. 41, February, pp. 80–94.

Trist, E. and Bamforth, K. W. (1951) 'Some Social and Psychological Consequences of the Longwall Method of Coal Getting', *Human*

Relations, vol. 4, no. 1, pp. 331–58.

Turcotte, W. E. (1974) 'Control Systems, Performance and Satisfaction in Two State Agencies', *Administrative Science Quarterly*, vol. 19, no. 1, pp. 60–73.

Wilson, J. (1966) 'Innovation in Organizations: Notes Toward a Theory', in *Approaches to Organizational Design*, ed. J. Thompson (University of Pittsburgh Press) pp. 193–218.

Woodward, J. Editor. (1970) *Industrial Organisation: Behaviour and Control* (Oxford University Press).

Zaltman, G. R., Duncan, R. and Holbeck, J. (1973) *Innovations and Organizations* (New York, Wiley/Interscience).

Further Reading

The following are included as examples of the literature available on the application of open-systems theory:

Beer, M. and Huse, E. F. (1972) 'A Systems Approach to Organization Development', *Journal of Applied Behavioral Science*, vol. 8, no. 1, pp. 72–101.

Kast, F. E. and Rosenweig, J. E. (1974) *Organization and Management – A Systems Approach* (New York, McGraw-Hill).

Katz, D. and Kahn, R. L. (1966) *The Social Psychology of Organizations* (New York, Wiley).

Mauerer, J. G. (ed.) (1971) *Readings in Organizational Theory: Open Systems Approaches* (Wayne State University/Random House).

Thompson, J. D. (1967) *Organizations in Action* (New York, McGraw-Hill).

4
The Social Organisation of Work

In the late 1970s and early 1980s serious efforts were, and are being, made by more and more managers, and union and government officials, to come to terms with the question of control over industrial affairs. The Bullock Report (1976) is a major statement outlining the future shape and form of industrial democracy in Britain. Worker participation has become a major focus of attention on the subject of work organisation and regulation (Banks and Jones, 1977; Brannen *et al.*, 1976; Daniel and McIntosh, 1972; Guest and Fatchett, 1974; Jacques, 1978; Pace and Hunter, 1978).

Participation can be defined as the act of sharing in the formulation of policies and proposals, a process in which two or more parties influence each other in making certain plans, policies and decisions (French *et al.*, 1960). Collective bargaining and joint consultation are probably the most common instances of participation by employees and unions in company matters. Various means of joint consultation and participation are invoked by management in an attempt to improve the reliability and functioning of companies, as (for instance) in introducing changes in production plans, methods of operation and technological developments. An increasing number of companies provide consultation and enter into collective bargaining on matters of payment systems, discipline, safety, production schedules, hours of working, etc.

Participation in Operation

Autonomous work groups have been found to operate successfully in coal-mining, textiles, motor-car firms, chemical and steel industries

(Rice, 1958; Taylor, 1973a; Trist *et al.*, 1963; Walker and Guest, 1952). The Swedish car firm Volvo, for instance, introduced opportunities for greater internal powers and responsibilities among work groups for assignments, training and supervision, which has cut down on labour turnover and absenteeism, and raised productivity, morale and job satisfaction.

A number of companies have set up project teams to investigate and recommend changes in existing company practices and procedures. At Vosper Thorneycroft Shipyard, Southampton, the company brought in changes in the manning and scheduling of work, in work-booking and preparation of detailed inventory control. Briefing groups have been adopted by some senior managements in discussion with employees on varying issues related to day-to-day events within and relating to the company and job content. Fred Olsen Shipping Lines is one company that has undertaken these briefings on matters related to the terminal operations of ships (Taylor, 1973b). Norwegian works councils have formally defined powers over major changes in production plans, methods, development of products and plans for expansion, contraction or reorganisation, where they affect employees or their working conditions.

Research Findings on Participation

A participatory style of management in the social organisation of work is strongly advocated on the grounds that it improves job performance and raises the commitment of the persons involved to their organisational task. However, research on the subject is divided on the subject.

The Hawthorn experiments in 1927–33, Coch and French (1948), Blumberg (1968), Hackman and Lawler (1971) and Taylor (1973a) echo the view that participative management raises worker performance and commitment to the job. However, Brayfield and Crocket (1955) and Powell and Schlacter (1971) challenge these findings. There is a body of informed opinion both in Britain and the United States (Dubin, 1958 and 1975; Zweig, 1961; Goldthorpe *et al.*, 1968; Russell, 1975; Strauss, 1963) which contends that the majority of the work-force do not wish to be involved in the management function.

This is very much so in the case of blue-collar workers, in lower occupational groups and socio-economic levels (Bonjean and Vance,

1968; Friedlander, 1966; Friedlander and Walton, 1964). For women, commitment to work is secondary to family and home, particularly in the case of poorly paid and routine work (Beynon and Blackburn, 1972). However, the recent research findings of Wall and Lischeron (1977) in local government, private industry and the health service suggests that there is a strong desire to be involved in management decisions. A study was undertaken of workers' attitudes towards participation in different decision-making areas in order to establish whether attitudes towards participation were common across diverse populations or whether they varied according to the different individuals, jobs and organisations involved. The majority of all the workers interviewed exhibited a strong desire to influence decisions which directly affected them in their job, in terms of how jobs were to be scheduled, how duties were to be allocated, and work autonomy generally. However, in the case of less-skilled workers, such as nursing auxiliaries, little say about their own jobs was desired; they preferred, to leave medical and nursing decisions to those best trained. Unskilled industrial workers had mixed views. They expressed a strong interest in decisions affecting their bonus earnings and thus in bonus schemes and work-study methods but not in the purchase of materials.

Yet over all a majority of workers in all the organisations studied expressed a wish to influence managerial decisions which affected employees generally, such as the choice of new personnel, purchase of new materials, equipment and recommendations for training and promotion. Because of the low degree of perceived influence associated with these decision areas, employees expressed the strongest desire to participate in these activities. However, French *et al.* (1960), Kay *et al.* (1962) and Juralewicz (1974) found little evidence of improved worker attitudes as a result of increased participation. The study undertaken by Juralewicz in a Latin American clothes manufacturing organisation reported that an increase in participation by workers in decisions concerning work methods was achieved but did not affect attitudes towards the job itself, the company, supervision or the 'motivated feeling of being valued'. On the other hand, Morse and Reimer (1956) found that greater participation led to increased satisfaction with superiors and the organisation but not with the job itself. Ritchie (1974) points out, however, that research is beset with difficulties and unresolved dilemmas. Likert (1961) argues that research often neglects the lag between changes in behaviour and that of the climate of working in the organisation. Franklin (1975) identifies time as a crucial element in the description of linkages between social (psychological forces across levels of hierarchy. Measurement over time is needed because the relationship between variables may well change (Marrow, 1972). Morse and Reimer (1956), for example, indicate that authoritarian supervision may lead to production increases in the short run but not necessarily in the long run.

It is difficult in survey research to distinguish between 'real attitudes', socially desirable answers (usually assumed desirable to the boss), the climate of working relations and supervisory behaviour. Ritchie (1974) states that the dimensions of the problem are reflected in the limited evidence which establishes a direct link between attitudes and behaviour (Michaelson, 1972), the inconsistent perceptions of superiors and subordinates (Miles, 1964) and conflicting reports of a supervisor's behaviour from his superior and subordinates (Nealey and Owen, 1970).

Another issue Ritchie cites is the *criterion problem*. What do we measure in determining effectiveness. According to French *et al.* (1960), the study of Lewin, Lippitt and White (1939) revealed that children showed better interpersonal relations, higher morale, and greater productivity under a democratic style of leadership than in an autocratic atmosphere. In contrast, Vroom (1964) argues that 'the highest level of productivity occurred under autocratic leadership'. These conflicting conclusions come about because of the different criteria used to evaluate productivity.

A drawback in research is the difficulty of knowing in which direction the principal causes and effects work. A close correlation between participative management and productivity does not necessarily confirm a causal relation between the major variables. There may well be an unmeasured intervening variable which has brought this correlation about. More motivated and productive workers may well evoke more participative behaviour from their superiors. Lowen and Craig (1968) found that those supervisors responsible for a subordinate with poor performance adopted closer and less considerate styles of management than those in charge of a subordinate with good performance. A similar finding was made by Crowe *et al.* (1972).

Higher levels of motivation, morale and work performance and lower levels of absenteeism and labour turnover reported in studies of participative management may in fact be due to any one or more factors.

Factors Motivating Individuals

Research undertaken on the influence of personality characteristics upon people's attitudes to different management styles reveals that individual differences may play a significant part in how people respond in terms of job satisfaction and work performance. O'Reilly (1977) found that individual differences explained work attitudes and behaviour in cases where a differentiation could be made between people with a need for achievement and personal growth and those wishing greater job security and high financial reward. High achievers placed in low-challenging jobs showed lower commitment, were dissatisfied with their job and produced lower performances. Low achievers in highly challenging jobs responded equally unfavourably.

Certain people prefer clear directives and laid-down instructions to work to, because of either a dependency on authority or a need for security. On the other hand, other individuals wish to determine for themselves how they can set about a particular job and are a lot more independent of authority, and work effectively alone and unsupervised (Tannenbaum and Schmidt, 1958); Goldthorpe *et al.*, (1968). Vroom (1960) found that autocratic personalities tend to work harder under supervisors who are equally autocratic, while democratic personalities work harder under more democratic supervisors. However, Tosi (1970), and Searfoss and Monczka (1973) have failed to replicate these findings. At the same time, research demonstrates that the attitudes and behaviour of individuals may be more directly related to task characteristics, for example skill variety (Stone and Porter, 1975), the individual's position in the organisational hierarchy (O'Reilly and Roberts, 1975), or related to aspects of organisational structure (Herman, Dunham and Hulin, 1975), rather than to individual differences in personality.

The motivating influence of job characteristics

Hackman and Lawler (1971) claim that to establish the conditions for internal work motivation a job must: (i) allow workers to feel personally responsible for an identifiable and meaningful portion of the work; (ii) provide work outcomes which are intrinsically meaningful; and (iii) provide feedback about performance effectiveness. If the job is to meet the above requirements, it needs to rank high on skill variety, autonomy, task identity and feedback (Hackman and Oldham, 1976). A job-redesign study by Lawler, Hackman and Kaufman (1973) of telephone operators revealed that neither job satisfaction nor motivation improved after job changes in which skill variety and autonomy were very low. Similar findings were made by Hackman, Pearce and Wolfe (1978) in a study of redesigned clerical jobs in a bank. Wall, Clegg and Jackson (1978) found that with employees in blue-collar jobs in a sweet production factory internal motivation was low, because of low skill variety, task identity and task significance, and as such was a critical factor likely to affect job satisfaction, work performance, absenteeism and labour turnover.

The person's position in the organisational structure

Dieterly and Schneider (1974) argue that differences in perception of management styles and openness of decision-making is a function of organisational position and role. Jago and Vroom (1977) and Heller (1971) found that lower-level management in an organisation tends to disbelieve that higher management approves of participation in spite of views held to the contrary by higher management and immediate subordinates. This is partly due to the fact that middle managers tend to pass down the decisions which have been reached in the form of an instruction or order. At the same time, lower-level management is invariably faced with implementing decisions upon which it has had little or no influence, even though higher levels of management may have been involved. The desire of lower-level managers to advance themselves by modelling their behaviour upon an incorrect perception of higher management's style of leadership may lead to more autocratic behaviour.

These differences in perception affect the 'psychological' climate of work and organisational relations. Decentralisation of decision-making would serve to decrease the number of levels through which communication would travel downwards, providing those most affected by the outcome of the decision with more involvement in, or at least more knowledge of, the decision process used. This would serve to make expectations about participation more reality-orientated. Each level of management can also provide their staff with more explicit, unambiguous information about the decision process chosen to evolve policies and solve problems that cannot be devolved further down the organisation hierarchy. This would help to minimise misperceptions. It would also serve to prevent middle managers protecting their own status by giving the appearance that the original decision came from them. Managers may be more inclined to be more open about the constraints upon their decision-making discretion if the organisational costs or penalties are removed.

The impact of technology

Commitment to the job and one's colleagues is said to be significant to the performance of the enterprise only under certain kinds of technology, and is possible only if people have certain personality characteristics needed to adapt to certain alienating work conditions (Aronoff, 1967; Blauner, 1964; Fullan, 1970; Rouseau, 1977).

Blauner (1964) attempts to show that the worker's relationship with the technological organisation of the work process, and with the social organisation of the factory, determines whether or not he experiences in his work 'a sense of meaningful purpose rather than isolation', and a sense of 'spontaneous involvement and self expression as opposed to detachment and discontent'. A study was made of four industries with different types of work environment and systems of production and how they affect the extent of meaning and purpose which manual workers experience in their jobs. For example, in the printing industry the essential feature of craft technology is the lack of standardisation of the work process. The work of the printer is varied and involves the application of individual skill and judgement. Because of the low level of mechanisation and sub-division of work, the printer is directly responsible for much of the technical process and is very much involved in deciding on how the production system will operate.

The basic production processes in the textile industry are carried out by highly mechanised power machinery. The worker's control over the immediate work process is minimal. The constant work pressure, the inability to control the pace and rhythm of his work activity, lack of choice of work techniques, and the absence of free physical movements, all create powerful alienating work conditions.

The main feature of the motor-car industry is mass production of vehicles and automation of the work process. The narrow field of work and the specialisation of people's jobs along the assembly-line subject the work-force to the alienation of meaninglessness. The car worker is directed and controlled by the pace of the work process. His actions and initiatives are severely constrained by the process of mechanisation and automation.

The chemical operator works in a continuous-process industry, one which is automated to a high degree. The operation of the equipment requires extensive technical know-how and expertise for dealing with different plants, products and processes. The major task is monitoring and controlling the technological process. The chemical operator has a wide range of responsibilities, and exercises considerable discretion in his job. He is not only closely involved with supervision and management in decisions relating to methods and modes of operation, but actively chooses to take on responsibility for monitoring and reviewing operational control. Job satisfaction is much higher as a consequence of the responsibility and authority which the job carries.

What is Participation?

In view of the conflicting evidence as to the value of participative forms of management certain fundamental questions need to be asked about the nature and outcome of them. An understanding should also be sought as to how people respond to this style of management.

We need to establish more precisely what is involved in participation and in what form it appears. What occurs in practice, and what are people's notion of it? For what reason is it applied, and what is understood to be the purpose of it? Is it seen to be relevant or feasible by the parties involved? Who really desires management by participation, and for what purpose? How is it received? What are the long-term consequences and implications of worker participation?

It is important to be clear as to what participative management entails. To some managers it means little more than informing the employees of current decisions, while others see it as the first step in worker control. Participation may involve consulting employees over working conditions, facilities or work organisation, while management reserves judgement on the possible findings. Management thus determines what, if any, decisions need to be taken. However, is consultation in advance of decision-making enough, or must the subordinate take part in the decision-making process if he is to influence the decisions made and the course of action taken?

Participation may involve working parties or project groups enquiring into alternative courses of action necessary to deal with a particular problem or issue raised by higher management. While it may provide an element of choice in determing what decisions should be reached, there may in fact be little if any choice for the person affected by the decisions made. An older employee of a company faced with technological and administrative change may be forced to choose between two eminently less desirable, less satisfying and less responsible tasks than he held previously. For such employees their bargaining powers are limited in situations involving this kind of participative decision-making.

However, there are instances of more personal and direct participation which have lead to greater job satisfaction and motivation for employees. At I.C.I., for example, where several studies of job enrichment were undertaken, design engineers were given greater responsibility and authority over work standards, cost control and the use of resources, and were found to have a sense of greater responsibility and commitment to their work (Paul and Robertson, 1970).

Participation may arise from a manager's efforts to resolve a particular problem which affects his work-force, such as the manning and scheduling of shift work, or the lay-out of a new product line requiring special methods. He may invite questions and discussion in order to assess the level of commitment to the decisions he has carefully arrived at and to reduce the uncertainty in his mind of whether or not the initiatives he is taking are acceptable. He may, on the other hand, present his own views of the changes, and outline his own proposals, in an attempt to solicit support for his ideas. However, his prime motivation may be to ensure conformity and compliance with his own proposals and desired intentions. Underlying the manager's actions are his motives. These will determine whether participation is sought and what level of involvement is being asked for.

The failure of job enrichment

Job-design changes, which have formed the basis of job-enrichment programmes, have invariably failed to upgrade the task and quality of work performed by employees. Changes in task responsibilities have not produced the desired level of individual autonomy and discretion. Managers have invariably reasserted control whenever any uncertainties or problems have arisen. Some individuals have lost valued skills and work interest in the job changes. Increasing the scope and responsibility of a person's job does not overcome dissatisfaction with pay, supervision and job security. Managers often lack the commitment to undertake the process of educating people to accept change, partly because changes are required in his style of management and in his own role as a manager. Unless the impact of job-design changes upon other departments is accepted, it will often nullify the benefits anticipated. The work of Frank and Hackman (1975) and Plant (1972) highlights some of the problems involved (as opposed to the successes) which rarely come to light.

Levels of involvement

A manager may present a problem to his work-force and seek suggestions concerning its resolution. He may then make his own mind up and pursue his own course of action. Could one really say that the work-force participated in the decision-making process? If so, to what extent? On the other hand, we may have a superior who is very willing for his subordinates to influence the decisions to be reached on certain issues, problems and tasks and who is prepared to act on suggestions made to him. While some subordinates will air their opinions and make suggestions, others may not feel free to do so. To what extent could one say an individual has participated who has not directly contributed?

Inevitably all suggestions and proposals cannot be taken up. If some are taken up and others are not, under what circumstances will the individual work to implement a decision to which he is opposed or which he has not significantly influenced? Again, one is more likely to be guaranteed commitment and responsibility from people for a course of action to which they were not a party if it happens to coincide or further their own interests.

Conditions for participation

There are no really clear or definitive answers to such problematic issues. In the first instance an outline is given showing the different conditions under which participation is conducted by organisations, and some of the problems of working under them are highlighted. Then an assessment is made of the types of management by participation which might lead to greater motivation and commitment to the job and thus serve organisational ends.

In most instances of participative management in which two or more parties seek to influence each other in making certain plans, policies and decisions, there are well-defined limits within which mutual influence and joint negotiation may take place.

In the capacity of a management adviser and consultant to a group of companies, the present author found that the managers involved were very much constrained by the plans, policies and decisions already made at higher-management levels. For example, the company, in pursuing a policy of rationalisation of its industrial operations, with plans afoot for

  (i) a cut back on expenditure and product ranges,
 (ii) economy in the use of resources (human, material and financial),
(iii) tighter cost controls and higher performance standards demanded of employees,
(iv) a maximisation of productive capacity available for particular product ranges at the expense of other ranges,

was laying down some specific and clear conditions for, and requirements of, participation and the areas for decision.

In this situation the persons involved were asked to assess how best to achieve the objectives set within the technological, organisational and financial constraints before them. They were faced with evaluating:

(i) how to optimise their existing resources – labour, plant and machinery – and prospective financial resources that would be made *less* available;
(ii) how to direct their efforts in maximising the high-growth sectors of the company's product operations;
(iii) how to schedule and allocate tasks and work loads more effectively;
(iv) how to meet the target dates and performance standards required, in the light of changes in priorities in company operations and revised plans and product development; and
(v) how to control costs and systematise task and operational requirements, which allowed for an effective review and control of the necessary plans, responsibilities and results of individuals and departments.

Participation of this nature will inevitably have an influence on the manner in which it is received by participants. Uncertainty over what can be achieved, and whether the decisions reached can actually be realised with the resources available and the constraints foreseen, evoked defensiveness, frustration behaviour, anxious concern and apprehension. Cynicism and sceptism grew as the extent of the problems and difficulties emerged more clearly. While some participants were keen to influence decisions, take on responsibilities and have the opportunity to shape and develop their jobs, others were more anxious to preserve their existing responsibilities and authority, and were clearly concerned by prospective changes in their position and standing which they would have no control over.

Discussion and debate brought disagreement and open conflict over

(i) what the organisation's needs and objectives were;
(ii) which were the problem areas and what were the means of problem resolution;
(iii) the identification and definition of constraints;
(iv) what potential performance levels and standards were required;
(v) the realism and attainability of targets and plans outlined; and
(vi) the validity of the whole exercise (see Brooks, 1973).

Management by edict

It is not surprising, therefore, that managers invariably avoid or withdraw from participative decision-making and revert to authoritarianism by informing the employees of their decisions. By this means they can make decisions more speedily and get the work performed more quickly and, in their eyes, more efficiently. Thus time spent on inducing people to co-operate, in seeking to reconcile different views, could be more profitably spent on doing the job for which they were appointed.

Conditions for greater motivation

Now, an assessment can be made of how management by participation might lead to greater motivational commitment to the job.

Participative decision-making which determines what action should be undertaken in a work situation increases job interest and satisfaction where individual skills are recognised and considered as valued resources by the work group and manager. In promoting a higher sense of personal worth and importance it can stimulate a greater sense of responsibility and commitment to the task at hand (Likert, 1967).

Direction, control and restriction of people's initiatives are forms of regimentation which invariably induce dependent behaviour and deter initiative, creative thinking and commitment to a course of action (Argyris, 1964).

Numerous studies have shown that individuals who view their performance outcomes as determined by themselves exhibit more initiative in their attempts to control their work environment than those who consider it to be controlled by outside forces (Lefcourt, 1966; Phares, Ritchie and Davis, 1968; Rotter, 1966; Seeman, 1963). Ruble (1976) found that individuals who feel that they have personal power to influence the results of their work performed better when provided with the opportunity to plan their work than when they were instructed what to do. In cases where individuals had feelings of powerlessness performance may suffer under participative management in the short run. This may well discourage further attempts to involve workers in the planning of their jobs.

There is evidence to suggest that employees are:

(i) more motivated and committed to decisions they have contributed to which are of intrinsic interest;

(ii) work more effectively towards goals they have contributed which reward them for their productive efforts; and

(iii) operate more competently using methods and plans they have devised for themselves (Bowers, 1964; Frost and Mahoney, 1976; French *et al.*, 1958; Likert, 1961; Mann, 1957; Morse and Reimer, 1956; Marrow, Seashore and Bowers, 1967; Seashore and Bowers, 1963).

The research of Coch and French (1948), in examining the effects of participation upon an organisation undertaking technical innovation, is one of the few systematically and scientifically researched pieces of work which establishes the relationship between different levels of participation and organisational productivity, cost-effectiveness, turnover, job satisfaction and morale. The research was undertaken at a clothing factory owned by the Harwood Company in the United States. Increasing production costs and market competition made a new production design imperative. In the control group of workers an outside engineering firm worked out new flows and handling procedures and the changes were introduced by management through formal channels of communication. Productivity rose slightly aue to technological improvement. A second group of workers were more closely informed and consulted over the matter. Productivity was higher than in the control group. The experimental group were given a complete picture of the cost squeeze and were asked to work with the design engineers in solving the problem. The contrasting rise in productivity was significant, after initial downturns in production, when retraining of operatives was required so as to enable them to change to the new methods of operation.

Motives for willing participation

If organisations provide employees with greater freedom to determine a course of action, and/or to determine the necessary plans and methods of achieving them, what conditions are necessary for an individual or a work group to be willing to participate in furthering the ends of the organisation? What in the nature of participative management is likely to increase performance levels and general motivation among participants?

When tasks are directed and controlled by higher authority, an individual may feel few opportunities exist which allow him to shape and develop (influence) the nature of his work. If participation allows the individual to determine how best to perform his duties, it may bring greater motivation where resentment and frustration existed previously.

Participation which allows people to ventilate grievances,problems and felt injustices may rid individuals of pent-up emotions and frustrations which had previously reduced work motivation. However, action must be seen to be taken in removing the sources of discontent and dissatisfaction. This may not be easy except in the long run because of organisational, financial and administrative constraints.

However, the opportunities presented by participation for ventilating grievances and felt injustices are often circumscribed by social and political inhibition. Emotionalism of this kind threatens hostility and ill-feeling in working relationships. It therefore tends to be witheld or disguised. Co-operation and support is feigned, while antagonism, anger and frustration are felt. At the same time, the quality of decision-making is adversely affected under conditions of goal conflict over pay-offs. (Rapoport and Cvetkovich, 1970; Cosier and Rose, 1977).

Participation may permit the subordinate to feel that doing the job well provides him with an opportunity to demonstrate skills which he values – that is, participation provides him with an opportunity for deriving achievement from his work.

If participation is seen in terms of group operations it subjects the individual to group pressures to implement the group decision, particularly if he values being in the group. Work groups with high levels of cohesiveness, of mutual influence, of tolerance of conflict and differences of views, as well as commonality of purpose, will be more committed to joint decision-making and experience a greater sense of individual and collective responsibility and commitment to the task. On the other hand, the individual whose opinions are rejected may become alienated from the group and from participation as a system of management.

An exchange relationship

Given participation, the subordinate may feel that an exchange relationship has been set up – one of mutual influence and concern for the task each is responsible for. If the manager now acts on the subordinate's problems, the subordinate may feel obliged to reciprocate by putting more effort and being more conscientious in his work. This obligation may be enforced by the subordinate's concern that if he does not work harder, the opportunity to participate may be withdrawn (Mangham, 1970).

If participation leads work groups to feel that they have higher status from control and influence over organisational decision-making, they may then value the organisation's policies more highly and be more receptive to its operating norms and over-all performance goals.

The demands put on managers by participation

The manager who invites participation must ensure that the objective of the exercise is clear, what the task is, and what decisions have been reached. The participants need to be informed of the situation in which they find themselves, of current developments and their possible effects in order to minimise the anxieties, doubts and confusions which may dissuade participants from committing themselves to performance improvements which appear unrealistic or problematic.

In situations of uncertainty there is a need for more closely defined objectives. An individual's task and the responsibilities it entails may need to be more closely defined. Clearly defined and agreed targets and performance standards are likely to leave people less confused and more sure of what they have to achieve. Specifically challenging goals (e.g. 'produce 190 units') are more helpful than general ones (e.g. improvements in output). (See Meyer *et al.*, 1965; Locke, 1966 and 1968.)

How to plan, organise, control, what has to be done, by when, in what stages, with what resources, at what cost, and with what degree of risk, all these are fundamental considerations in implementing change. A manager must ask himself how people's efforts are to be co-ordinated in the interests of achieving his plans and objectives.

What procedures, systems and methods are necessary to see that resources (human, material and monetary) and information are utilised to maximum advantage within the framework of a plan?

How are the stages of the plan to be controlled and what control systems are needed to ensure that plans are coming to fruition? At what stage should it be decided (by continuous review) that plans need to be modified? Control and feedback systems are necessary in order to review and appraise the progress of tasks, their stages of completion, and to pinpoint problems and delays. Where people are uncertain of their role, there is a need for better organisation.

Where individuals feel oppressed or repressed in terms of inadequate authority to carry out responsibilities, or have insufficient resources to achieve over-optimistically set targets and performance standards, there is a need for a review and reappraisal of task situations and objectives. The changes that are necessary in plans and responsibilities must be systematised and review procedures arranged accordingly, allowing for joint problem-solving and decision-making.

Objectives and plans reached by participative decision-making must be seen to be realistic and feasible in the circumstances. Failure to achieve objectives and plans set may reduce the motivation and commitment of a work-force to any future attempts at participation For objectives and plans reached by participative decision-making to influence an organisation's operations, the decisions reached must take account of the responsiveness of non-participants and how effectively to secure the support and co-operation of relatively uncommitted parties. This may well necessitate extending participation to previously uninvolved personnel; for unless the rewards and influences which motivate the decision-makers apply equally to those not consulted, for example other departments or the shop floor, then almost certainly a lower level of motivation and commitment in the implementation stage will be found.

Skilled workers and participation

If the degree of motivation is to be sufficient to make participation effective, the participant must:

    (i) place some personal value on his work;

(ii) derive a sense of greater achievement in doing his job more effectively;

(iii) receive adequate recognition for such achievements;

(iv) have control over those aspects of his job for which he is responsible;

(v) feel that he has the need and the ability to decide and influence the nature and scope of his work; and

(vi) derive satisfaction and a sense of accomplishment from the responsibility and authority delegated to him in the accomplishment of his task.

Thus it might be predicted that participation, particularly the delegation of responsibilities and authority, would work more effectively with skilled workers (who value their particular skills) than with unskilled workers.

At the same time, the individual must obtain some reward from his work efforts; otherwise he is unlikely to respond positively to greater autonomy and work skills to his job (Steers and Porter, 1974). Participation will not be particularly effective where the work is not intrinsically satisfying.

In Sweden, it has been found that with a highly educated, trained and skilled population, unskilled, menial and repetitive work, such as assembly-line work, is unsatisfying, frustrating and anethema to people's occupational wants. High wages and increasing job security have failed to stem these feelings.

As the level of education and training grows, Britain is also having to face these problems. Increasing numbers of man-hours are lost by absenteeism, lateness, high labour turnover and industrial action or unrest. Industrial strikes represent growing demands for adequate compensation for dissatisfying work, shorter working hours and improvements in working conditions in the shape of extrinsic payment for intrinsic need deprivation.

However, opportunities for organisations to redesign job and work-flows so as to increase the various forms of job satisfaction, such as autonomy and achievement, may not be viable on economic grounds and in the face of competition and the need to maintain profitability. Such problems have been found at the Volvo motor-car plants in Sweden when attempts were made to redesign assembly-line work.

The technology of many operations, particularly on the shop floor, does not allow much discretion in terms of job responsibilities and authority, as all essential decisions are centrally programmed. There are few opportunities in industry for participation which allow for the shop-floor worker to influence and shape the nature of his or her work. Until jobs in the manual spectrum are enriched or enlarged, so as to provide a greater sense of achievement and satisfaction, participative management is unlikely to raise the motivation and commitment of a work-force performing unskilled and intrinsically dissatisfying jobs.

References

Argyris, C. (1964) *Integrating the Individual and the Organization* (New York, Wiley).

Aronoff, J. (1967) *Psychological Needs and Cultural Systems* (New York, Van Nostrand).

Banks, J. and Jones, K. (1977) *Worker Directors Speak* (London, Gower Press).

Beynon, H. and Blackburn, R. M. (1972) *Perception of Work: Variations within a Factory* (Cambridge University Press).

Bonjean, C. M. and Vance, G. G. (1968) 'A Short-form Measure of Self-actualization', *Journal of Applied Behavioral Science*, vol. 4, pp. 297–312.

Blauner, R. (1964) *Alienation and Freedom* (University of Chicago Press).

Blumberg, P. (1968) *Industrial Democracy: The Sociology of Participation* (London, Constable).

Bowers, D. G. 'Organizational Control in an Insurance Company, *Sociometry*, vol. 27, no. 2, pp. 230–44.

Brannen, P., Batstone, E., Fatchett, D. and White, P. (1970) *The Worker Directors – A Sociology of Participation* (London, Hutchinson).

Brayfield, A. H. and Crocket, W. A. (1955) 'Employee Attitudes and Employee Performance', *Psychological Bulletin*, vol. 52.

Brooks, E. (1973) 'Worker Participation – The Fundamental Issues', *Journal of Industrial and Commercial Training*, vol. 5, no. 9.

Bullock Report (1976) Committee of Inquiry on Industrial Democracy, Cmnd 6706 (London, H.M.S.O.).

Coch, L. and French, J. P. R. (1948) 'Overcoming Resistance to Change', *Human Relations*, vol. 1, no. 4, pp. 512–32.

Cosier, R. A. and Rose, G. L. (1977) 'Cognitive Conflict and Goal Conflict Effects on Task Performance', *Organizational Behavior and Human Performance*, vol. 19, no. 2, pp. 378–91.

Crowe, B. S., Hochner, S. and Clark, A. W. (1972) 'The Effects of Subordinate Behavior on Management Style', *Human Relations*, vol. 25, pp. 215–37.

Daniel, W. W. and McIntosh, N. (1972) *The Right to Manage: A Study of Leadership and Reform in Employee Relations* (London, MacDonald & Jane).

Dieterly, D. L. and Schneider, B. (1974) 'The Effect of Organizational Environment on Perceived Power and Climate: a Laboratory Study', *Organizational Behavior and Human Performance*, vol. 11, no. 3, June, pp. 316–37.

Dubin, R. (1958) *The World of Work* (Englewood Cliffs, N.J., Prentice-Hall).

Dubin, R., Champoux, J. and Porter, L. (1975) 'Central Life Interests and Organizational Commitment of Blue-collar and White-collar Workers', *Administrative Science Quarterly*, vol. 20, pp. 198–212.

Frank, L. L. and Hackman, J. R. (1975) 'A Failure of Job Enrichment: the Case of the Change that Wasn't', *Journal of Applied Behavioral Science*, vol. 1, no. 4, pp. 413–36.

Franklin, J. L. (1975) 'Down the Organization: Influence Processes across Levels of Hierarchy', *Administrative Science Quarterly*, vol. 20, no. 2, June, pp. 153–64.

French, J. R. P., Israel, J. and As, D. (1960) 'An Experiment in a Norwegian Factory', *Human Relations*, vol. 13, pp. 3–19.

French, J. R. P. *et al.* (1958) 'Employee Participation in a Programme of Industrial Change', *Journal of Personnel*, November–December, pp. 16–29.

Friedlander, F. (1966) 'Importance of Work versus Non-work among Socially and Occupationally Stratified Groups', *Journal of Applied Psychology*, vol. 50, pp. 437–41.

Friedlander, F. and Walton, E. (1964) 'Positive and Negative Motivations towards Work', *Administrative Science Quarterly*, vol. 9, pp. 194–207.

Frost, P. J. and Mahoney, T. A. (1976) 'Goal Setting and the Task Process: an Interactive Influence on Individual Performance',

Organizational Behavior and Performance, vol. 17, no. 2, pp. 328–50.

Fullan, M. (1970) 'Industrial Technology and Worker Integration in the Organization', *American Sociological Review*, vol. 35, December, pp. 1028–39.

Goldthorpe, J. H., Lockwood, D., Bechhofer, F. and Platt, J. (1968) *The Affluent Worker* (Industrial Attitudes and Behavior, Cambridge University Press).

Guest, D. and Fatchett, D. (1974) *Worker Participation: Individual Control and Performance* (London, Institute of Personnel Management).

Hackman, J. R. and Lawler, E. E. (1971) 'Employee reactions to job characteristics', *Journal of Applied Psychology*, vol. 60, pp. 259–86.

Hackman, J. R. and Oldham, G. R. (1976) 'Motivation through the Design of Work: Test of a Theory', *Organizational Behavior and Human Performance*, vol. 16, no. 2, pp. 250–79.

Hackman, J. R., Pearce, J. L. and Wolfe, J. C. (1978) 'Effects of Changes in Job Characteristics on Work Attitudes and Behavior', *Organizational Behavior and Human Performance*', vol. 21, no. 3, June, pp. 289–303.

Heller, F. (1971) *Managerial Decision-making: a Study of Leadership Styles and Power-sharing among Senior Managers* (London, Tavistock).

Herman, J., Dunham, R. and Hulin, C. (1975) 'Organizational Structure, Demographic Characteristics and Employee Responses', *Organizational Behavior and Human Performance*, vol. 13, no. 2, pp. 206–33.

Jacques, E. (1978) 'A General Theory of Bureaucracy' (London, Heinemann).

Jago, A. G. and Vroom, V. H. (1977) 'Hierarchical Levels and Leadership Style', *Organizational Behavior and Human Performance*, vol. 18, no. 1, pp. 131–45.

Juralewicz, R. S. (1974) 'An Experiment on Participation in a Latin American Factory', *Human Relations*, vol. 7, no. 27, pp. 627–37.

Kay, E., French, J. P. R. and Meyer, H. H. (1962) *A Study of the Performance Appraisal Interview* (New York, General Electric Company).

Lawler, E. E. (1969) 'Job Design and Employee Motivation', *Personnel Psychology*, vol. 22, pp. 426–33.

Lawler, E. E. and Hackman, J. R. (1971) 'Employee Reactions to Job

Characteristics', *Journal of Applied Psychology*, vol. 55, no. 3, pp. 259–86.

Lawler, E. E., Hackman, J. R. and Kaufman, S. (1973) 'Effects of Job Redesign: a Field Experiment', *Journal of Applied Social Psychology*, vol. 3, no. 1, pp. 49–62.

Lefcourt, H. M. (1966) 'Internal versus External Control of Reinforcements: A Review', *Psychological Bulletin*, vol. 65, pp. 206–20.

Lewin, K., Lippitt, R. and White, R. K. (1939) 'Patterns of Aggressive Behavior in Experimentally Created Social Climates', *Journal of Social Psychology*, vol. 10, pp. 271–99.

Likert, R. (1961) *New Patterns of Management* (New York, McGraw-Hill).

Likert, R. (1967) *The Human Organization* (New York, McGraw-Hill).

Locke, E. A. (1966) 'The Relationship of Intentions to Level of Performance', *Journal of Applied Psychology*, vol. 50, no. 1, pp. 60–6.

Locke, E. A. (1968) 'Toward a Theory of Task Motivation and Incentives', *Organizational Behavior and Human Performance*, vol. 3, no. 2, pp. 157–89.

Lowen, A. and Craig, J. R. (1968) 'The Influence of Level of Performance in Managerial Style: An Experimental Object-lesson in the Ambiguity of Correlational Data', *Organizational Behavior and Human Performance*, vol. 3, no. 1.

Mangham, I. (1970) 'Management by Participation', unpublished paper, Leeds University.

Mann, F. C. (1957) 'Studying and Creating Change: a Means to Understanding Social Organisation', in *Research in Industrial Human Relations*, ed. C. Arensberg (Madison, Wisconsin).

Marrow, A. J. (1972) *The Failure of Success* (New York, Amacom).

Marrow, A. J., Seashore, S. E. and Bowers, D. G. (1967) *Management by Participation* (New York, Harper & Row).

Meyer, H. H., Kay, E. and French, J. R. P. (1965) 'Split Roles in Performance Appraisal', *Harvard Business Review*, vol. 43, pp. 123–9.

Michaelson, L. K. (1972) 'Leadership Orientation, Leader Behavior, Group Effectiveness, and Situational Favorability: an Extension of the Contingency Model', Technical Report, Ann Arbor, Michigan, University of Michigan, Institute for Social Research.

Miles, R. E. (1964) 'Conflicting Elements in Managerial Ideologies', *Industrial Relations*, vol. 4, October, pp. 77–91.

Morse, J. J. and Reimer, N. (1956) 'The Experimental Change of a Major Organizational Variable', *Journal of Abnormal and Social Psychology*, vol. 52, pp. 120–9.

Nealey, S. M. and Owen, T. W. (1970) 'A Multitrait-Multimethod Analysis of Predictors and Criteria of Nursing Performance', *Organizational Behavior and Human Performance*, vol. 5, no. 2, pp. 348–65.

O'Reilly, C. (1977) 'Personality–Job Fit: Implications for Individual Attitudes and Performance', *Organizational Behavior and Human Performance*, vol. 18, no. 1, pp. 36–46.

O'Reilly, C. and Roberts, K. (1975) 'Individual Differences in Personality, Position in the Organization and Job Satisfaction', *Organizational Behavior and Human Performance*, vol. 14, no. 1, pp. 144–50.

Pace, D. and Hunter, J. (1978) *Direct Participation in Action: The New Bureaucracy* (Farnborough, Saxon House).

Paul, W. and Robertson, K. B. (1970) *Job Enrichment and Organisational Change* (London, Gower Press).

Phares, E. J., Ritchie, E. and Davis, W. (1968) 'Internal–External Control and Reaction to Threat', *Journal of Personality and Social Psychology*, vol. 10, pp. 402–5.

Plant, R. (1972) 'Releasing Supervisory Potential', *Journal of European and Industrial Training*, vol. 1, Spring, pp. 34–42.

Powell, R. M. and Schlachter, J. L. (1971) 'Participative Management: a Panacea?', *Academy of Management Journal*, vol. 14, no. 2, pp. 165–74.

Rapoport, L. and Cvetkovich, G. (1970) 'Effects of Reward and Structure and Cognitive Difference in a Mixed Motive Two Person Conflict Situation', *American Journal of Psychology*, vol. 83, pp. 119–25.

Rice, A. K. (1958) *Productivity and Social Organisation: The Ahmedabad Experiment* (London, Tavistock).

Ritchie, J. B. (1974) 'Supervision', in *Organizational Behavior: Research Issues*, ed. G. Strauss, R. E. Miles, C. C. Snow, A. S. Tannenbaum (New York, Wadsworth Publishing Co.).

Rotter, J. B. (1966) 'Generalized Expectancies for Internal versus External Control of Reinforcement', *Psychological Monographs*, vol. 80, no. 609.

Rouseau, D. M. (1977) 'Technological Differences in Job Characteristics, Employee Satisfaction and Motivation: a Synthesis of Job Design Research and Socio-Technical Systems Theory', *Organizational Behavior and Human Performance*, vol. 19, no. 1, pp. 18–42.

Ruble, T. L. (1976) 'Effects of One's Locus of Control and the Opportunity to Participate in Planning', *Organizational Behavior and Human Performance*, vol. 16, no. 1, pp. 63–73.

Russell, K. J. (1975) 'Variations in Orientation to Work and Job Satisfaction', *Sociology of Work and Occupations*, vol. 2, no. 4, November, pp. 299–323.

Searfoss, D. G. and Monczka, R. M. (1973) 'Perceived Participation in the Budget Process and Motivation to Achieve the Budget', *Academy of Management Journal*, vol. 16, no. 4, pp. 541–54.

Seashore, S. E., and Bowers, D. G. (1963) *Changing the Structure and Functioning of an Organization*. Report of a Field Experiment (Ann Arbor, Michigan, Institute of Social Research).

Seeman, M. (1963) 'Alienation and Social Learning in a Reformatory', *American Journal of Sociology*, vol. 69, pp. 270–84.

Steers, R. M. and Porter, L. W. (1974) 'Task Goal Attributes in Performance', *Psychological Bulletin*, vol. 81, pp. 434–52.

Strauss, G. (1963) 'Some Notes on Power Equalization', in *The Social Science of Organizations*, ed. H. J. Leavitt (Englewood Cliffs, N.J., Prentice-Hall).

Stone, E. and Porter, L. (1975) 'Job Characteristics and Job Attitudes', *Journal of Applied Psychology*, vol. 60, no. 1, pp. 57–64.

Tannenbaum, A. S. and Schmidt, W. H. (1958) 'How to Choose a Leadership Pattern', *Harvard Business Review*, March–April.

Taylor, L. K. (1973a) *Not by Bread Alone: an Appreciation of Job Enrichment* (London, Business Books).

Taylor, L. K. (1973b) 'Management of Change', *Journal of Industrial and Commercial Training*, vol. 5, no. 1; no. 4; no. 5.

Tosi, H. (1970) 'A Pre-examination of Personality as a Determinant of the Effects of Participation', *Personnel Psychology*, vol. 23, pp. 91–9.

Trist, E., Higgin, C., Murray, H. and Pollock, A. (1963) *Organisational Choice* (London, Tavistock).

Vroom, V. (1960) *Some Personality Determinants of the Effects of Participation* (Englewood Cliffs, N.J., Prentice-Hall).

Vroom, V. (1964) *Work and Motivation* (Harmondsworth, Penguin).

Walker, C. R. and Guest, R. H. (1952) 'The Man on the Assembly Line', *Harvard Business Review*, vol. 38, no. 3, May–June.

Wall, T. D. and Lischeron, J. A. (1977) *Worker Participation* (New York, McGraw-Hill).

Wall, T. D., Clegg, C. W. and Jackson, P. R. (1978) 'An Evaluation of the Job Characteristics Model', *Journal of Occupational Psychology*, vol. 51, no. 2, June.

Zweig, F. (1961) *The Worker in the Affluent Society* (London, Heinemann).

5
Changing the Structure of Organisational Operations

While it is generally accepted that changes in the social organisation of work should have the support and commitment of the persons affected, serious thought must be given to the impact and influence of such changes on the structure and functioning of the organisation.

All organisations seek to ensure the smooth running of their systems of operation by controlling and predicting the actions of their members. For instance, organisations apply hierarchical authority relations, formal rules and regulations, mechanical and administrative procedures and enforce various performance measures which prescribe the bounds of people's activities.

Organisations must be able to function and achieve their desired objectives in spite of changes in people, and therefore in policy, plans and procedures. One way an organisation can attempt to ensure stability is to specify the roles and responsibilities of its members. Each position in the organisational hierarchy carries a certain authority which provides individuals with the means for ensuring task accomplishment. At the same time, certain performance·expectations and responsibilities are built into each position so as to ensure that the operation of an organisation is effectively co-ordinated and controlled through the execution of certain rules, regulations and procedures.

The authority system (chain of command) places people in a position to make these decisions and to delegate such responsibility further down the line. It also puts those same people in a position to accept direction and undergo certain specified work.

Yet there are situations when compliance to duties, responsibilities and work objectives are obstructed and hindered by the administrative and hierarchical system. When the information available to the person and that which is required for the fulfilment of one's job is incongruent, role ambiguity, expressed in terms of uncertainty and confusion, arises (Kahn *et al.*, 1964). It stems from a situation where the individual cannot anticipate the consequences of his own actions, or is not aware of, or influential in, the determinants of key events which directly affect him in his job.

When, in such circumstances, the execution of a task becomes removed from the planning and decision-making processes, organisational control over task performance is very suspect and problematic. The prime management function in such instances, of effectively co-ordinating and controlling the principal operations of the organisation, may well be undermined by possible malfunctions and defects in the system of operation.

Malfunctions in Systems of Operation

The following study made in an oil refinery, illustrates something of the nature of the problem, in spite of full prior consultation and collective involvement, in an operational decision of key members of supervision responsible for plant maintenance and resource deployment and efficiency.

A new work-order-priority system was introduced by engineering maintenance in order to deal with a well-recognised problem of competing and conflicting demands for insufficient maintenance resources which led to production losses being suffered because mechanical failures were not attended to promptly enough. The work-order system was suitably revised to reflect more appropriately the demands imposed on the system. For instance, 'B' and 'C' priorities were omitted on the grounds that few, if any, jobs were recorded in these categories. 'B' priorities were reclassified as normal routine maintenance, and 'C' priorities as shutdown work. 'A' priorities were redefined as work requests which were necessary to avert immediate production losses. However, the 'A' priorities rapidly began to encompass work of varying degree of risk of production losses. With a high volume of different 'A' priorities, it became extremely difficult to decide on the relative merit of one urgent job as opposed to that of another. At the same time, the onrush of 'A' priority jobs frustrated advanced planning, serving to disrupt work organisation and scheduling. Planned maintenance programmes had to be cut back in order to cope with the urgency of work demands. Operations and engineering fell into dispute over this and in the cross-questioning of one 'A' priority over another. Management then responded to the failure of one work-order system by substituting it with another. However, it soon realised that it had failed to resolve the problem of providing an effective answer to the maintenance of plant operations and resource demand.

What had to be carefully considered and examined was the use and abuse to which the work-order system was put in relation to the demands of the operating system and the pressures and influences upon the individuals called to use it. It was agreed that changing existing attitudes to management controls and procedures was necessary to avoid abuses of the system. Making people aware of the impact and repercussions of their own actions and motives upon the viability and operability of a system intended for their benefit helped to establish the hidden costs involved in distorting and falsifying information fed into work-order systems originally designed for systematically planning, controlling and predicting resource-allocation requirements.

The Structural Divisions in Organisations

There is already well-documented evidence on the dysfunctions of bureaucratically devised administrative systems (Merton, 1957; Dubin, 1965; Gouldner, 1955). What is highlighted here is that management by participation by way of the decision-making process may well entail commitment on the part of those concerned to implement a new system of working, but it does not necessarily ensure a high probability of success.

Selznick (1949), for example, on the basis of a study of the Tennessee Valley Authority, showed that Weber's formal description of an efficient bureaucracy left out the dysfunctions which must occur when the top administrators in a large organisation inevitably delegate some of their authority. They do so differentially, and this has several consequences. As intended, it increases the specialised competence of the various groups which now have authority over the different parts of the organisation's functioning. But, at the same time, it also has the unintended effect of increasing departmentalism and underlining the differences of interests between different parts the organisation.

Each department soon develops its own goals and values, and conflict between departments ensues with consequently greater identification of the individual with his own department and lesser identification with the organisation. A man's career appears to be best served by conforming to his department's interests, rather than by pursuing the over-all organisation's good, if this means undermining his own department.

Conflict and Competition

When operational decision-making involves the working relationship between different sections of the enterprise, the pursuit of separate objectives can produce conflicts of interest and competition over the control and influence of resources, services and company plans. Concerns for control over decisions and actions to be taken express strong needs to preserve functional and departmental autonomy. Disputed areas of authority and responsibility lead departments and groups to struggle for their control. Attempts by certain groups to raise their level of power and authority within the firm compromise vested interests and privilege. Tight control and influence can be effectively combated and neutralised by withholding information and technical support necessary for managers to determine adequately decisions and courses of action.

Open confrontation and problem-solving among sections of the enterprise may reflect greater attempts to criticise, discredit and expose the problems of others than to engage in problem resolution and joint decision-making. Such phenomena are particularly evident in companies where one particular function has assumed increasing control over another. With the hierarchic structure of organisations, most organisational problems are resolved by appealing to higher authority or by exerting power and influence over those with whom one is in dispute, whereas the requirements of a supportive and collaborative environment for participative decision-making (which minimises status differences, technical prestige, functional preserves, privileges, vested interests, problem avoidance and withholding information) can render the situation extremely problematical. Unless all the sections of the enterprise work together successfully for the accomplishment of its commercial task, then participation is likely to cause operational difficulties.

The Impact of Change in Working Relations

An increasing amount of effort is being put by management into gaining acceptance and agreement on the need for the organisation to cut back on expenditure and ensure tighter cost controls, higher performance standard and maximisation of productive capacity.

Participation within this context inevitably has an influence on the manner in which it is received and how participants will respond. Uncertainty over what can be achieved, and the consequences of not realising the decisions made, evoke defensiveness, frustration, anxiety and apprehension. As the outcrop of problems and operating constraints emerge, disagreement and conflict may produce deadlock. Learning how to deal with such tension and stress is essential. Hilgendorf and Irving (1976) support this view in their research.

Changes in Human Organisation

Introducing participative management inevitably involves an element of change in working relations, and therefore in an organisation's functioning. Any significant change in human organisation involves a rearrangement of power, association and status. While some may benefit by it, others may lose control and influence over resources and other functions.

Most management strategies outlining the conditions under which worker participation may lead to greater motivation and commitment to the job focus on the individual or his immediate work group (Hertzberg, 1968; McGregor, 1960; Paul and Robertson, 1970). The arguments which are put forward are that the motivated individual places more personal value on his work, derives a greater sense of achievement in doing his job more effectively, receives adequate recognition for such achievements and derives satisfaction and a sense of accomplishment from the responsibility delegated to him in the accomplishment of his task.

Such a strategy denies the organisational forces and pressures acting on people. There is no guarantee that a responsible individual with discretionary power and influence in deciding the scope and nature of his task will be able to act in the best interest of the company.

Sometimes the changes brought about in an individual or work team fail to establish themselves because there are no fully and carefully worked out organisational arrangements to ensure co-ordination with other interacting parts of the system. In such cases it may be because the changes usurp or undermine the interests of a different department which has crucial links with that part of the system undergoing such changes.

Improving Organisational Performance

The chief factors deemed to make a difference in the contribution which management by participation can make in the performance of an organisation are as follows:

(i) securing support and commitment to over-all organisational goals;

(ii) improving collaboration and joint problem-solving among different functions and operating units;

(iii) resolving the conflicting interests and needs of different parties;

(iv) establishing effective leadership and control over the outcomes of change initiatives;

(v) overcoming resistance to change and enabling the people involved in the change to adapt to new systems of operation and organisational arrangements;

(vi) improving the utilisation of human resources;

(vii) raising of level of communications and improving the quality of information flow; and

(viii) developing the expertise and capability of managers to initiate and implement organisational change.

Introducing participative management requires organisations to improve the interpersonal competence of their managers, as well as effecting a change in values so that human factors and feelings come to be considered legitimate, developing increased understanding among and within working groups to reduce underlying tensions, discord and defensiveness, developing 'team management' (and better methods of conflict resolution than suppression, denial and the use of unilateral powers), and viewing the organisation as an organic system of relationships marked by mutual trust, independence, shared responsibility and conflict resolution through training or problem-solving (Bennis, 1965).

Planned Organisational Change

A strategy which can be successfully adopted in dealing with these issues is one of planned organisational change and development applying behavioural-science theories and methods Blake, and Mouton 1964; Goldstein, 1978; Guest, 1962; Jacques, 1952; Kimberly and Nielsen, 1975; Rice, 1958; Seashore and Bowers, 1963). It is deemed most applicable to the organisation's needs in that it is a planned programme involving the total system. Top management is aware of and committed to it and it is related to the organisation's main objectives. Interventions and activities are action-orientated in that organisational member participation is invoked for the diagnosis of operational ills and in the implementation of improved working practices. It focuses on changing attitudes and/or behaviour and ultimately affects the performance of people in the organisation. It usually relies on some form of experienced-based learning activity. The reason is that if an objective is to change attitudes and behaviour, then it is necessary to examine interpersonal relations and working practices, test alternative approaches and begin to practise modified but improved ways of working.

Defining an Organisational Development Framework

The over-all objective is to develop within the organisation self-generated improvements within the management of the system in order to foster the conditions needed to effect organisational change and development. In setting out an organisational development approach there are certain prerequisites for success:

 (i) In the long run the organisation will manage its work against jointly agreed objectives and plans for achieving improved working practices and procedures.

 (ii) Human resources are so organised and managed that operational problems are investigated and tackled on a regular and systematic basis.

(iii) Personnel responsible for improving working conditions are entrusted with the responsibility and discretion necessary to take, where necessary, corrective measures.

(iv) Individuals are more open and challenging about current organisational practices, procedures and about possible alternatives.

(v) Concern is expressed at all levels to treat potentially problematic issues as deserving closer collaboration and joint problem-solving efforts.

(vi) Personnel are able to recognise and perceive a need for closer collaboration and joint problem-solving on organisational matters.

(vii) Individuals and groups by way of the management system report back on and act upon the changes needed to be taken to improve organisational performance (Beckhard, 1969).

In order to be able to explain and evaluate the functioning of organisations and the impact of changes in an organisation's structure and functioning a behavioural approach is deemed to be necessary. The reason underlying this is that only by determining and affecting individual and collective beliefs and actions can managerial policies and decisions be realised. Behavioural science provides an important basis for understanding and analysing organisational behaviour and its impact on task performance.

A behavioural-science approach to understanding and effecting organisational change involves an appraisal and diagnosis of interpersonal or group relationships and the implications of these for changes in technology, structure and task. The focus is on adapting and developing the human-resources system in the sense of making better use of the people in the organisation to meet the changing demands of the external (business) environment upon the internal system of operation. The key variables which assist in understanding and influencing organisational behaviour are the values, norms, goals, interpersonal relationships, climate of working and the problem-solving activities of individuals and work groups. These variables provide a means of analysis and the data for evaluating the outcome of alternative organisational change strategies aimed at changing individual and group relations for purposes of improving an organisation's performance.

Theories and Methods of Studying Organisational Change

In order to establish how improvements in interpersonal and group relationships may be realised for purposes of raising organisational performance, the contribution which various approaches to planned organisational change have made to an understanding of the changes needed in the structure and functioning of organisations is now examined.

Organic system of management

The organic model of organisational functioning recognises the complex interdependence required of people by the organisation's task and the importance of ensuring effective communication, operational control and decision-making networks. The principal method of effecting an organic system of management is one of redistributing power based on overlapping responsibilities, task interdependence and multi-functional liaison and collaboration. Any conflicts of interest must be resolved by the use of bargaining and joint problem-solving rather than by resorting to unilateral arbitration or competition. Arbitration involves some sort of compromise and loss of face which does not meet the needs of either party, while competition is destructive in the sense that the parties concerned will seek to undermine the other's position and defeat its initiatives and efforts. The organic model has been developed and outlined by, among others, Shepherd and Blake (1962), Burns and Stalker (1961) and Davis (1967).

Methods of changing social structures

Resistance to change is a central focus of study in investigations conducted into planned organisational change. The tension and anxiety which stems from people's expectations and insecurities about change is seen as expending and consuming energy, and this diverts people's efforts unproductively away from the primary task of the organisation.

The reduction of tension, particularly of those forces tending towards lowering the level of production, for example anxieties, hostilities, role conflicts, various threats to self-esteem, communication distortions, etc., is considered as a means of effecting change (Sofer, 1972).

The target of change is the social structure, because the tension reflects itself in the particular working relations (social structures) people build up and preserve. Resistance to change occurs because it arouses people's defences against the anxiety brought about by a fear of failure, or a loss of, say, status and authority from the present system. Effective social change is likely to require analysis of the common anxieties and unconscious collusions underlying the resistance to change and the defences people put up (Jacques, 1956).

By an examination of tension-increasing situations, the consequences of the social structures/relations and defensive patterns adopted become more visible, and thus more controllable and amenable to change. The strategy of the change agent is to obtain consensual validation among the parties involved of the realism or otherwise of their expectations of one another's roles, responsibilities, authorities and accountabilities in order to achieve more effective working relations.

Approaches to changing human interaction and organisations

There are numerous organisational change efforts which can help managers examine and face up to organisational and interpersonal issues, for example team-work development and laboratory training (Blake and Mouton, 1964; Bradford, Gibb and Benne, 1963; Friedlander and Brown, 1974; Schein and Bennis, 1965; Rice, 1965).

By closely examining and appraising their own behaviour and actions on a work-related issue, organisational members can come to understand the dynamics of group behaviour, e.g. decision-making processes, leadership, norms, roles, communication distortions, influence patterns, etc. This enables them to become more aware of the process of human interaction and its impact on managerial/supervisory performance in organisational settings. Such training provides the basis for the first two phases of Blake's (1964) organisational change programme. By phase 3 of this programme the key members of the organisation will have undergone training designed to achieve better integration between functional work groups and various organisational divisions such as staff and line, sales and production. The purpose of this is to create a climate of working whereby outstanding problems and stumbling-blocks can be resolved.

In phase 4 senior managers get together to set over-all goals, identify key issues, and plan strategies for a total organisational change effort. Phase 5 is one in which the group members work through the implications of the planned initiatives and think about how to overcome major problems and obstacles such as inadequate co-ordination and control of service support to mainstream operations. By stepping back, management can carefully consider what is the best course of action to pursue in order to obtain changes it desires in organisational practices and procedures. Phase 6 is directed at stabilising the changes brought about earlier. The main effort is directed at ensuring the maintenance of the organisation's new improved functioning and to guard against it reverting to its former state.

A Study in Organisational Change

The research case study that follows illustrates the application of a planned approach to organisational change and performance improvement. The study serves to show what effects the various change interventions adopted had on the system of operations and to show how organisational relations were affected. By identifying the problems and obstacles facing the organisation, the success of management's efforts to initiate performance improvements can be guaged. The result of changes made will be assessed; and the contribution which increased communication and interfunctional problem-solving and joint collaboration on change initiatives make, and what changes can be made in the organisation's structure and functioning, will be made clear.

The adaptability of the organisation's system of operation to change is viewed in terms of the system of management that was adopted and how much more capable it was to respond to the needs for change after the intervention of the change agent. The study highlights several fundamental issues about managerial behaviour and control which directly affected the degree of support and commitment to the organisational change.

Improving the management of performance

Ineffective working practices and administrative procedures have bedevilled many organisations in terms of lost productive capacity and performance efficiency. Personnel and training departments have sought to create a climate of renewed consciousness of the problem through publicity and training. Work study, organisation and methods, and ergonomics have all been techniques adopted at one time or another. For instance, in spite of a vast amount of time, energy and resources put into reducing safety hazards and the incidence of accidents, safety is still a major problem, which (potentially) can be of the magnitude of Flixborough and Seveso.

The present author was called in by the management of a chemical company who were concerned by the absence of safety in their plants. A week earlier a production unit had exploded. Following initial discussions on the gravity of the incident and the need for improved working practices in the whole organisation – though research and development, production and maintenance personnel were particularly involved – the author felt that an *organisational development approach* was the most effective organisational and attitudinal change mechanism.

A strategy for the management of change

The initial strategy was to initiate a planned change programme which allowed for the following:

  (i) a systematic diagnosis of the organisation and its work; i.e. procedures and practices, in order that it might allow for a clearer definition of the problem and needs facing the enterprise;

 (ii) an analysis of the possibilities and limitations for change in attitudes and behaviour (this would determine the system's readiness, capability and potential for change);

(iii) a development of an action plan for initiating and maintaining the safety programme; and

 (iv) a continuous evaluation and review of its progress.

The client consultant relationship began with the definition by top management of safety as an area where management performance could be improved.

The decision as to where to begin in the organisation and the suitable point of leverage or influence fell on senior managers, production supervisors, senior maintenance, and research and development personnel. It was felt that they had the best communications link with the rest of the system, experience of the safety problem and the existing situation at hand, as well as sufficient influence and management authority for promoting safety improvements.

The initial work we undertook within the organisation was to set up a series of performance-improvement programmes given to the above personnel.

The motivation and response to interviews reflected a high level of concern and consideration for safety and positive attitudes to overcoming safety hazards. Many views were put forward which presented investigators with several concrete and immediate proposals and ideas for safety improvement.

However, there was an element of strong feeling in regard to inconsistent actions and attitudes among supervisors over safety, and this made some disinclined to follow safe practices themselves. Criticism was laid at the design of plant technology and the absence of sufficient consultation of plant personnel in safety matters. Various safety hazards were attributed to poor management with respect to the scheduling and control of finished processes. Again, grievances were expressed regarding the lack of real opportunities for consultation and the lack of workers' influence on the work-flow and their own areas of work.

Constraints on improved safety

Production, and research and development personnel spoke of an absence of communication between themselves in the various stages from the inception of a new-product idea to its commercial development and manufacture. This was reinforced by the feelings of first-line management and shop-floor personnel who felt that many safety hazards stemmed from insufficient co-ordination and integration of work efforts by the various organisational departments and specialist functions. There was a strong belief that production, financial and organisational considerations overrode safety considerations.

The company's policy of rationalisation of plant, equipment and manpower resources was seen as constraining safety-improvement considerations. The running down of plant utilisation and the threatened future obsolescence of plant gave first-line and middle management a cynical view to the organisation's real intentions. A feeling of general uncertainty, intensified by inadequate and often ambiguous and misleading information, had given rise to queries as to how improving safety stood in relation to over-all company policy, and its place in it.

Top management's concern for safety was seen as encouraging and motivating personnel to strive more conscientiously to reduce accident risks and potential safety hazards. However, more hardened and cynical personnel felt it would only serve to prolong the life of run-down antiquated plants, which in the short term were to be maintained, and in the future made obsolete.

The company's policy of rationalisation inevitably meant a running down of the work-force, which made the various necessary safety considerations more difficult to ensure.

The overriding concern for safety attached by top management could not be expected to be strongly held by a work-force who felt aggrieved by the fact that complaints of safety hazards were very rarely acted upon by first-line and middle management. The neglect of certain essential practices and procedures among the work-force was rapidly emerging as a consequence of managerial/supervisory attitudes and behaviour.

The investigations revealed further problems of communication and co-ordination of activities across departmental and functional boundaries. They also revealed problems of a hierarchical nature.

The influence of organisational sanctions

Production targets set by higher management were considered to be sought at the expense of safety considerations. Middle management felt constrained by pressures and directives from above in maintaining and improving safety practices by the work-force.

The need to meet customer demands in a changing and fluctuating market brought overriding pressures and sanctions to bear on production management to meet production deadlines set by higher management.

On the other hand, there were strong incentives to the work-force to maximise output in order to raise bonus earnings. It was frequently said by several operatives that safety was risked in order to boost earnings and in order to meet production pressures exerted by management. Rush jobs (assignments) tended to be undertaken with insufficient regard to safety by management. While a manager's lack of motivation and concern to act promptly upon, and initiate, safety improvements may have been influenced by antipathy to the company's policy of rationalisation, an important constraint felt by middle management was the financial resources available for safety improvements.

Many extensive schemes proposed to reduce safety hazards had been eliminated from consideration in the past by the necessary expenditure and absence of adequate budgets to cover projected costs. Proposals and schemes which were submitted to higher management met with delays and closure as other more pressing matters, e.g. cost control, resource utilisation, production targets and raising plant capacity, were given priority. Major proposals were thus shelved for lack of financial resources and because of the pressing claims of other concerns.

Factors eroding managerial responsibility

Initially there was a strong body of sceptics and cynics among the management investigation groups who could not see that the company policy on safety was meant to be a practical reality. In their experience they found it difficult to see how they could influence and affect safety conditions in operational terms with the many financial, organisational and production restraints overriding safety considerations.

The concern for safety expressed within the over-all company policy was not readily transmitted to the investigation groups, in spite of general powers of responsibility and authority vested in them to take corrective actions to improve safety practices in the company.

The system of operation and management in the company was still seen to one opposing the implementation of safer working practices and conditions. Motivation and commitment to an investigation of safety were restricted by an inability to see recommended changes and corrective proposals being readily and easily implemented. Such feelings tended to allow individuals to escape from responsibility for change in that the source of frustration was with the system of operation and management in the company over which they claimed they were able to exert little influence.

The management of change

Each person seemed fairly sure of the general responsibilities of his job and what it was necessary to do in order to ensure it ran well and safely in a technical sense. There was, however, little evidence of initiative to act in a way as to cause improvements in performance (there was a tendency to accept the status quo). Here again there was a suggestion of acceptance of constraints even though the constraints were ones imposed by the system's own inadequacies. For instance, although there was much discussion of financial constraints bearing on improving safety, there was little evidence of accurate and detailed cost estimations being made in order to assess budgeting requirements, i.e. the likely costs entailed in proposals and recommendations for improved safety. The exact funds available were not ascertained, nor were priorities clearly established or outlined.

The study groups, while consulting with line management and operatives, were reluctant and at the same time uncertain of how to tap the knowledge and resources of the safety department. The latter was seen as ineffective and not fulfilling its responsibilities adequately. Typical of many line–staff relations, responsibilities and authorities were not clearly identified and recognised as being mutually supportive.

The management study group failed to derive from the safety department accurate measures of the costs of accidents – which were important data for presenting a case for certain financial resources to be made available in order to overcome reduced performance of employees and losses of production through accidents and worker absenteeism. In general a cloud of suspicion hung over operations and service support relations, and this reduced incentives for mutual support and co-operation.

Obstacles to change

While the investigation groups were anxious and able to communicate downwards through the hierarchy, they were less anxious and able to communicate laterally outside the group and were reluctant to communicate with superiors. This was evident by the diligence with which they conducted the surveys among plant operatives and first-line management, the time they took to produce and follow up on their reports and by the low level of personal communication with senior management.

No formal outline of plans, procedures and recommendations had been presented to senior management for improving safety. While voices were raised concerning the possible assistance, support and encouragement from higher management, and the absence of initiative and responsibility from the top, little or no advice had been sought. This created a situation in which the project groups were acting without over-all direction and guidance from above, a position in which they had largely put themselves but which also they resented.

The dissenting and sceptical elements used this situation to shed their responsibilities for the change programme and to reinforce their view of an absence of two-way communication, the isolation and distance of higher management and thus the absence of an opportunity to influence goal-setting and decision-making on matters affecting them in their own working environment effectively. Although communications presented a problem in terms of the will to communicate upwards, this of course varied with individuals and was largely based upon a lack of managerial confidence and understanding of why and when it was necessary to communicate upwards and a lack of a system of communication where face-to-face contact was routinised.

It proved essential, therefore, to introduce a series of team-work development sessions over a period of time with full involvement of senior management in small work groups to examine some of the operational problems and how they could be tackled. The value of this exercise was that it did not explicitly centre on communications improvement but rather on job improvement. Improved communications were one of the results. There was the problem, however, that some individuals had deeply entrenched ideas about what they were allowed to do and what they were prevented from doing which may well have negatively influenced attitudes towards task performance. In such an organisational environment these attitudes spread and influenced others and needed to be changed. By having more clearly defined objectives and regularly discussing the degree of achievement and the necessary levels of responsibility with senior management in a planned fashion, such attitudes, and indeed the performance, of individuals and work groups can be materially affected for the better.

Summary

In summary the overriding objective of the research was to improve safety within the organisation at three separate sites by improving management performance. A planned strategy for action was adopted by the project management group in order to enable them to plan, and implement safety improvements in the work situations set against specific organisational objectives at their level of authority conscious of the integrated nature of departmental practices and procedures and the need to involve different functions and all levels of management, supervision and the work-force.

While significant steps and actions were taken to resolve safety hazards, certain factors were likely to impair the management of safety. There was a need to open up communications between top and middle management, in order to promote mutual influence in areas of decision-making and review the perceived controls felt to be exerted upon middle management from above. This would allow a more effective planning of changes in working practices and procedures, in the light of fuller information and raise levels of motivation and commitment to improvements in organisational performance.

Organisational Developments necessary for Improving Management Performance

In planning an organisation development programme for an organisation there is a need for the active involvement of key line and staff management in its planning and execution. Personnel with a perceptive awareness of the needs for performance improvements and with influence in the organisation are needed in the initial problem identification and planning of the change initiative.

A systematic diagnosis of the particular changes needed in the organisation's system of operation requires expert problem-solving skills. An investigation and examination of operational problems and needs necessitate interpersonal skills which enable the researcher or manager to be receptive and responsive to feedback from organisational personnel. Guidance and training in these two areas may be required in the early stages of such a project before the decision-making process gets too far underway and action is taken based on an inadequate or misinformed understanding of the problems facing the organisation.

Changing attitudes and behaviour may require changing an individual's perception and view of his or her job, away from the parochial and technical aspects, and more towards organisational change and project management.

There may be a need for open problem-solving communication across the organisation, and for placing decision-making responsibilities lower down the organisational hierarchy. Managers and supervisors need to see themselves as managing change if they are to feel at all committed to job-improvement programmes. This could involve personnel functions in investigating perceived organisational constraints, in recommending improvements in organisational performance and in outlining which changes are needed in systems of operation and in the management of them. Management training and development may be identified as necessary for facilitating such change initiatives.

The rewards and sanctions inherent in the system of operation must be in alignment with the job improvements desired from personnel. In the above case study managers voiced the view that production considerations overrode other requirements. Plant operatives, on the other hand, felt that concern for safety could reduce bonus payments as far as production incentives were concerned. The development of managerial expertise derived from training programmes is nullified by the sanctions which compel people to conform to less than effective working practices. Personnel departments should investigate with their line management what particular impact the management system has upon working practices and the degree of flexibility which can be built into work systems and procedures without jeopardising safe working practices and conditions.

In attempting to implement job-improvement programmes operating functions should first diagnose the existing management and communications system and the climate of working, in order to establish what obstacles may confront new change initiatives, and how they might be overcome. At the same time, one will have a clearer picture and assessment of what possible performance improvements can be realised by the organisation.

Whether or not management and supervision are able or willing to improve their current working practices is much more of a problem than communicating and reinforcing the need for it through management training and project work. This can be readily deduced from considerations of the constraints operating on different individuals in their working environment.

Of ultimate importance is obtaining the full understanding, commitment and involvement of senior management in a strategy for performance improvement within an organisational change and development context. A key to the success of any change programme is obtaining a willingness and receptivity of participants to want to do things differently back on the job in so far as initiating improvements in working practices is concerned.

However, the commitment to do so is very much dependent upon the degree to which participants see change initiatives responded to and performance improvements realised.

References

Argyris, C. (1962) *Interpersonal Competence and Organizational Effectiveness* (Homewood, Ill., Dorsey Press).

Beckhard, R. (1969) *Organization Development – Strategies and Models* (Reading, Mass., Addison-Wesley).

Bennis, W. (1965) 'Theory and Method in Applying Behavioral Science to Planned Organizational Change', *Applied Behavioral Science*, vol. 1, no. 4.

Blake, R. R. and Mouton, J. S. (1964) *The Managerial Grid* (Houston, Texas Gulf).

Bradford, L. P., Gibb, J. R. and Benne, K. D. (eds) (1963) *T-Group Theory and Laboratory Method: Innovation in Re-education* (New York, Wiley).

Burns, T. and Stalker, G. M. (1961) *The Management of Innovation* (London, Tavistock).

Davis, S. A. (1967) 'An Organic Problem-solving Method of Organizational Change', *Journal of Applied Behavioral Science*, vol. 3, January, pp. 3–21.

Dubin, R., *et al.* (1965) *Leadership and Productivity* (San Francisco, Chandler).

Friedlander, F. and Brown, L. D. (1974) 'Organisation Development', in *Annual Review of Psychology*, ed. M. Rosenzweig and L. W. Porter, vol. 25.

Goldstein, S. G. (1978) 'A Structure for Change', *Human Relations*, vol. 31, no. 11, November.

Gouldner, A. W. (1955) *Patterns of Industrial Bureaucracy* (London, Routledge & Kegan Paul).

Guest, R. H. (1962) *Organization Change: the Effect of Successful Leadership* (Homewood, Ill., Dorsey Press).

Hertzberg, F. (1968) 'One More Time – How do You Motivate People?', *Harvard Business Review*, January–February.

Hilgendorf, E. L. and Irving, B. L. (1976) 'Workers' Experience of Participation: the Case of British Railways', *Human Relations*, vol. 29, no. 5, May, pp. 471–505.

Jacques, E. (1952) *The Changing Culture of a Factory – a Study of Authority and Participation* (London, Tavistock).

Jacques, E. (1977) 'Social Systems as a Defence against Persecution and Depressive Anxiety', in *New Directions in Psychoanalysis: Significance of Infant Conflict in the Pattern of Adult Behaviour*; ed. M. Klein *et al.* (London, Karmac, 1977).

Kahn, R. L., Wolfe, D. M., Quinn, R. P. and Snoek, J. D. (1964) *Organizational Stress: Studies in Role Conflict and Ambiguity* (New York, Wiley).

Kimberly, J. R. and Nielsen, W. R. (1975) 'Organization Development and Change in Organizational Performance', *Administrative Science Quarterly*, vol. 20, no. 2, June, pp. 191–206.

McGregor, D. (1960) *The Human Side of Enterprise* (New York, McGraw-Hill).

Merton, R. K. (1957) *Social Theory and Social Structure*, 2nd ed. (New York, The Free Press).

Paul, W. and Robertson, K. B. (1970) *Job Enrichment and Organisational Change* (London, Gower Press).

Rice, A. K. (1958) *Productivity and Social Organisation: The Ahmedabad Experiment* (London, Tavistock).

Rice, A. K. (1965) *Learning for Leadership* (London, Tavistock).

Schein, E. H. and Bennis, W. C. (1965) *Personal and Organizational Change through Group Methods* (New York, Wiley).

Seashore, S. E. and Bowers, D. G. (1963) 'Changing the Structure and Functioning of an Organization', in *Organizational Experiments: Laboratory and Field Work*, ed. W. M. Evan (New York, Harper & Row).

Selznick, P. (1949) *T.V.A. and the Grass Roots: A Study in the Sociology of Formal Organizations* (California University Press).

Shepherd, H. A. and Blake, R. R. (1962) 'Changing Behavior through Cognitive Change', *Human Organization*, vol. 21, Summer, pp. 88–96.

Sofer, C. (1972) *Organisations in Theory and Practice* (London, Heinemann).

6
Developing a Learning Organisation

The Context of Organisational Change

A major responsibility of management is ensuring that the operation of an organisation is effectively co-ordinated and controlled. Various procedures, rules and regulations serve as controls in ensuring that working practices comply with normal efficient operations. Information systems are operated so that individual tasks may be more effectively co-ordinated and controlled and organisational performance can be more effectively monitored and reviewed.

Whenever there is a questioning of the bases of current operational efficiency in a company, a need is being recognised or felt for some form of internal change. Managerial initiatives in organisational change terms spring from either a dissatisfaction with existing methods and modes of operation or a belief that they are either no longer feasible or are limiting performance and are thus less than effective in fulfilling their original purpose. External influences act as a stimulus for organisational change, and management has to face up to the impact of changes in the business environment. For instance, rising operating costs, fluctuating market demand and price re-straints, all call for tighter cost controls. Malfunctions in the use to which the cost-control system is put expose and undermine an organisation's ability to regulate its cash flow and to administer a policy of cost-effectiveness in its daily operations.

Managers more readily appreciate the need for change when pressures, problems and difficulties beset them in their task of having to work under technical, financial or human constraints which limit or undermine their capacities, efforts and energies for achieving an acceptable level of operational performance. Competing and conflicting demands and expectations between separate departments cause barriers to go up which undermine and erode an organisation's need for co-ordination and control of the work-flow.

Managers attempt to adapt and improve the organisation's structure and the workings of its various systems so as to be able to respond effectively and quickly to changing business needs, dictated by changes in the direction of company policy or enforced by external pressures and constraints. Yet a manager's primary concern is to ensure smooth, uninterrupted, trouble-free operations. The management of change is therefore the manager's biggest risk facing him and is his most difficult challenge.

The Development of a Learning Organisation

In that managers need to learn how best to cope and adapt to the pressures and demands for change an important consideration is whether the organisation is capable of responding by providing the necessary set of conditions for organisational change problems to surface and for enabling the management system to act upon them.

Figure 6.1 traces the source of organisational change problems back to the competing and conflicting demands and expectations of the individual in relation to the needs of the organisation for rules, regulations, procedures and control systems. This is set against a background of a changing and uncertain external environment which imposes constraints on an organisation's need for growth and development in certain desired directions. In having to respond to pressures and demands for change managers face another set of additional problems concerning the implementation of change. The diagram outlines a number of outstanding problems which impede organisational change. The next essential consideration is whether the problems facing an organisation are being identified and examined by the various departments and managers concerned. The diagram suggests that an organisational search and investigation is required about current operational performance to see how far short it falls of desired levels, measured in terms of performance improvement. A process of information-gathering, analysis and diagnosis is required initially. The next stage is for various decision-making bodies to embark on planning and devising alternative change strategies. The diagram puts forward the steps necessary. At the same

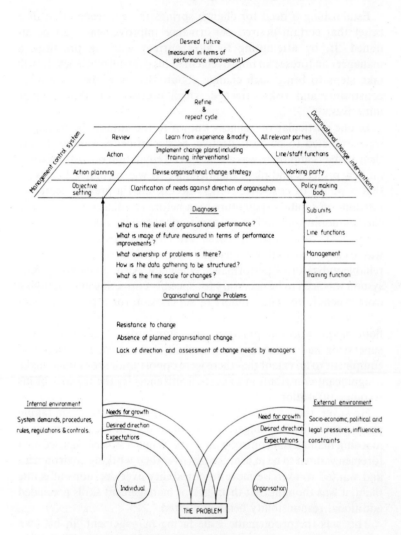

Desired future
(measured in terms of
performance improvement)

Refine
&
repeat cycle

Management control system

Organisational change interventions

Review	Learn from experience & modify	All relevant parties
Action	Implement change plans (including training interventions)	Line/staff functions
Action planning	Devise organisational change strategy	Working party
Objective setting	Clarification of needs against direction of organisation	Policy making body

Diagnosis

Sub units

What is the level of organisational performance?
What is image of future measured in terms of performance improvements?
What ownership of problems is there?
How is the data gathering to be structured?
What is the time scale for changes?

Line functions

Management

Training function

Organisational Change Problems

Resistance to change

Absence of planned organisational change

Lack of direction and assessment of change needs by managers

Internal environment

System demands, procedures, rules, regulations & controls.

External environment

Socio-economic, political and legal pressures, influences, constraints

Needs for growth
Desired direction
Expectations

Need for growth
Desired direction
Expectations

Individual

Organisation

THE PROBLEM

FIGURE 6.1   *The development of a learning organisation*

time, there should be careful monitoring and reviewing of progress at each stage in the change process.

These, then, are the conditions which are seen as being instrumental in creating and developing a learning organisation in which managers can cope and adapt to the needs for change.

Establishing a need for change springs from a recognition or a belief that certain desired performance improvements can be attained. If, by attempting to alter current working practices, a manager can foresee an improvement in his over-all efficiency, he will take steps to bring such change about. However, there are often constraints and risks attached which preclude or abort change initiatives.

In one particular oil refinery known to the author the managers were exhorted to be cost-effective, as departments were exceeding their budgets and there was a widespread escalation of costs incurred on new projects and plant maintenance. It was recognised early on that a policy of cost-effectiveness necessitated a greater degree of restraint on capital expenditure than before and that it needed more careful monitoring and speedier action taken when deviations from acceptable cost control appeared. An effective cost-control system was seen as essential and changes were needed to make it a more reliable indicator of performance efficiency. Also, an early-warning system was seen to be necessary for speedily correcting and rectifying over-expenditure. The support of supervision for a policy of cost-effectiveness was essential because of its direct impact on the shop floor upon working practices and standards of efficiency. The supervisor had significant responsibility over men, materials and equipment to an extent that there were opportunities for him to make a significant contribution to cost-effectiveness by the manner of his resource utilisation.

However, there was little confidence expressed in foremen taking on responsibility for budgetary control because of the risks involved in losing managerial control over costs. While it was recognised that foremen wanted to be in firm control over their working environment and wanted to exercise more responsibility over decisions affecting them, it was thought that their lack of management skills precluded additional responsibility being conferred.

This was the problematic issue facing management. In his own defence the supervisor claimed he was unable to control operating costs any more effectively than management could, attributing some of the reasons to management's own lack of commitment to cost-effectiveness and the others to the constraints under which he worked, such as the lack of authority in disciplining or dismissing members of the work-force whose work was not of an adequate standard.

Establishing the Change Relationship

A consequence of unresolved issues and expectations between levels of management is that divisions are set up between people, and barriers build up which undermine trust and confidence in others' efforts to introduce change. Problems can come to be attributed to the other party, thereby absolving people of their own responsibility for problem resolution.

Tensions in the system are therefore evident when the bases of current organisational ills are seen differently, and contradictory reasons attributed to them, for a feature of organisational life is that departments and functions have competing and conflicting objectives and interests.

The establishment of a working party or project group whose task it is to investigate and explore new alternative methods of operation may enable the organisation to set about tackling outstanding problems which adversely affect business performance and operational capability. It provides a forum which encourages relevant collaboration and management of differences as far as the perception of organisational ills and the bases for them are concerned. Dissatisfaction expressed about the present methods and modes of operation serve to highlight the complexity and multivariate nature of the different issues, concerns and demands facing an organisation. The management of differences therefore requires a long and continuous process of relationship-building. This can begin with a listing of problems drawn up from the claims and counter-claims brought out in different departments. An examination of the underlying causes to the dissatisfactions expressed enables certain problem areas to be defined more accurately and understood more clearly by all parties.

Diagnosing the Bases of Organisational Problems

In sharpening the views and opinions expressed, working parties can assist in substantiating known facts and uncovering individual ways of thinking and responding to current problems which existing control systems may hide or neglect.

At the same time, in allowing for shared perceptions and interpretations of the major areas of common concern, it enables a working party to agree on what the constraints currently are on effective action-taking and decision-making in the resolution of organisationally based problems. In that issues of concern relate to an individual's own experience of them in terms of the direct impact they have on him at his own level in the organisation, he is more likely to be committed to achieving an effective resolution of the major problems in a responsible fashion. In examining the bases for different interpretations of the problems and concerns voiced the working party is required to assess what more rigorous ways and means there are for looking at the major areas of concern in order to work through the essential differences in assumptions, beliefs and definitions of the problems besetting them and the organisation.

Once there has been more complete understanding of the differences, the working party is then able to sit down and establish what the priorities are for resolving the outstanding issues and concerns. In this way it establishes the ground for joint working and collaboration in key organisational areas in the pursuit of some commonly framed policy, such as resource development and cost-effectiveness. The task of the working party may be to establish how a more effective deployment of manpower can be secured in order to maximise productive capacity and minimise resource development costs. One means of improving manpower efficiency and cutting cost is by improving work standards. An important contribution can be made by management training in upgrading the skills and capabilities of individuals in their job.

The Contribution of Training to Change Management

What, therefore, is the contribution which management training can make to facilitate organisational change?

First, it ought to provide individuals with better understanding and clearer insight into human behaviour and its influence on organisational relations. A fundamental aspect of improving operational efficiency is changing working practices. Understanding the different response patterns of individuals to management controls and work systems can make a significant contribution to the success of changes implementation.

Dealing with organisational problems and ills requires problem-solving and decision-making skills. At the same time, there is a need to understand how problems recur and what the underlying basis for them is.

One of the aims of the training may be to change behaviour so as to alter working relations which currently detract from an individual's job performance and the organisation's effectiveness in achieving the necessary co-ordination of functions on jointly undertaken operations.

In setting out certain desired performance improvements an organisation is implying the need for altering current working practices. Such changes may require extensive training in the process of management and the skills needed for coping and dealing with constraints on action.

Establishing Training Objectives by an Operation/Training Needs Analysis

Once the major problem areas acting as stumbling-blocks to job performance and organisational effectiveness are established, training needs can be identified.

An assessment of what exactly are the needs for change can be more clearly defined when it is realised what current performance is. This involves an examination and a reappraisal of:

   (i) core activities and problematic interfaces;
  (ii) working practices and relations across key interfaces;
 (iii) human influences operating in a problematic situation; and
 (iv) management skills needed to deal with operational problems.

Training can provide a manager with skills and knowledge to contribute to his greater understanding of the forces and influences acting upon job performance and to deciding which behavioural tactics and strategies are available for coping with and adapting to organisational problems, and for attaining certain performance improvements measured in terms of job results.

Establishing Job Performance Improvements

By means of an operational performance assessment as outlined above, the manager can begin to define his particular training needs in terms of the key issues affecting his performance in relation to his departmental and organisational responsibilities.

To illustrate, a senior engineering maintenance manager recognised the need to develop more sensitivity, understanding and skill in handling his staff in the face of growing pressures and demands from operating plants for engineering to improve the quality and efficiency of its maintenance service. The manager also recognised the need for proper judgement to be exercised as to when to intervene in a situation of conflict between his staff and operating departments and how best to intervene in order to avoid blame and recrimination leading to diminished responsibility at the individual level for overcoming the interface problem.

A particular personal objective of this manager was to understand the full impact and influence of his own leadership style upon his staff at the problematic interface. In terms of improving organisational effectiveness by way of obtaining better job results the manager recognised the need to reduce the amount of fire-fighting and trouble-shooting between his own and other departments by engaging relevant people more often in planning and anticipating operating problems.

Training can therefore assist the manager to re-evaluate his role and responsibilities for the management of his relations with his staff and other departments and to be aware of what changes are necessary in current practices and procedures.

Criteria for Success in Training

In devising a strategy for management training within an organisational change effort there are certain necessary conditions which need to be fulfilled for the training part to be effective. First, the manager should be able to recognise and establish the value and contribution of the training to his job needs and problems. Unless this is the case, the individual may not be motivated to learn ways of managing change more effectively. Second, there is the actual testing of relevant skills, understanding and attitudes to change related to current working practices adversely influencing job performance. Third, a stage which is at the heart of achieving organisational change, is recognition of how the learning can be applied on the job. The fourth stage involves the receptivity and response of people in his working environment in so far as they allow him to apply the knowledge and skills he has acquired. For this to be possible the learner has to have adequate resources in himself to behave differently, and to this end his behaviour must be reinforced by appropriate support and recognition from higher management. There must not be sanctions from within the system which deter putting the new learning into effect and which compels the individual to conform to less efficient working practices.

The Role of Developmental Training

Training can play a significant part in creating the conditions needed for organisational change efforts to succeed in that it is concerned with the development of the skills and understanding of those people charged with the application, interpretation and operation of new policies, procedures, regulations, systems and controls which accompany new organisational change initiatives.

The question is: how can management training assist the organisation to manage more effectively and to move towards a climate of working in the future which enables it to respond quickly and appropriately to internal and environmental changes in the furtherance of its primary task, without adversely affecting performance efficiency?

Setting and carrying-out training objectives

The following illustrates, once training needs have been identified and carried out, the contribution they make to facilitating organisational change efforts. The organisation under study was seeking to achieve tighter cost control as a means of overcoming its shortfall in working capital in order to pay for the rapidly increasing costs of its operations.

A working party met to discuss ways and means of achieving greater cost-effectiveness in its operations by obtaining better management control of expenditure. The meeting decided on developing the managerial skills and attributes of engineering maintenance foremen. An examination was made of the management functions necessary for maintenance efficiency at the supervisory level.

The foremen were then set certain field assignments where exercising cost control was essential, which would serve to deepen their understanding of the management process and the management responsibilities they could effectively exercise for controlling costs. The aim of the supervisory development/training plan was to bring about a re-examination and appraisal of the foremen's supervisory role in the engineering function and in their relations with the total organisation, such as operations and service departments.

The proposed approach was to set up working parties who would report back on their findings and recommendations on performance-improvement opportunities in terms of current operational problems, the system's needs and alternative plans for refining and modifying existing operating procedures and practices necessary for achieving more adequate cost control.

The desired outcome of the training programme was to have a supervisory force who were more able and ready to understand the managerial demands for their job, more understanding of the reasons for current managment practices, procedures and controls, and more informed and questioning about present methods of operation, procedures adopted and controls available.

The process of managing change

Each individual, prior to the training sessions, carried out an examination of a specific function. The purpose of this was to highlight what the aim of each principal activity was and to define the present system of operation. The work-flow analysis of each main activity was presented so as to outline the steps presently taken to achieve the main task. This was intended to give the work teams an appreciation of the activities involved and where their own contributions fitted into the over-all scheme of support activities required from people.

Steps were then taken to examine how best to get the work done with the back-up and resource support available. This served to define support needs and areas of joint responsibility more clearly where previously responsibility relations had become confused or blurred.

In examining the work-flow of a particular function it enabled the work team to recognise the problems and difficulties caused along the route from work origination to inception and execution. It helped to predict potential trouble-spots and allerted people to possible problem areas. It also served to highlight inadequate management control due to a lack of understanding of the impact of individual actions, as well as that due to serious omissions.

The diffusion and stabilisation of organisational change

The investigations undertaken by the small task forces involved the foremen in gathering cost information, identifying key operating variables and deviations from normal practice and procedure, problem identification and evaluation of various working practices and procedures being adopted to meet the system's needs.

A task of the working party was to co-ordinate and control any change initiatives which were agreed to emanating out of the recommendations and proposals which were made from the investigations of the task forces. In this way it was hoped to reinforce and develop the skills and attributes of supervision back on the job.

The undertakings by foremen of investigations into current practices, procedures and controls served to influence and set the direction of thinking in departments about how the particular demands of the system could be realised more effectively in their own jobs. The investigations served to highlight where there were ways and means of further improving existing working practices. It was found that feedback up the line on specific issues encouraged more open and direct problem-solving.

After a period of six months the evidence was that foremen were now more capable of taking on managerial responsibility in their own job: they were now tackling some of the outstanding cost-control problems faced by the organisation. The contribution they were making to improved operational efficiency became more apparent by the number of cost-saving schemes adopted.

Evaluating the impact of management training interventions within an organisational change programme must be related to the degree of success achieved in improving operating efficiency as measured by normal indices and standards of performance such as increased production, lower operating costs or improved quality of product. In specifically evaluating the training contribution it is reasonable to judge whether or not the skills and capabilities of individuals to manage change are evident in their ability to adapt to and initiate change as well as manage the change process successfully.

Training in Human-resource Management

Six years ago a large oil refinery and chemical plant embarked on a management training and development programme as part of an over-all strategy to improve the management of its human resources. The purpose underlying this strategy was to create the conditions in which employees at all levels would be encouraged to develop and realise their potentialities while contributing towards the company's objectives.

There had been an awareness in the refinery for some years of the need to improve the skills of its managers in dealing with people. At the time senior management wanted to encourage middle managers to consult the shop floor more and operate in a participative style in order to bring the industrial work-force closer to management and thereby improve the process of resolving work-related matters of importance.

A working party was set up in 1970, with a brief to examine and make recommendations for management training, and it drew up what it believed to be the conditions for effective man management, namely: (i) the participation and involvement of subordinates in the affairs of the department; (ii) a critical and yet enquiring review of established procedures and practices for getting work done; (iii) open and frank communications with others on the different needs and problems faced at work; and (iv) the development of subordinates by delegation of authority and responsibility and by establishing realistic work goals with them so as to give people a sense of achievement and motivation to improve their own job performance.

A general appreciation course in management behaviour was developed in order to foster these conditions. It covered the following subject-areas: awareness of own interpersonal competence; motivation theories; styles of leadership and their impact; understanding work-group behaviour and people's part in it; and decision-making and interactive skills needed to solve problems. The aim of the training programme was to develop an awareness among managers of the importance of their working relationships in the solution of work-related problems. At the end of the course the manager should have examined and established some of the possibilities of bringing about improvements in his job performance and what steps he needed to take in terms of organisational change initiatives.

Evaluation of Management Training

Three years after the inception of the training in the oil refinery, attempts were made to evelute its effectiveness in contributing to the best use of human resources in the solution of business and operating problems. Managers claimed that they more consciously involved their subordinates in decisions, inviting feedback on their own plans, in order to get more ready acceptance and commitment to improved methods of working. Involving subordinates in the decision-making process, it was reported, enabled managers to delegate responsibility for tasks which at times went by default. However, there were several strong messages running through the reported interviews, which illustrated the problems of transferring and applying the learning derived from the course back on to the job. The training programme highlighted for many young managers and graduates the high degree of resistance to change they encountered and the rigidity of outlook which foremen and supervisory staff had in looking at a problem in a different way. The tendency was to adapt to the low level of influence and support by withdrawing initiatives and conforming to current practices and procedures. Concern was expressed about the quality of working relations because the conflicting demands and expectations of functions reinforced the need for closer team work than the two departments would admit being responsible for. Although it was claimed that involving staff in the decision-making process was desirable, it was not always possible to ensure accountability from people for their actions. In many instances there was a tendency to 'play it safe' and avoid responsibility in areas of risk, as (for example) in handling industrial-relations and disciplinary matters. Outside pressures imposed on supervisory staff or managers were observed to produce a high degree of defensiveness, a covering-up of mistakes and a careful avoidance of problematic issues. While the need for encouraging frankness and honesty with staff was recognised, it was seen as particularly difficult with some individuals because of the attacking and blaming stance they adopted and the reluctance to recognise any personal limitations. Over all, attempts to examine and question working practices and procedures constructively were inhibited or suppressed by a denial and concealment of problems and issues. In such a climate of working, errors and misjudgements not infrequently led to mistrust, ill-will and rancour.

Three years on from the inception of the training programmes this particular strategy of improving the management of human resources by creating the conditions for effective man management did not appear to have succeeded. While the training programme certainly enabled more managers to appreciate the impact of their working relations in the resolution of problems, the efforts made to move in the direction of examining working relations, management procedures and practices back on the job were very much less supported – in fact, were frustrated or avoided – in the follow-up to the course. The value of continuing with the training in its initial form with the current organisational climate of working was decidedly questionable. First, the particular needs and benefits derived from management training were insufficiently aligned to the company's business needs and to operating problems which directly impacted on the efficiency of the refinery in its day-to-day operations. Second, the course brought people together from all over the refinery whose operating concerns and working relationships could not be effectively examined without also examining those people directly or indirectly concerned in the individual's task, i.e. those people who had control and influence over what the individual did and how he did it. General training for a diffuse spread of people can only lead to an examination of a generality of concerns with no determined 'payback' or measure of results. The attitudes and behaviour of managers cannot be changed in isolation from the problems faced back on the job, nor divorced from those who control or influence that problem situation. People's performance and capability in a job is influenced less by a one-week, off-site programme and more by the people they have to work with and their understanding of what is wanted, and more particularly those who exercise control by authority or influence on the system. Third, an individual's attempts to improve work systems and operating procedures, and in this way exerting an influence on operating costs, must involve questioning organisational practices and problems as much as individual be-haviour and problems of motivating subordinates or influencing colleagues.

A principal finding of the management training report as regards the transfer of learning back on the job was that there could be little if any visible payback from the training when there was a widespread of opinion from managers and supervisors that little apparent concern was placed or action taken to initiate an examination in departments and between them on improving working relations in the solution of business problems. Yet there are many major organisational difficulties which managers experience in their job which directly affect their performance, and occupy their thinking and problem-solving energies on the training programme. For example, the continued use and abuse of the work-priority system was frequently referred to on the training programme. So, too, was the resistance of technical and managerial staff to improved operating procedures and work systems, such as universal maintenance standards in information systems as measures of manpower efficiency and utilisation. The fact that these problems remain with the company and others emerge as a consequence, such as unnecessary breakdowns and equipment failures which could have been prevented if the priority system was more reliable, means that there is room for improvement in the use of human resources in the solution of business and operating problems. The contribution that a general appreciation course can make to such problems can only be incidental, and yet if the course is to have a visible payback the training and development needs of managers and supervisors must be tailored to meet their demands for resolving operating problems. A further important aspect is that the training objectives were drawn up very largely without the knowledge and commitment of the functional managers, with the exception of the administration manager. The effectiveness of management training programmes in aiding people's capability to resolve operating problems faced on site could not easily be demonstrated to senior management in their present form.

If, going back to first principles, the relevance of developing the company's human-resource potential in solving its business problems is determined, then the strategy which evolves will directly contribute to organisational effectiveness. In the first instance one of the routes which can be taken is to meet jointly with senior functional managers in order to establish what management training needs there are in relation to the organisational problems faced in meeting business objectives on an operational basis. For instance, behaviour which is evidently of concern to senior management is the level of responsibility and accountability felt down the line for operating problems.

This is witnessed by the reluctance of personnel to take initiatives. There is also a concern to play it safe and avoid the risks involved in owning problems. There is a low level of commitment in several instances to enter into joint examination and responsibility for the resolution of operating problems, an example being the problems of technological impovements to service support operations. There is a heavy dependence on higher management for action to support them. There is a strong element of wanting to be told what to do and wanting the limits of responsibility to be clearly defined. A feature of this dependency and conformity is an absence of questioning and challenging of ineffective practices and any dysfunctional activities. One of the consequences of this situation is senior management's time-consuming efforts to tighten management controls and the heavy investment of time from middle managers in monitoring and providing control information. One of the consequences of this are the efforts of managers to avoid shared responsibility where problems have arisen on work assignments where blame can be attributed to them. This serves to harden existing boundaries between functions and reduces the prospects of achieving integration.

Management Training Alternatives

By identifying the training needs of area teams and work groups with senior managers, the sort of training needed and for whom, can be established in certain outstanding operating problem areas. Examining the nature of the problems involved and the behavioural techniques available, certain desired outcomes can be established and a strategy for training developed in response to the manager's needs on the job. The training identified may be a one to three day team-building event, a decision-making skills programme for managers concerned over responsibility and commitment for a certain course of action, or a communications course in order to improve working relations and co-operation between departments. If it is recognised by the managers involved that the training experience off site has been devised in order to allow for an examination of the many facets and complex elements to an existing problem area, a crucial and necessary element will have been recognised of follow-up work back on the job with those persons involved. Only in this way can training provide a real payback and secure the genuine commitment of managers and supervisors. Management training programmes would thus be developed and run to meet identified training needs in relation to operating problems and the demands of the working situation facing the manager responsible for the training initiative. This would then provide the most effective use of training resources for developing people's potential to resolve operating problems.

Unless a planned, managed, systematic process for changing the climate of organisational working is devised, then an improvement in the organisation's effectiveness in solving its problems and achieving its objectives will not materialise. Until there is a personal commitment from managers at the top to the systematic setting of goals and plans for achieving them, and to the providing of responsible leadership in terms of policy direction on human-resource management, management training programmes will have limited impact on organisational effectiveness and on the management of business operations.

Organisational Developments in Human-resource Management

With changes in the business environment, including fluctuating market demand and rising costs and the demands this puts on an organisation, adaptation to change is a necessary part of a manager's job. An effective ongoing service function requires a continuity of management in terms of a felt sense of responsibility for and control of the unit's operational performance and capability. However, change threatens control, in that it creates uncertainty and imposes new demands on people to act differently. Over a period of time people develop set ways of working and establish certain controls in which they have confidence and which enables them to cope with predictable pressures and problems by adopting methods of resolution which have been safely tried and tested. New methods of working, in the short run at least, require adjustment and adaptation. Errors and misjudgements will inevitably occur and teething troubles will arise with the introduction of a new system. Individual and work groups therefore become reluctant to adopt new methods and modes of operation for fear of new problems and difficulties besetting them, which may mean sanctions being invoked against them.

Constant work pressures preclude significant amounts of time being available to devote to the education, training and development of supervisors and managers, for there is a heavy expenditure of time involved and any tangible results are usually long term. Taking on added job responsibilities creates greater confidence in people to perform more exacting work. However, there is a certain degree of reluctance in managers to risk delegating responsibility for fear of losing managerial control. At the same time, there is some frustration on the part of managers with the support effort and capability of supervisors. One of the reasons why supervisors are not always able to fulfil the pressing demands of their job is because of constant work pressures created by the system and imposed by management. Each supervisor has to respond to competing and conflicting objectives which cannot always be readily reconciled.

Quite naturally people become less and less willing to accept responsibility for deficiencies in operational performance over which they do not have direct control and influence. Unless management adopts a planned and systematic process for changing such a climate of organisational working, then they will not be able to improve the organisation's effectiveness in resolving such problems and in achieving its performance objectives.

This chapter has attempted to set out some recent developments made in a large refinery and chemical plant of fostering a climate of working which integrates system demands with individual and work-group needs as part of an over-all strategy for organisational change and development. Implicit in this approach is an organisational framework for human-resource management.

The strategy shown in Figure 6.2 sets out the means of changing an organisation's climate of working by improving the human-resource management performance of managers, directed towards solving an organisation's problems which currently frustrate performance objectives.

Why Human-resource Management is Necessary

A manager's task must be to ensure that his staff respond to the changing needs of the business situation with a sense of personal responsibility and a feeling of control and influence over his or her working environment. In situations of uncertainty, as in the economic climate of Britain recently, there may well be a lack of clearly defined expectations and a consequent need to clarify the present

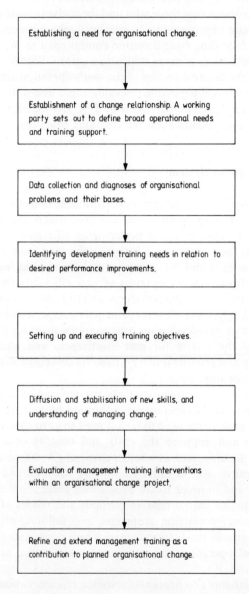

FIGURE 6.2 *An integrative strategy for organisational change and management training*

demands of the system and the contribution of work teams to it in order not to demoralise those who find themselves constrained to act on and initiate improvements in current working practices.

Without providing clear direction commitment to organisational goals and objectives is more difficult to secure. Without an understanding of the future direction of the unit's operation and their part in it individuals will be unable to evaluate and assess their performance in career-development terms and be less inclined to identify potential improvements in current working practices.

The Needs of the System

In an endeavour to realise certain performance objectives set by the organisation managers introduce controls which enable them to review and appraise levels of performance efficiency. The primary purpose of these controls is to measure and record: (i) cost-effectiveness in terms of resource utilisation and expenditure; (ii) levels of productivity in terms of how efficiently the resources were converted into finished products; and (iii) the quality of output. Correspondingly, there are three principal managerial controls which are adopted in manufacturing organisations in order to meet the demands of the system for cost-effectiveness and high levels of productivity and product quality – namely, cost control, production control and quality control.

For instance, cost-control systems are imposed so as to regulate and control levels of expenditure authorised by managers. Various accounting procedures need to be followed so as to enable managers to evaluate and appraise the costs and benefits of a particular investment decision, such as whether to spend £X, 000 on a new piece of equipment or not, in order to improve the level and quality of production and in order to cut production costs.

In an effort to ensure reliable methods and modes of operation which prevent production stoppages and failures, organisations impose systems of production control which necessitate that certain standards of operation and equipment maintenance are properly adhered to.

In their attempts to maximise resource efficiency, managers and supervisors are required to use a system of advanced planning for ordering service support work, as a means of enabling management to co-ordinate and control resource demands in relation to resource availability. A system of recording and scheduling work orders enables an organisation to decide on the relative merits between the demands and priorities of one manager or department with those of another in view of the cost of meeting resource demands.

The Needs of the Individual and the Work Group

Because of the diverse and complex tasks which individuals and work groups perform, there is a need on the part of managers to co-ordinate and control the efforts of different people. Individuals have many varied responsibilities which are tied to the specialist skills and 'know-how' required of them to fulfil their particular jobs. Because people have to work closely together in achieving a particular task, it is essential that they have available to them the information and support required from others with whom they have to liaise, in order to fulfil their contribution to the over-all task of the organisation.

The different roles and responsibilities of individuals need to be co-ordinated. Differing practices and procedures need to be accommodated and different ways of working need to be looked at closely in order to achieve more effective team-working. The establishment among a work group of commonly agreed ways of working together helps to promote a greater predictability of desired performance outcomes and encourages more efficient methods or modes of operation.

In a work situation which is ambiguous with respect to the location of responsibility and authority it cannot be expected that individuals can perform their duties effectively. If people are uncertain of their responsibilities and of the authority which they have, they may exceed their duties or use their uncertain powers ineffectively. If people are unsure who to go to obtain a decision on what course of action to take in a situation, they may be misled into taking the wrong steps. Each person's responsibilities and authority must be carefully understood and recognised by those with whom he has to work, if he is to achieve the assistance and support needed to fulfil his task. Individuals require sufficient autonomy and discretion in their jobs in order to overcome some of the constraints which may impede their efforts to correct or modify faults in the system. For example, inflexibilities in certain administrative procedures and regulations can detract from an organisation's level of performance efficiency. Enabling an individual to exercise personal initiative may assist him to overcome some of the problems besetting him and frustrating his performance.

Figure 6.3 illustrates the inter-linked aspects of the manager's own working environment which he has to attend to in successfully managing his operating unit. System demands tend to place a restraint on individuals and work groups. The manager is the more successful, however, in adapting to change and responding in a coherent, planned fashion, the more integrated system needs are with the needs of the individual and the work group involved.

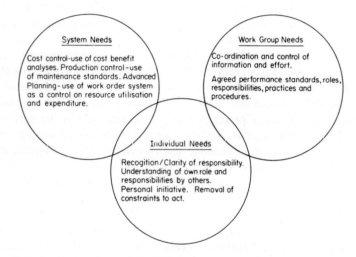

FIGURE 6.3 *Integrating system demands with individual and work-group needs*

The following illustrates this in its application to a service maintenance function responsible for planning and carrying-out large extensive plant closures two to three years in advance at the cost of many thousands of pounds.

System needs. Advance planning for closure preparations as a control on costs, work schedules, completion dates and use of manpower.

Work-group needs of engineering administration function. The co-ordination and control of closures across the site.

Individual need of engineering manager. A reliable information system which provides an accurate guideline for a maintenance resource plan needed to ensure proper labour allocation and availability of labour to all shutdowns.

Key constraints on the system. Lack of recognition for centralised planning function from operating departments.

Key constraints on the individual. Lack of information on future business operations and changes in plant operation. Insufficient commitment from operations' managers to adhere to the concept of centralised site-wide planning for closures and the labour required.

Desired outcome for system and the individual. Removal of some of the constraints imposed on centralised planning. Planned closures with maximum available resources at minimum cost.

The closure of a production unit in order for maintenance work to be carried out involves a significant loss of sales revenue. An overriding concern of management is to complete the necessary overhaul and repair of machinery and equipment on the production unit as speedily as possible so that production may resume.

Because of the rising cost of labour and materials, the cost of maintenance work on a production unit can escalate dramatically if the job is not completed on time. In an attempt to control and regulate the cost of such operations a system of advanced planning is adopted so as to measure and record the efficiency of resource utilisation, cost expenditure on plant maintenance and over-all levels of performance efficiency on each single item of work undertaken on the production unit.

The adoption of a system of advanced work planning provides managers with a means of preparing and scheduling the multitude of both small and large, complex and routine jobs necessary on a maintenance closure. At the same time, a system of cost control enables management to keep a check on how far maintenance costs, work schedules and other measures of manpower efficiency such as job-completion times deviate from the over-all plans laid down for effecting the closure as speedily and efficiently as possible.

Various departments in the engineering function provide support to the central maintenance unit responsible for executing the work programme. The task of the engineering administration function is to co-ordinate and control successfully all the various closures which

occur over the year. This requires the co-operation of both production managers and maintenance engineers in establishing the
scope and nature of the work to be undertaken. Information needs to
be generated on what new pieces of equipment and machinery require
ordering and placing in stock. In order to establish what resources
will be needed to complete the maintenance programme a breakdown
of information is required on what each job involves. Estimates of
how long the work takes enables management to decide what
manpower is necessary in order to complete the work programme by
the scheduled date. Thus, for a system of advanced work planning to
succeed, agreement and support must be reached between production, engineering maintenance and engineering administration departments on measures of performance efficiency, standards of
performance, working practices and operational procedures.

The individual needs of the administration manager is for reliable
information and feedback from production and engineering departments which enables him to derive an accurate estimate of the
manpower and material resources required for overhauling plant
machinery so as to ensure that the maintenance plan that has been
drawn up can be realistically attained and yet still be cost-effective.
Because of the rising costs of labour and materials required for plant
maintenance the system demands that an efficient allocation of
labour and other resource needs be achieved. There are also controls
imposed by the system on the availability of labour which the
engineering administration manager must carefully consider in
drawing up work programmes and plans.

A major constraint on the effective operation of an advance
planning system is the lack of recognition and support for the
centralised planning function from production personnel who believe
that the system inhibits flexibility of operations, and from engineering maintenance personnel who believe that the system does not
adequately reflect the complex and variable demands of the job and
the resource support required to complete a closure in the time
available. What management needs to do is examine and appraise the
different constraints which exist and take steps to overcome them.
This requires a process of joint problem-solving which recognises the
interdependence of system needs with work-group and individual
needs.

Examining Changes in System Demands and Individual Needs

Changes in the organisation's environment have an impact on company policy, administrative procedures and managerial control systems. For instance, rising costs of raw materials and government restraint on price increases on consumer goods has meant that more and more organisations have had to impose tighter controls on plant expenditure and on costs of production – by calling on managers to exercise stricter controls on all costs related to maintaining systems of operation at desired levels of performance. With such changes in policies and procedures, managers have been made responsible for fulfilling new system demands. For example, tighter costs controls mean that each manager's performance is judged more strictly in terms of cost-effectiveness for his own operations. One index, or measure of performance, is the figure on manpower utilisation and efficiency, expressed in terms of productivity per man-hour.

The model for integrating system demands with individual and work-group needs provides a framework within which managers and work teams can usefully open up and explore questions about the benefits and advantages of existing ways of working in the light of present and future business needs. An internal examination within the team of system needs, work-team needs, and individual needs, i.e. their interrelationship and impact on one another, enables a systematic review of individual (job) needs in relation to the needs of the system. The initial focus is on a particular system of operation in force and how the demands of that system can be met without constraining individual performance and work-group efforts. By making an examination of the underlying constraints imposed by the system of operation, the management team can identify which constraints need to be removed and how those constraints might be overcome. In enabling individual team members to discuss their view of the different control system in force and the possible demoralising impact or influence of them, understanding and recognition may be· achieved on how managerial systems and administrative procedures could be adapted or improved to meet changing business needs and system demands.

Any examination of system demands and work-group or individual needs has to be done in the light of the changes which have occured in:

    (i) managerial policies, operational practices and administrative procedures;

   (ii) industrial-relations agreements;

  (iii) climate of industrial relations, e.g. the impact of restrictive practices on unit performance;

  (iv) resource structure – skill distribution and composition of the labour force;

   (v) cost of operations – equipment values and replacement costs;

  (vi) management policy on service support provision; and

 (vii) operational flexibility of service support functions to mainstream operations.

In trying to establish more effective systems of operation management has to take into consideration what has *not* changed, such as attitudes, ways of thinking, conflicts of interest, and the industrial-relations climate. In this way management can assess what level of understanding there is on these matters and what further efforts are required to improve the implementation of managerial control systems and team-member working. In examining and exploring system needs in comparison with individual needs the team will then be in a position to be more understanding of differences in thinking and more receptive to reaching agreement on, say, departmental objectives, standards of operating performance, priorities, modes of operation, levels of operating efficiency, and over-all levels of responsibility and accountability.

Controlling the Cost of a Company's Operations

A major concern of organisations is with controlling and regulating operating costs. Various cost-accounting systems are adopted by companies so as to provide management with an accurate estimate of expenditure incurred by its personnel in maintaining the operation of the business and in executing their own tasks. However, cost-control systems can be either maladaptively applied or ill-conceived to a degree such that they no longer serve the purpose for which they were intended.

By reviewing the needs of the system for cost control in relation to individual or work-group needs for cost-effectiveness in their own jobs, a method can be devised for enabling managers to identify what can be done to imrpove the operation of the cost-control system for purposes of deriving more efficient systems of operation.

The scheme shown in Figure 6.4 provides managers with a way of examining and evaluating the operation of cost-control systems. It sets out initially to present managers with a means of looking at what the needs of the system are and how those needs can be met. The scheme provides managers with the opportunity to review and appraise how the system is intended to be operated and how different it might be in practice. The purpose of this examination is to establish how a system of cost control could be adopted more effectively, having identified what problems and constraints there are in the use to which cost-control systems are put. By the end of this exercise management and staff should be more able to decide on how best the demands of the system can be met for achieving and maintaining appropriate levels of cost-effectiveness in the running of their operations. The first step is to assess and evaluate (in terms of cost-effectiveness) what the needs of the system are in relation to those of the individual and the work group involved in accomplishing a particular task.

There are various indicators of performance efficiency which managers can use in examining and appraising the cost-effectiveness of unit operations and of those persons responsible for resource expenditure. Expenditure on plant maintenance can be stabilised and even reduced without undermining the efficiency of production among operating units if, by installing new equipment or modifying modes of operation, a saving can be made on engineering maintenance because fewer technical failures and production losses occur.

The adoption of information systems which highlight the cost of equipment failures and record the history of that particular piece of equipment helps management to identify the frequency and gravity of production losses and to establish what improvements are necessary in terms of plant reliability and operability. If reliable estimates can be made of the costs and benefits of investing in new machinery or equipment, for purposes of improving the productive efficiency of unit operations, then managers will be able to secure more money from the budgets which are allocated to departments. In this way cost-control systems can help managers and supervisors to present good economic grounds for larger sums of money being made available for improving business operations.

Because cost-control systems can highlight instances when devi-

System needs	Measures of operating costs	Managerial control systems	Describing problems with the operating of the system	Projecting desired improvements in the operation of the cost control system
Cost control	Overtime payments	Cost information system	Inconsistent feeding in of cost information	More reliable and accurate provision of cost information in terms of schedules
	Production costs	Budgetry control system	Infrequent use of cost data	Uniformity of working to cost standards
	Maintenance expenditure		Different interpretations put on cost information	Early management identification/correction of deviation in costs from operating norms
			Disparity of cost control information	
			Absence of proper cost estimates	

Individual needs	Measures of personal success	Demands of cost control system	Identifying the constraints acting upon the present system	Desired improvements in the use to which cost control systems are put
Control over expenditure	Cost savings	To allocate costs correctly to projects	Cost control may deter capital investment projects which promote cost savings	Recognition and clarification of cost control responsibilities
Powers of authorisation over expenditure on equipment and machinery	Improved levels of output and quality of production from new equipment	To highlight costs incurred	Lack of cost accountability	Rationalisation/authorisation of the different levels of expenditure
			Authority levels for approving expenditure are inconsistent and ineffective as basis of planning and estimating project expenditures	Obtain agreements with operating departments on policy of cost effectiveness
				Ensure reliable cost/benefit analysis made before expenditure incurred

FIGURE 6.4 *Financial control systems and the needs of managers*

ations from cost estimates arise, it is possible for managers to act quickly on the information which it receives. However, the system of cost control may be operated in such a way that it fails to be a realiable indicator of the expenditure that is incurred. It is important that any such malfunction of the system is identified and remedied. At the same time, if the different cost-control systems are to present an accurate picture of expenditure, then the constraints and obstacles which frustrate or impede the persons who have to employ it, and also are affected by it, need to be examined and dealt with.

Once the various problems associated with the system of cost control can be identified, improvements can be made to the operation of the system. For example, one of the desired improvements in the system might be the establishment of uniform methods for correcting deviations in costs from operating norms. A clarification of responsibilities and accountabilities for different forms of expenditure would then help in establishing uniform practices and procedures in the use to which cost-control systems are put.

The following strategy outlines the steps a manager can take to improve the performance of his unit by bringing more closely together the needs of the system with the needs of the people who have to work within it – in the way just outlined.

Intervention strategy

(1) Setting of goals by the manager and his work team for the purposes of improving cost-effectiveness of unit operations.

(2) Examination of system demands in relation to individual and work-group needs.

(3) Identification of operational issues, managerial concerns and organisational problems.

(4) Examination and evaluation of the effectiveness of cost-control systems and the constraints imposed by them on task performance.

(5) Planning and implementation of changes in the operation of cost-control systems.

(6) Review and appraisal of managerial practices and procedures in relation to unit performance, measured in terms of costs of production.

Goals of strategy

The managerial change strategy above has five principle aims associated with it:

(1) Individual and group planning and commitment building to act on an issue which is seen to have a realisable payback in terms of performance improvement.

(2) Removing bottlenecks in the system which serve as constraints upon individual initiative and endeavour.

(3) Clarifying and managing differences in the interpretation and operation of systems and procedures for purposes of 'improving' working practices and unit operations.

(4) Rationalising systems, procedures and managerial controls.

(5) Improving the task (job) performance of individuals and work groups in relation to the needs of the system.

Establishing a New System of Working

Now it will be shown how these goals can be realised in practice. The following account describes how a new system of working was successfully established in a large company. A series of system development meetings were convened by the manager responsible for engineering maintenance, and all his managers and supervisors attended. Each individual, prior to the management system development meetings, carried out an examination of a specific function. The purpose of this was to highlight what the purpose of each principal activity was and to define the present system of operation. A work-flow analysis of each main activity was presented so as to outline the steps currently taken to achieve the main task. This was intended to give the work teams an appreciation of the activities involved and show where their own contributions fitted in to the over-all scheme of support activities required from people. Steps were then taken to examine how best to get the work done with the back-up and resource support available. This served to define support needs and areas of joint responsibility, more clearly, where previously responsibility relations had become confused and blurred.

Examining the work-flow of a particular function enabled the work team to recognise the problems and difficulties caused along the route from work origination to inception and execution. It helped to predict trouble-spots to be avoided and alerted people to potential problem areas. It also served to highlight inadequate management control due to a lack of understanding of the impact of individual actions and because of serious neglect in people's responsibilities. In reviewing each principal activity in the work flow the work group can make an assessment of the case for and against that activity in its present form and decide whether there is any justification for doing a job in a different way in order to meet the constraints of the system.

One of the aims of the exercise is to identify problem areas not previously tackled or performance deficiencies which require a co-ordinated and systematic examination and evaluation of the steps which need to be taken to improve operational performance. For instance, records were kept but were not being used to spot the potential hazards to production of defective equipment on plants based on information and reports handed in by safety inspectors or plant operatives. This form of work appraisal can help identify and define areas of activity with other service supports, such as inspection and operations, where there is an essential degree of overlap in responsibilities which may have previously become blurred or neglected due to weak lines of communication or on account of the absence of a co-ordination and control function.

Impact on the Climate of Working

Each team member is better able to understand what each individual's responsibilities are, the importance of their respective contribution to the total effort, and what constraints from within a department and outside of it frustrate initiatives due to an inability to act. A greater awareness and appreciation can be had of one another's support needs and commonality of objectives. In this way it helps to establish a common sense of purpose. Success in fulfilling system demands builds up a belief in a work group that there is real mutual benefit in openness and sharing of common concerns and matters of importance. It is important in such an exercise for the manager to be seen to understand and support his team's efforts, in order to increase their sense of responsibility and accountability towards their jobs.

Any possible misconceptions and false assumptions about management being unwilling to act on the constraints imposed by the current system of operation can be cleared away when the various interpretations of managerial control systems and their intentions are put to the test.

Conclusion

An examination and reappraisal of changes in system demands in comparison with individual and work groups needs can, if managed successfully, foster a climate of working whereby management is more able to adapt to and influence the broader working environment and achieve the desired performance improvements demanded by the business climate. By encouraging a more critical and realistic view of current working practices among his staff a manager will be able to motivate and develop the use of human resources in meeting changing business needs more effectively.

By integrating system demands with individual and work-group needs managers may be able to reduce the defensiveness and overcome the reluctance to examine more openly the problems, concerns and obstacles facing an organisation. In encouraging task groups to review new ways of looking at and tackling the constraints felt to be imposed on them, this aids the efforts of managers to spot job improvement and change opportunities which enhance the organisational performance of managers.

7
Managerial Strategies of Organisational Control

Managerial Systems of Control

All organisations employ a management system of one kind or another for directing and controlling the operations of its different specialised functions and units. At the simplest level it involves senior management deciding on what it wants to achieve, issuing orders and making sure that these are consistently and reliably carried out. With the increasing size of organisations and the complexity of operations associated with the division of labour, a more extensive and elaborate control system is necessary to ensure that patterns of human behaviour align with the demands and responsibilities of the job and that people comply to certain desired norms of behaviour related to organisational standards.

One of management's prime tasks is to exercise sufficient control and influence over others in order to fulfil the performance objectives and plans expected of them. At the same time, the enforced adaptation and change of unit operations to new organisational policies and strategies call for more sophisticated management control systems. The essential aspects of managerial control are objective-setting, planning, execution and control. Objectives have to be set in relation to the task of the organisation; in particular in the case of a manufacturing business decisions have to be made about the nature of the product and the market. A sequence of activities might then be planned in order to achieve these objectives. Orders have to be given for the plans to be executed and for information, through which results can be assessed, to be generated. If the results are unsatisfactory, corrective action might be taken or objectives modified in the light of these results (Woodward, 1970).

An effectively functioning management control system enables units to (i) establish their own objectives in line with over-all company policy; (ii) define and agree responsibilities and tasks; (iii) set and agree performance standards; and (iv) define and outline operating constraints, and outline and implement plans and object-ives. A primary function of management is to balance different unit objectives and decide on priorities, to relate sub-goals to the over-all task, and to get these sub-goals accepted by the organisation's members (Drucker, 1954). In that managerial control systems serve as measures of organisational performance, their effectiveness in conditions of economic uncertainty and market instability needs to be examined. In such circumstances can managerial control systems ensure that modes of operation and resource utilisation match up to changing business performance objectives?

Hierarchical Control

Managerial control has traditionally been exercised through the delegation of authority and responsibility down the organisational hierarchy from senior to middle management. This hierarchical system of authority conferred upon managers gives them the power to lay down terms and conditions of work and to prescribe desired levels of performance. The power vested in a manager's position in the organisational hierarchy gives him the right of enforcing compliance if necessary. Sanctions may be used to ensure that the required tasks and prescribed roles of people are enacted, and that new methods and modes of operation are being carried out. Sanctions may involve depriving a department or an individual of certain rewards such as promotion, overtime, merit money or by disciplining and/or dismissing employees as punishment for deviat-ing from accepted performance norms and standards. However, compliance and conformity can be obtained from people only if sanctions can be strictly applied and management is able to regulate and control individual and work-group actions by such means.

Impersonal Forms of Managerial Control

As organisations grow in size, operational control tends to move from line management to staff functions, i.e. from control exercised by shop-floor managers to specialists in personnel departments who exert more impersonal forms of control. As technology develops, more and more of the control system is made up of procedures dictated by standardisation of routine activities and the new specialists who devise the procedures, rules and regulations (Pugh, Hicks and Hinings, 1969). Strictly speaking the manager is accountable to his immediate superior for the work allocated to him and therefore for the results he has achieved, and he refers back to his superior on the problems which he cannot resolve himself. With increases in organisational size and technical complexity, it becomes more difficult for separate operating units to exercise direct hierarchical control over their staff.

Since specialised functions exercise responsibility for particular facets of the organisation's operation, for example product planning, designing, costing, programming and scheduling, line management no longer has firm control and influence over all the various specialised and complex technological processes and administrative procedures which are inherent in the task of the organisation. To avoid the danger of losing control over the multiplicity of sub-tasks allocated to subordinates down the organisational hierarchy, management build into it impersonal processes of control to influence and regulate the work behaviour of those who have been delegated authority and responsibility to manage financial and material resources. The feature of these impersonal controls is that they are intended to regulate and adjust the inflow of resources and outflow of products in relation to unit and organisational objectives. The procedures, rules and regulations which are devised for these purposes may be administrative or mechanical. They encorporate such elements as complex programmes for production planning, and measurement as in the case of cost-control systems or automatic controls of machine-tools and continuous-flow production plants. The assumption underlying scientific management thinking, i.e. that managerial control can be exercised effectively through a pyramid of hierarchical authority, becomes increasingly invalid as a firm moves more towards mechanical and administrative forms of control.

Control mechanisms are adapted by management so as to ensure that deviations from acceptable modes of operation and performance levels can be accurately predicted and dealt with in advance as part of the planning process. Line managers and supervisors increasingly cease to concern themselves with day-to-day operations in relation to work-flow activities and function primarily as regulators and adaptors of the control processes tied to the work-flow.

Blau and Scott (1962) have suggested that the significance of management is no longer that of being at the apex of a system of personal control but rather that of being the designer, in association with technical staff specialists, of administrative controls of the impersonal kind involving the work-flow system (see also Woodward, 1970). However, the co-ordination and control of the organisation's major unit operations is much more problematic when, say, the design and programming of tasks is separated from the execution of them. By divorcing responsibility for policy-making from the implementation of them, a serious control gap may be set up, in that greater reliance is placed on impersonal control mechanisms and on those personnel who devised the rules and regulations which were designed to regulate and determine the work behaviour of relevant others.

What exists in large organisations are a growing multiplicity of control systems with different performance criteria (standards), of which one or more may be in direct conflict with others.. If and when a manager's or a supervisor's attempts at satisfying each of the control criteria fail, because the different control systems cannot be continuously reconciled, he has to accept that his performance objectives may be jeopardised on one or more performance criteria. Whether due to rational or irritational acts, the imposition of such controls may well be subverted, and managerial controls may well become ineffective devices for measuring, predicting and deciding on corrective courses of action in relation to the central work-flow.

While an increase in the number of staff functions has served to improve mainstream operations by means of the knowledge and expertise which can be brought to bear on the key performance objectives of an organisation, there is not always a ready acceptance or adoption of specialist advice. Also, many decisions have to be made without adequate information. The uncertainties and vagaries of the business environment may preclude accurate forecasts being made of what actions to take or decisions to make. The pressing nature of operational problems frustrate longer-term thinking about alternative approaches to problems. However, scientific measures of performances are often criticised and thrown out on the grounds that the information on which they are based does not explain or recognise abnormal or changing operating conditions which are tied to the particular mode of operation, equipment and personnel involved. Managers are reluctant to face up to doing things differently when staff department recommendations are seen as constraining historical practices and procedures which have taken root.

Different organisational units and personnel prize their freedom of action and are resistant to any outside interference or unfavourable judgement being made about the way that the unit may be organised and managed. At the same time, the central concern of each line manager is to fulfil his targets and to realise his regular ongoing performance objectives first and foremost, to the exclusion of 'expert' opinion and pressures to modify and adapt ways of working which may promise to raise levels of performance but which may also jeopardise normal performance levels. Dalton (1959) observed that staff units valued stability because change reflected unfavourably upon, or inconvenienced, them. Staff units were also strongly committed to preserving the integrity of control and rule systems, whereas line personnel believed they could be more effective by flexible reinterpretation of control and incentive schemes and by ignoring many discipline and safety violations. The essential prerequisites of managerial control may therefore be undermined in such circumstances.

Questioning the Bases of Managerial Control

There are inevitably a host of problems and issues facing managers who endeavour to achieve the necessary control over their own unit operations. Control imposed by hierarchical authority or the power of technical specialist experts is evidently problematic and uncertain. An alternative approach is to enable individuals to be responsible for control over unit operations and be involved in influencing the direction of unit operations. By such means individuals can be held more accountable for their actions and performance, and this gives an organisation a greater capacity to formulate and realise its policies and plans.

Underlying this thinking is the belief that acceptance and commitment to managerial change initiatives are necessary prerequisites for success. This, however, involves management establishing a climate of working which produces a set of attitudes, relationships, values and skills which are supportive of performance improvement and the changes necessary. In assessing the capability of the people in the organisation to adapt to new performance demands, it is important to examine and evaluate the impact of the hierarchical structure on how people work and how the management system of control operates.

In doing so, the key factors which affect, or rather constrain, an individual's efforts at attaining performance objectives should be identified and assessed. Power, authority, work norms, rewards and sanctions are some of the key factors which affect work groups and their actions. Other important variables for consideration are technology, administrative rules, management culture and working environment, and their interaction upon one another and their influence on working relations and performance levels. The focus of this chapter will be on how past practices have determined current levels of performance and what changes are necessary in order to realise performance improvements.

The Management of Change

Adaptation to change is an essential feature of a manager's job when faced by demands and pressures put on him by his organisation to improve the operating capability and performance efficiency of his unit because of changes in the business environment, e.g. fluctuations in market demand.

An effective ongoing organisation requires a continuity of management to cope with and adapt to change, in terms of a felt sense of responsibility for, and control over, current performance efficiency and future operating capability. This in essence is what organisational growth and development is about. How to achieve this in practice is altogether a different matter and a very much more difficult proposition.

There are few general conclusions which can be applied by a manager to his own work situation. However, what has become evident from research is that managers and consultants need to work with a much more complex model which includes both the internal and the external environment in which change takes place, the process by which organisational change is brought about, the particular role played by change agents and the perceived impact of a change upon the balance of power between the various interested parties (Bowers, 1973; Buchanan, 1971; Franklin, 1976; Greiner, 1967).

Current notions about the management of change tend to lack a unifying perspective. Much of the literature on change reveals that strong resistance and even failure is often encountered in efforts to change only the organisational structure (Dalton, 1965), only the technology of the organisation (Trist and Bamforth, 1951), or only the individual (Campbell, 1971; Campbell and Dunnette, 1968; Fleishman, 1953; Friedlander and Greenberg, 1971). For instance, both organisational *process* and, organisational *structure* are concerned with authority, communication, decision-making, goal-setting and conflict resolution. But *process* implies the implementation of these as dynamic behavioural events and interactions, whereas *structure* describes these as ongoing sets of durable roles and relationships. Attitudes and behaviour are clearly affected by both process (Miles *et al.*, 1969) and structure (Porter and Lawler, 1965). Since structure and process are embedded in each other, it is almost impossible to create lasting change in one without modification of the other (Friedlander and Brown, 1974).

Organisational changes that are focused on increasing the autonomy and influence of lower-level employees without taking account of the role changes or needs of employees one level higher up are not long lasting because of the resistance to change by those whose position or standing in the organisation has been undermined or has seen to have been attacked. Part of the reason for the resistance or opposition to change is due to the feelings of role ambiguity and dissatisfaction with participative decision-making, when supervisors (for instance) find that their traditional roles and decision-making prerogatives in respect of production setting and changes in production technology are being invaded by the lower-level members of the organisation (Nadler and Pecorella, 1975). There is additional support for these findings in the study made by Lawler, Hackman and Kaufman (1973), who reported of the mixed success in a job-redesign experiment due to problems arising with supervisory personnel who felt their jobs were threatened by the intervention. In another study by Lawler and Hackman (1969) a participative approach was used to develop a new pay incentive plan. In a follow-up study (Scheflen, Lawler and Hackman, 1971) it was found that in two of the three original participative groups the plan had been dropped despite favourable results (i.e. low rates of absenteeism). The supervisors in those groups who had not participated in designing the new pay plans felt neither ownership of, nor commitment to, the plans, and thus discontinued them at the first opportunity. Thus the conclusion reached is that long-lasting change can only be effectively brought about when the changes are accepted and 'owned' by all those in the organisation who are affected by new work programmes and systems of operation.

If we can therefore understand and predict more effectively the forces which facilitate and restrain the management of organisational change, then it is possible to devise appropriate intervention strategies which assist management to influence successfully the direction and outcomes of organisational change initiatives. A key role of the change agent is to develop and define the processes of change which have to be undergone for an effective implementation of change to take place.

The concern of management in a changing and uncertain environment is to maintain effective control over the performance efficiency and the operating capability of the organisation. Various control systems are devised and implemented by management so as to enable individual departments and their managers to carefully monitor and review their performance, and in the light of that performance to modify and change their policies, plans and decisions so that the organisation can attain its over-all business objectives. This chapter examines and appraises the barriers to planned organisational change, in terms of the behavioural responses of people to management control systems. Evidence suggests that changes in perceived organisational climate (human-resource development, communications flow, motivational climate, decision-making practices, technological readiness and lower-level influence) directly influence the impact of different change strategies; without positive changes in the climate of working in an organisation interventions had very little positive effects (Bowers, 1973).

An adaptive change strategy is therefore devised which fosters a climate of working, facilitating organisational change and development.

Barriers to Management-imposed Change

Management by objectives (M.B.O.) is a managerial device for laying down the organisation's goals, aspirations and development plans and for establishing the success of the organisation in terms of these objectives. M.B.O. enables a manager to establish and define a plan of operation for attaining the organisation's performance objectives. Each manager is accountbale for realising certain performance objectives which are tied to the particular role and responsibilities he has. M.B.O. serves as a measure of an individual's efforts in executing his task and enables the manager concerned to identify whether he has achieved the performance objectives expected of him. In this sense M.B.O. is a system of control over a manager's activities in that it specifies how a manager should perform this job.

The middle managers in one particular oil and chemical products company had been very reluctant to commit themselves to performance objectives and production targets proposed by their supervisors for fear of not attaining them. Fear and anxiety arose because, whenever unsatisfactory results were highlighted by the M.B.O. system, the manager's own shortcomings were now exposed since ne was formally held accountable for his actions through regular performance reviews with higher management. On the other hand, some of the factors influencing his performance were considered to be outside his immediate control and influence. These factors included: limitations on resources (financial, human and material), inflexible administrative procedures, an absence of co-ordination and control of service support, and an absence of authority over the departments upon whom he was dependent for service support.

Management may in these circumstances be obliged to make policy decisions without any reliable and accurate feedback about the realism of its plans and targets, which invariably leads to management becoming increasingly divorced from operating needs and problems. For instance, the practical difficulties experienced in implementing new cost-control systems and procedures were not brought to management's attention for fear of sanction and blame. Personal errors and misjudgements in applying new procedures and systems were also kept hidden from management who were seeking new suggestions and improvements to the evidently imperfect operation of the system. This was evident from a misallocation of expenditure and from several incidences of departments going over budget. The problems of implementing managerial performance objectives were disguised in the form of acceptable grievances; excuses were offered for the constraints in the system as a means of problem avoidance. In order to beat the constraints of managerial control systems various alternative informal networks and associations were developed. As the various procedures and systems became more and more untenable, so management imposed tighter and tighter controls on staff so as to ensure they adhered to them.

The failure of communications

In large organisations the need for accurate and reliable performance information is particularly necessary when there are many different hierarchical levels which removes higher management from contact with operating problems and from close contact to or surveillance over employees (Blau, 1963; Brewer, 1971). Certain unfavourable information of performance is suppressed or distorted when the sender distrusts the use to which it is put (O'Reilly and Roberts, 1974 and O'Reilly, 1978; Friedlander, 1970; Zand, 1972). Insecurity, fear and anxiety induce people to distort upward communications, particularly in situations where individuals have competing and conflicting objectives (Asthanassiades, 1973), and where poor performance is suspected (Ouchi and Maguire, 1975).

In such situations management loses the ability to discriminate between relevant and irrelevant indicators of performance which significantly affect the quality and reliability of decision-making (Chervany and Dickson, 1974).

M.B.O. – a failure in control

There are very real problems in the superior–subordinate goal-setting process in terms of the adequacy and reality of participation by the subordinate in formulating and adhering to work plans agreed with his boss. The impetus is often the threat of sanctions, which pressurises him to react defensively to change demands, without sufficient powers to realise these demands. The process of objective-setting and attainment then becomes ineffective. Clearly, changes in the authority control structure need to be made. Levinson (1970),

Raia (1965) and White (1973) have questioned the research done on management by objectives and have challenged their findings. In fact, White (1973) found more support and application of M.B.O. where it was perceived to contribute significantly to internal communications which enhanced organisational problem-solving and improved decision-making at higher levels.

Organisational maintenance or change?

Managerial policies, plans, operational procedures and working practices which prove inadequate in bringing about the resolution of problems pose a threat to the maintenance of the productive system currently in operation. There are forces inside the organisation which endeavour to maintain the status quo, and these are expressed in strong resistance to change and forces for organisational growth and development which provide the necessary impetus for adaptation to change needs. A resolution of these opposing forces only emerges from the struggle for power and control.

The diffusion of control

Organisations are controlled by those who control the organisation's most problematic dependencies. In Blau's (1963) terms organisations give compliance to those upon whom they are most dependent, namely the key sources of authority both within the hierarchy and outside of it. The more that the controllers of power and influence in an organisation are divided and widely dispersed, the less able will they be able to exercise control over the organisation (Jacobs, 1974). The more divided an organisation is, the less it will be in each individual's interest to participate in any attempt to organise in order to seek collective or indivisible benefits (Olsen, 1968).

Organisational Crisis and Change

A study undertaken by Purcell (1979) of nine companies which had a record of strikes and internal conflicts indicates that some of the improvements in working relations could be attributed to the traumatic effect of these events or crises. Management's threat of closure or withdrawal of investment and the renewed disruption of production by the work-force forced both sides to look realistically at the implications of these actions with respect to the survival of the company and people's jobs. Neither side could win adopting such tactics. Senior management and union leaders realised that they had the power to destroy each other: 'We had to learn to live together.'

Purcell believes that a crisis or 'trauma' can reverse a declining spiral of misunderstanding, forcing the two sides to begin to trust each other in order to survive. The urgency and gravity of a crisis compells the two parties to find a joint solution which reinforces the new relationship. The study sees generation of trust as the first step towards tackling the underlying structural problems of industrial relations. In the successful cases of adaptation and change in companies which suffered crises management took the initiative in accepting a larger role for the unions and expanding the scope of collective bargaining, while shop stewards responded by taking on the increased responsibility by viewing management with less suspicion, and defending bargains made with the union members they represented.

The key to sustained improvements in the climate of labour relations which is indicative of the receptivity or otherwise of the work-force to technological innovation and to changes in working practices and procedures seems to lie in good leadership of different interest groups, with 'negotiators of change' having control over their organisation so that they could be trusted as bargaining agents (Hildrew, 1978).

Conditions Necessary for Planned Change

There are certain key factors which contribute to the success of planned change. Management must recognise that change is possible and that choices exist in the form of alternative courses of action. The central conflict must be located and the antecedent problems analysed (Alschuler *et al.*, 1977). One of the major parties must be highly committed to collaboration and to the people involved in order to maintain the change process, especially if the system is out of balance in terms of accountabilities and entitlements (Appleby and Winder, 1977). Commitment from top management is important. Skills of effective participative decision-making are required. Developing support systems and networks through the use of working parties or steering groups for sustaining commitment to the task of change are necessary. Resistance to change needs to be respected and time is needed before attitudes change. Also, the surrender of power and control over resources is required (Trist, 1977; Finch, 1977).

Key Aspects to the Implementation of Change

Evidence from the particular organisational change projects so far discussed indicates that there are four basic concerns or hurdles that have to be negotiated by management in order to implement performance improvements successfully. An acceptance is required of current operational problems, needs and opportunities to adapt and modify some aspects of the organisation's mode of operation and system of administration. The principal issue at stake is the acceptance of a need to question existing working practices and arrangements. Once this is agreed to constructive efforts can be made to reassess the use to which human, technical and financial resources are put. Only then are the issues which divide people about the aims and outcomes of change amenable to open and meaningful examination and resolution through joint problem-solving.

A key to the success of any change programme is obtaining a willingness and receptivity of participants to want to do things differently back on the job as far as initiating improvements in working practices is concerned. However, commitment to do so is very much dependent upon the degree to which people see change initiatives responded to and performance improvements realised.

It is critical at the early stage of the proceedings for management to recognise and accept that implementation problems will arise when people have to adjust and learn new ways of working. Responsibility must also be taken by management to review the progress of change initiatives and if necessary take corrective measures for dealing with changing business fortunes and unforeseen developments which impose constraints on operational needs.

Another major hurdle is obtaining the full understanding, commitment and involvement of key people or authority figures who control and influence the system of working. The various issues, needs, problems and opportunities for performance improvement need to be carefully examined and fed back to all relevant parties. Feedback is necessary because it creates an enlarged understanding of the need for change – which more readily encourages people to enter into a fruitful dialogue and a realistic examination of current working practices and arrangements and of what performance improvements may be needed to cope with and adapt to changing business demands.

For management to decide on an effective course of action, the bases for such decisions are reliant on accurate and reliable information being generated and fed back up the line. Feedback is important for identifying problems which constrain performance improvements. Through a careful and informed diagnosis and evaluation of the changes required in current working practices and procedures, management can anticipate previously undetected problems in the implementation phase of a change initiative.

A major factor of concern is the potential impact and consequences of the changes upon the position and standing of the persons concerned. What, for instance, will changes in the nature and character of the individual's job mean, and how will this affect his ability to meet the demands of the system in terms of the performance criteria he is judged on? Another issue of fundamental concern to all persons involved is the degree of control and influence which individuals and departments may gain or lose. What is of paramount concern in the 'negotiation' stage is how much control and influence can be exerted on the impact that any decisions or changes in management policy will have on the job an individual is expected to perform. Will there be changes in the task of the manager/supervisor or his work-force which undermine or potentially enhance individuals' capability of carrying out their changed responsibilities? Will they have the authority necessary to ensure that their new accountabilities can be met?

Taking into consideration these basic hurdles that have to be considered by managers initiating change, a model has been devised for the purpose of assisting organisations to predict and identify the basic forces and influences which restrain and facilitate organisational change (see Figure 7.1). The model establishes a conceptual framework of socio-emotional issues which help to explain the behavioural phenomena which have a fundamental influence on the problems and obstacles experienced by management in implementing change.

Primary Concerns (expressed in socio-emotional terms)	Cause of Concern	Symptoms of Unresolved Concern	Symptoms of Resolved Concern
Acceptance Security	Uncertainty about the impact of change on an individual's position in organisation Concern as to whether change promotes or frustrates an individual's needs and aspirations	Fear of change Anxiety Distrust of, and opposition to, change	Acceptance of needs, problems, and opportunities for change Trust and confidence in change initiatives and the motives and intent of managers
Feedback Self esteem	Lack of influence in the decisions which bring about change in organisation roles and responsibilities Risk of previous performance failures being exposed	Secrecy Lack of reliable information available to make decisions Organisational change plans divorced from operating needs and problems	More reliable information flow and two way communication of problems and concerns Greater commitment to initiatives of people affected by change
Goal integration	Competing and conflicting performance objectives Absence of shared goals Failure to reconcile individual needs with organisational goals	Competition Conflict of interests Lack of commitment to organisational goals and objectives	Joint problem solving Commonality of objectives Reconciling and managing differences in priorities and performance objectives
Control and influence	Imposition of change from higher management Centralisation of authority Lack of autonomy among individuals and work groups Changes in the balance of power and authority	Resistance and opposition to authority Frustrated initiatives due to lack of authority to act Avoiding accountability and ownership of problems Hardening of boundaries between functions	Participation and involvement in change Delegation of responsibility and authority Coordination and control of change Reconciliation of unit goals and interests

FIGURE 7.1 *Stages of organisational change and development*

A Model of Organisational Change

In their attempts to intervene within the organisation's system of operation managers often fail to recognise the underlying problems involved in implementing change. The model shown in Figure 7.1 serves as a diagnostic aid for evaluating the appropriate intervention strategy needed to tackle the causes and consequences of the restraints upon organisational change. The model helps to establish four major areas of concern to managers in implementing change and the causes of these concerns to organisations undergoing change. It also illustrates why in general these concerns are widespread and common to most organisations. There are four primary concerns in the model which are believed to constrain significantly management change initiatives:

  (i) a lack of acceptance of change from the people involved;

 (ii) inadequate information on which to base decisions as to what changes need to be made;

(iii) an inability of people to perceive the mutual benefit that might be derived from organisational changes because of the absence of shared goals; and

(iv) the need for an organisational structure (division of labour and system of management) which enables individuals, groups and functions to retain or obtain sufficient control and influence over the changes which alter their working lives and destinies.

The causes of concern are only resolved when management has recognised what the unresolved concerns are and has overcome them successfully. The column showing how the four areas of primary concern to management may be resolved represents a set of objectives for managing organisational change. The degree to which any one of the four modal concerns is capable of being resolved is limited by the degree to which the modal concern preceding it has been resolved.

Acceptance of change is seen as a basic requirement for success. The degree of acceptance determines the willingness of people to provide relevant information about current operating problems, and what changes need to be made in the system of operation, if the organisation's objectives are to be realised. If the goals of management in the changes to be made are shared, then relevant structures can be formed to co-ordinate and control individuals, group and inter-departmental activities. Lack of personal acceptance of change is at the root of the behaviours mentioned in the unresolved column. In exerting pressure and compliance from people to implement changes in operational practices and procedures management may expend considerable energy without much, if any, results to show for it unless it can remove (understand and act on) the underlying forces or influences which are constraining the change attempts. The image of a tube of paste seems to clarify this matter: if the tube is squeezed near the nozzle, then only some of the paste will be forced out; continued pressure will not disturb the rest unless applied at an appropriate place.

Acceptance of change

An individual's support or opposition to change is dependent on the meaning of the change to him in his job and on his evaluation of the effect that the change will have on his aspirations and expectations. If he believes that the changes forthcoming in the organisation's system of operation are desirable, he will be motivated to accept the change. For example, if a person concludes that change will enable him to advance in the organisation, in terms of organisational status, career prospects, or financial gain, he is likely to welcome and support the change. If, on the other hand, the change is not seen as self-enhancing but rather detrimental to a person, he will oppose the change in every way (in terms of his power position) that he can. If there is no acceptance of change, either because employees distrust management's motives or because of the possible threat to people's job security, there is likely to be at least passive resistance to change. By putting up a polite, seemingly compliant, front employees do not readily assist management's efforts to identify and act on important operating needs and problems in its change plans. People's pride and sense of personal worth (self-esteem) is undermined when they are informed by higher management that their previous performance is no longer adequate or appropriate. People are naturally reluctant to risk having their shortcomings or failings exposed because this might then indicate that the person concerned is not able to hold down his job satisfactorily and carry out the full range of his responsibilities efficiently. Therefore, information which could incriminate an individual is either kept hidden or left undisclosed.

Feedback on organisational needs and problems

Poor information flow creates difficulties for management in progressing with change efforts concerned with identifying performance deficiences. The withholding or falsifying of information by people for fear of being sanctioned and held accountable for failures in the past creates a false picture as to what changes are really needed to improve performance efficiency and the operating capability of the system. It leads to a situation in which the views and opinions of a small number of powerful managers at the top of the organisation hold sway. They then decide amongst themselves what changes in policies, plans and actions should be taken, mindful of preserving their own vested interests when a change in the organisational status quo arises. Without consulting those people lower down the organisation who have to implement the changes, a situation builds up in which the changes planned become divorced from some of the critical operating needs and problems facing the organisation.

The need for trust

If the climate of trust is unfavourable, people will find it difficult to believe that changes in the organisation's system of operation will be of benefit to them. Under these circumstances management will need to demonstrate by their actions its concern for the individuals affected by any changes put forward, and will need to identify and outline how the steps being taken are compatible with the individual's goals and how the current change initiative is being handled differently from others in the past.

Resistance to change is often the consequence of people not being able to foresee the implications of change for their own needs and aspirations, rather than because of an outright rejection of it. If the demands that change makes and the effects that it will have on an individual are unclear and uncertain, an individual may well be fearful of impending changes because he is unable to see the relationsihip between the objectives of the change and his own goals.

In these circumstances opposition should alert management to the need for clarifying and amplifying further the meaning of the change for the persons concerned. When an individual is clear about the nature and form in which change will take place, he then feels he has more reliable information on which to decide for himself what change will mean to him and how he will be affected by it. He can then more ably and effectively decide on what grounds he can either support or oppose the change. With more reliable information available to an individual, he is then able to indicate to management what some of the critical problems faced by management are.

Management is then in a more informed position when it comes to deciding on what changes are necessary for improving the organisation's system of operation because it is more aware of the operational problems and difficulties which could not previously be foreseen and which would have obstructed or negated the original change plans. Organisational changes may now be made which are less likely to be divorced from operating needs and problems. With greater influence and say in the decisions which directly affect people's changing roles and responsibilities, an individual is more likely to feel a greater sense of responsibility for the success of the decisions to which he was a party. He is also likely to feel a greater sense of personal worth and importance (self-esteem) for having contributed his ideas to these decisions.

The Integration of Change Goals

An important aspect of securing support and commitment to organisational change from individuals, groups and departments is one of recognition and agreement from the parties concerned of the mutual benefits to be derived from the change initiatives of management. If departments and individuals have competing and conflicting goals and performance objectives, such as minimisation of production costs as opposed to maximisation of production, then each department's energies will be devoted to preserving its own interests at the expense of others.

Unless there is some understanding and reconciliation of the different priorities and performance objectives of speparate functions, then there will not be the joint collaboration and problem-solving required to resolve outstanding operating needs and problems.

If departments enforce different rules and regulations (administrative procedures), then inflexibilities arise in the system of operation which preclude close liaison and collaboration between them.

Unless departments have shared goals and common objectives, there is unlikely to be a constructive solution to problems or agreement reached on what change initiatives can be taken to improve organisational performance. Departments which provide service support to mainstream operations and attempt to introduce a more cost-effective service by streamlining and rationalising their mode of operation may find their change efforts resisted and opposed by production departments which argue that their own performance objectives are being undermined by the reorganisation of service support, and by the failure of the latter to provide the required service needs of production departments. This underlying conflict of interest can arise in spite of lengthy and prolonged consultation and involvement of mainstream operatives in the recommendations and plans which service support departments orginate. Managers soon become cynical or disenchanted with the notions of consultation and involvement in decisions when the failure to reconcile or manage conflicting differences become a recurring experience. Inevitably the information flow and the quality of organisational problem-solving are affected by attempts at control and influence of different departments seeking to exert power and authority in a change situation.

Because of a recurrence of these concerns it is not surprising that management efforts continue to be absorbed in improving data-retrieval systems and providing new administrative procedures and guidelines for dealing with operational problems, rather than in examining the lack of acceptance for change, the quality of inform-ation in the system for establishing the changes necessary, competing and conflicting goals between departments and the fight for control and influence over the outcomes desired from change. What all this reveals is that if a common sense of purpose between individuals and work groups is not achieved, the implementation of change will be undermined by efforts put into creating difficulties or hitting upon snags which serve to defeat or undermine the purpose of the change initiative.

The Diminution of Organisational Control

Increasingly control systems have proved to be necessary for organisations to have the information needed to act quickly and decisively on what courses of action to take in order to deal with competitive external market pressures and unforeseen changes in the business environment. However, the information has not always been a reliable indicator of performance demands because of the erosion and ineffectualness of control systems undermined by incomplete, false or inconsistent information fed upwards to policy-makers and key decision-makers.

Attempts can be made to enforce the people in the system to modify and adapt their ways of working and to devise new procedures for facilitating more efficient modes of operation. However, efforts concentrated on organisational problem-solving of this nature which are geared to improving managerial controls may only serve to raise opposition to management change initiatives when the underlying problems and concerns facing lower management effectively constrain or negate any attempts made to act on these initiatives.

When malfunctions in the work-flow system impose constraints on an individual's ability to respond and act on change initiatives, tighter management controls lead to greater efforts to avoid account-ability and blame for system shortcoming and performance de-ficiences. Efforts will be directed at providing higher management with excuses and in finding fault in other support units rather than in taking responsibility for difficulties and searching for resolutions to problems of a collective nature.

An inability to influence or change operating constraints creates a vulnerability and insecurity in managers and supervisors who are faced with pressure to improve results and performance. Accountability will be avoided for those problems which people consider to be outside their immediate control, avoided, that is, in order to protect and defend themselves against any failures or personal shortcomings which may reflect back on them in their jobs.

The fact that control systems are not necessarily effective as true measures and predictors of performance levels, and may not disclose how informal working practices and procedures sometimes under-mine and negate performance improvements, indicates that the underlying problems associated with implementing change may not be recognised or effectively dealt with by managers.

The model shown in Figure 7.1 above outlining the stages of organisational change and development, provides a conceptual framework for establishing the underlying causes and consequences of resistance to change and identifies what courses of action need to be taken by management in overcoming resistance to change. What the model shows is that acceptance of change is of paramount importance. If organisational change does not serve the purpose of those affected by it, then there will be a fight for control and influence over it which discourages the collaboration needed for overcoming the problems and difficulties associated with implementing change. Unless there is acceptance of a need for particular change initiatives, individuals will not respond effectively to them. If management seeks to impose tighter controls in the face of passivity or opposition to change, this may serve to constrain management initiative and tend to lower levels of personal responsibility felt for detecting and rectifying deviations from normal operations.

The question is to determine how an improvement in systems of operation and administrative procedures will improve working practices. What needs to be established are the attitudes which are supportive of change and encourage relevant collaboration over desired improvements in current working practices. Agreement is needed on the purpose of new systems and procedures as to how exactly they assist individuals and work groups to execute their jobs more effectively. Restraints on initiative in the form of inflexible procedures and systems of control imposed by management need to be carefully reviewed and reappraised so as not to frustrate or preclude potential improvements in work performance.

At the same time, management needs to reconcile competing and conflicting demands for, and expectations of, change. It has to overcome the conflict and dispute between individuals, groups and departments in their attempts to either maintain or alter the status quo in organisations in so far as control and influence over methods and modes of operation are concerned. Efforts have to be made to create a more effectively supportive and responsive change environment and climate of working which enables major unresolved issues such as a conflict of interest between functions and the impact of change on the balance of influence and power to be constructively managed.

Evaluating Organisational Change Needs

Because of the changing influences and pressures brought to bear upon organisational systems of operation, managers need to act quickly and effectively on the problems confronting them. An approach based on research and then action ('action research') is an effective method of enquiry in such circumstances in that it enables a specific organisational situation to be diagnosed and for plans to be drawn up in order to deal with the organisational practices and procedures which are problematic. This involves the manager in information-gathering, analysis and diagnosis (research phases), leading to action planning and implementation (action), the results of which are carefully evaluated (research). This evaluation provides data for further diagnosis and action in terms of developing problem solutions. This approach involves a continuous cycle of research and action which serves as a general model for organisational problem-solving and change management.

Action research can provide the means by which the parties concerned with a particular situation can secure fuller understanding and validation of the problem they are experiencing by way of feedback and discussion of diagnostic interpretation of the pre-liminary results of an enquiry.

Action research is a method of studying a social problem and then working to change the situation and modifying or changing the strategy of planned change by studying the effects of initiatives in the change situation.

A Strategy for Organisational Change

Having recognised and identified the underlying socio-emotional forces and the political influences restraining management change initiatives, a strategy needs to be developed for dealing with these same issues and problems which are impeding organisational change. A strategy is a pattern of objectives and purposes or goals which includes major policies and plans for achievement. It is an over-all multidimensional plan for action and achievement which also describes the style of operation and implementation tied to the organisation in question. The strategy is designed so as to enable the change initiator and the recipient of change to cope more effectively with, and adapt better to, the competing and conflicting pressures, demands and expectations they impose on one another in the process of negotiating the degree and extent of change (see Figure 7.2).

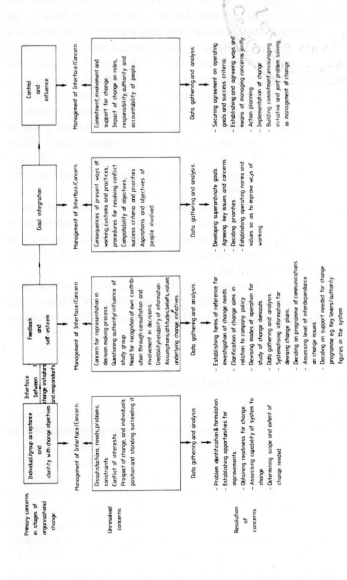

FIGURE 7.2   *A strategy for organisational change and development*

The strategy indicates that there are certain necessary stages of development in the negotiation process which are concerned with tackling and resolving certain fundamental concerns of those people affected by the change. The four primary concerns are: individual acceptance and identity with change objectives; feedback of, and involvement with, change initiatives; goal integration; and control and influence over organisational change. The strategy involves the change initiator and respondent examining and evaluating how unresolved concerns at different managerial levels can be dealt with by means of data-gathering, problem analysis and managerial decision-making. In practice this is what is meant by an action-research approach.

Learning how to undertake such an action-research strategy effectively requires examining and questioning the validity and accuracy of the information generated in each of the four stages of the process of negotiating and implementing change. At the same time, this would necessitate a serious review and appraisal of management's own mode of operation. By looking closely at the different underlying assumptions, norms and objectives which managers hold of the changes envisaged, greater understanding can be had of the potential conflicts and clashes of interest which might not surface but would still undermine or frustrate collective efforts at initiating and sustaining change initiatives. Argyris (1977) points out that any incongruities between what an organisation openly espouses as its objectives and what its practices actually are would need to be challenged, if managers were to learn how to overcome effectively the anxiety and fear of failure associated with tackling the problems and difficulties of improving desired levels of operational efficiency in an organisation.

The Climate for Organisational Change

Having identified the major concerns of organisations faced with implementing change, one can define more clearly the climate of working which is needed in order to foster the conditions under which organisational growth and development can occur with the strategy outlined above.

The following system of management is viewed as necessary for facilitating organisational change for purposes of performance improvement:

(1) Improving the quality and reliability of information flow which is necessary for accurate problem definition and resolution.

(2) Restoring a common sense of purpose between functions where operations have become fragmented, or a divorce in responsibilities for policy-making and execution of decisions has occurred down the organisation hierarchy.

(3) Ensuring that systems and procedures are flexible enough to allow individuals to carry out their essential tasks.

(4) Obtaining a commitment and sense of responsibility from individuals to operate systems and procedures for the purposes for which they were intended.

(5) Encouraging a sense of responsibility and initiative in people to look for methods and means of realising departmental objectives.

(6) Promoting a climate of working which enables people to face up to and tackle organisational malfunctions such as maladaptive procedures and working systems, and recurring organisational problems such as the management of inter-departmental conflict.

(7) Reviewing and reappraising the roles and responsibilities of a work team in order for members to fulfil the changing demands of their jobs effectively.

(8) Improving co-ordination, liaison and communication among people with different roles and responsibilities for a particular task which requires shared responsibility and close collaboration.

(9) Providing people with the responsibility and powers to take initiative and make judgements as to the best course of action to take in the face of organisational obstacles and operating difficulties.

(10) Fostering a more open style of managing conflict so that constructive attempts can be made to achieve its resolution based on dialogue and a proper understanding of the causes and consequences of conflict generation.

(11) Overcoming misunderstandings and managing differences which can become more imagined than real about prospect-

ive changes, by testing and refining opposing beliefs, values, assumptions, attitudes and stereotypes.

(12) Managing organisational change by gaining acceptance and support for the change initiatives such that people recognise the contribution they can make to improvements in their own job performance.

(13) Tackling outstanding problems which arise and the opposition or resistance to change, rather than imposing structural changes which may be out of step with the practical demands of ground-floor operations.

(14) Recognising and incorporating certain selected informal practices and procedures which help to overcome organisational obstacles such as inflexible procedures, rules and regulations that no longer serve the purpose for which they were intended.

References

Alschuler, A. *et al.* (1977) 'Collaborative Problem-solving as an Aim of Education in a Democracy', *Journal of Applied Behavioral Science*, vol. 13, no. 3, pp. 315–27.

Appleby, D. G. and Winder, P. (1977) 'An Evolving Definition of Collaboration and some Implications for Work Settings', *Journal of Applied Behavioral Science*, vol. 13, no. 3, pp. 279–91.

Argyris, C. (1977) 'Double Loop Learning in Organizations', *Harvard Business Review*, September–October.

Asthanassiades, J. C. (1973) 'The Distortion of Upward Communication in Hierarchical Organizations', *Academy of Management Journal*, vol. 16, no. 2, June, pp. 207–25.

Blau, P. (1963) *The Dynamics of Bureaucracy*, 2nd ed. (University of Chicago Press).

Blau, P. and Scott, W. R. (1962) *Formal Organizations* (San Francisco, Chandler).

Bowers, D. G. (1973) 'O.D. Techniques and their Results in 23 Organizations: the Michigan I.C.L. Study', *Journal of Applied Behavioral Science*, vol. 9, no. 1, pp. 21–43.

Brewer, J. (1971) 'Flow of Communications, Expert Qualifications and Organizational Authority Structures', *American Sociological Review*, vol. 36, June, pp. 475–84.

Buchanan, P. C. (1971) 'Crucial issues in O.D.', in *Social Intervention: A Behavioral Science Approach*, ed. H. A. Hornstein *et al.* (New York, The Free Press).

Campbell, J. P. (1971) 'Personnel Training and Development', *Annual Review of Psychology*, vol. 22, pp. 291–306.

Campbell, J. P. and Dunnette, M. D. (1968) 'Effectiveness of T-group Experiences in Managerial Training and Development', *Psychological Bulletin*, vol. 70, pp. 73–104.

Chervany, N. and Dickson, G. (1974) 'An Experimental Evaluation of Information Overload in Production Environment', *Management Science*, vol. 20, pp. 1335–44.

Dalton, M. (1959) *Men Who Manage* (New York, Wiley).

Drucker, P. F. (1954) *Practise of Management* (New York, Harper & Row).

Finch, F. W. (1977) 'Collaborative Leadership in Work Settings', *Journal of Applied Behavioral Science*, vol. 13, no. 3, pp. 268–78.

Fleishman, E. A. (1953) 'Leadership Climate, Human Relations Training and Supervisory Behavior', *Personnel Psychology*, vol. 6, pp. 205–22.

Franklin, J. L. (1970) 'Characteristics of Successful and Unsuccessful Organization Development', *Journal of Applied Behavioral Science*, vol. 12, no. 4, October–December, pp. 471–92.

Friedlander, F. (1970) 'The Primacy of Trust as a Facilitator of Further Group Accomplishment', *Journal of Applied Behavioral Science*, vol. 6, pp. 387–400.

Friedlander, F. and Brown, L. D. (1974) 'Organization Development', *Annual Review of Psychology*, vol. 25, pp. 313–41.

Friedlander, F. and Greenberg, S. (1971) 'The Effect of Job Attitudes, Training and Organization Climate upon Performance of the Hard-core Unemployed', *Journal of Applied Psychology*, vol. 55, pp. 287–95.

Greiner, L. E. (1967) 'Patterns of Organizational Change', *Harvard Business Review*, vol. 45, pp. 119–28.

Hildrew, P. (1978) 'Calm after the Storm of Industrial Crises', *Guardian*, 4 December.

Jacobs, D. (1974) 'Dependence and Vulnerability: an Exchange Approach to the Control of Organizations', *Administrative Science Quarterly*, vol. 19, pp. 45–58.

Lawler, E. E. and Hackman, J. R. (1969) 'Impact of Employee Participation in the Development of Pay Incentive Plans: a Field Experiment', *Journal of Applied Psychology*, vol. 53, pp. 467–71.

Lawler, E. E., Hackman, J. R. and Kaufman, S. (1973) 'Effects of Job Redesign: a Field Experiment', *Journal of Applied Social Psychology*, vol. 3, pp. 49–62.

Levinson, H. (1970) 'Management by Whose Objectives?', *Harvard Business Review*, vol. 49, no. 6, pp. 125–34.

Miles, M. G., Hornstein, H. A., Callahan, D. M., Calder, P. H. and Schiavo, R. S. (1969) 'The Consequences of Survey Feedback: Theory and Evaluation', in *The Planning of Change*, ed. W. G. Bennis *et al.* (New York, Holt, Rinehart & Winston).

Nadler, D. A. and Pecorrela, P. A. (1975) 'Differential Effects of Multiple Interventions in an Organization', *Journal of Applied Behavioral Science*, vol. 11, no. 3.

Olsen, M. (1968) *The Logic of Collective Action* (New York, Schocken Books).

O'Reilly, C. A. (1978) 'The International Distortion of Information in Organizational Communication: a Laboratory and Field Investigation', *Human Relations*, vol. 31, no. 2, pp. 173–93.

O'Reilly, C. A. and Roberts, R. (1974) 'Information Filtration in Organizations: Three Experiments', *Organizational Behavior and Human Performance*, vol. 11, pp. 253–65.

Ouchi, W. G. and Maguire, M. A. (1975) 'Organizational Control: Two Functions', *Administrative Science Quarterly*, vol. 20, no. 4, December, pp. 559–69.

Porter, L. W. and Lawler, E. E. (1965) 'Properties of Organization Structure in Relation to Job Attitudes and Job Behavior', *Psychological Bulletin*, vol. 64, pp. 23–51.

Pugh, D. S., Hickson, D. J., Hinings, C. R. and Turner, C. (1969) 'The Context of Organizational Structures', *Administrative Science Quarterly*, vol. 14, no. 1.

Purcell, J. (1979) 'The Lessons of the Commission on Industrial Relations attempts to reform workplace industrial relations', *Industrial Relations Journal*, vol. 10, no. 2, Summer.

Raia, A. P. (1965) 'Goal Setting and Self Control', *Journal of Management Studies*, vol. 2, no. 1, February.

Scheflen, K. C., Lawler, E. E. and Hackman, J. R. (1971) 'Long Term Impact of Employee Participation in the Development of Pay Incentive Plans: a Field Experiment Revisited', *Journal of Applied Psychology*, vol. 55, pp. 182–6.

Trist, E. (1977) 'Collaboration in Work Settings', *Journal of Applied Behavioral Science*, vol. 13, no. 3, pp. 268–78.

Trist, E. L. and Bamforth, K. W. (1951) 'Some Social and Psychological Consequences of the Longwall Method of Coal Getting', *Human Relations*, vol. 4, pp. 3–38.

White, D. D. (1973) 'Factors Affecting Employee Attitudes Toward the Installation of a New Management System', *Academy of Management Journal*, vol. 16, no. 4, pp. 636–46.

Woodward, J. (ed.) (1970) *Industrial Organisation: Behaviour and Control* (Oxford University Press).

Zand, D. E. (1972) 'Trust and Managerial Problem-solving', *Administrative Science Quarterly*, vol. 17, pp. 229–40.

8
The Management of Organisational Change

The Pace and Instability of Change

Organisations continually live with the uncertainty of not knowing exactly how changes in the external environment will affect its operating capability and performance efficiency. With the rapid pace of change emanating from the social, economic and legislative pressures which have built up in modern industrial society, the impact of external events upon an organisation prove increasingly more difficult to control and influence (Beer, 1975; Toffler, 1970).

The principal thesis of this chapter is that attempts by an organisation to improve its performance efficiency by reappraising its current operating capability to meet changing business needs demands a strategy for implementing organisational change whereby the organisation can maintain stability and cohesion in the face of economic uncertainty and fears of operational dislocation. This chapter sets out to outline how such a strategy for managing organisational change can be achieved.

In the face of changing business demands and environmental constraints imposed upon an organisation's operating capability and performance efficiency, management must be able to adapt its system of operation to meet the different needs and problems confronting it. Some of the adaptive processes involve monitoring and predicting environmental changes, acting on the environment concerned, and contending with fluctuations in the flows of resources across organisational boundaries (Norman, 1971; Starbuck, 1975 and 1976; Starbuck and Dutton, 1973; Thompson, 1967).

Externally imposed constraints on the performance efficiency of an organisation, such as rising costs of production, set up competing and conflicting pressures inside the system as regards the feasibility and desirability of new methods and modes of operation. However, various traditional practices and procedures may act as internally imposed constraints on the performance efficiency of an organisation and serve to frustrate the changes needed in the system of operation for improvements in the organisation's operating capability to be realised.

A major consideration in the growth and development of an organisation is the effectiveness of the system of management in enabling the organisation to cope with and adapt to such environmental constraints. Can management maintain the control and influence needed over the organisation's system of operation in order to respond to changing business demands?

The strategy for improving the system of management in organisations shown in Figure 8.1 provides management with the basis for identifying, planning and implementing the organisational changes needed to adapt to new methods and modes of operation.

Important Considerations in Managing Organisational Change

In a study of major organisational change some of the changes necessary in the system of management and organisational structure which foster innovation and the implementation of change can be identified. The task of those responsible for introducing change is to devise a plan that will bring together organisational objectives and individual goals. Such a plan should provide for a process of interaction whereby there is a gradual merging of the objectives of the organisational innovators and the goals and aspirations of the people who are affected by the change, and on whom the change is dependent for execution.

The relationships which exist between organisational units at the beginning of a change, particularly between those units which are most involved, will have important effects on the course of that change. For example, a projected change which will bring into closer contact two organisational units which formerly had little contact must be managed in such a way as to recognise the initial differences in operating procedures, norms of performance, expectations (and misgivings) regarding the other, and philosophies of management.

Major changes may require organisations to rethink the distri-

Establish impact of present policies on operating capability and performance efficiency

Highlight major organisational stumbling blocks to performance improvement

Establish how receptive management is to organisational change

Define the problems constraining management initiatives

Clarify understanding of key tasks, responsibilities, and operational objectives

Assess capability of the management system to meet its key tasks and responsibilities

Validate organisational plans with the operating needs of those lower down in the system

Establish changes needed in the climate of working and system of operation

Clarify how performance improvement plans can come about at the workface

Implementation of management change initiatives to enable the people system to fulfill its changed roles and responsibilities

FIGURE 8.1   *Strategy for managing organisational change*

bution of functions among divisions, to identify the essential objectives, to question ancillary ones that have been added during the years, and to assess the relative contribution of different units to the organisation's principal objectives.

Major changes usually call for the reallocation of responsibility among the functions concerned, and consequently a shift in power alignments within an organisation follows. For example, decisions made in one department may come within the province of another following changes in the roles and responsibilities of a particular function. On the other hand, personnel in one unit may come under the control of another after reorganisation. Such changes usually modify the amount of authority or power of key authority figures in the system, thus directly affecting the level of support and degree of commitment from different functions. The causes and consequences of organisational changes need to be carefully considered because they affect the position and standing of different departments and individuals, thus significantly affecting working relations and the outcomes of change initiatives. Also, major changes may require significant revisions in key policies or the development of new policies.

There is a need to reconcile the different aims and objectives of each department and to integrate activities which are closely linked. Problems of co-ordination and control of change initiatives arise, and these need to be worked through. When organisational changes alter relations between units in an organisation, there may arise ambiguous authority structures, unclear objectives and contradictory assignments of responsibility. The implementation of change will be assisted by opportunities for the parties concerned to work together in sharing information, ideas, modifying plans and establishing overall modes of operation which challenge traditional ways of working and incorporate new, more flexible and diverse initiatives.

One of the consequences of change will be competing and conflicting demands for redirecting resources, and rectifying imbalances because of new task initiatives called for in different departments and the decline and obsolescence of others.

In managing major change in an organisation the first-line supervisor plays a key role in conveying the organisation's objectives to subordinates in terms that they can understand and accept. However, new technological systems of operation may initially require debugging and fault-finding, which may lead to frustration and conflict, and this could limit the support necessary for change when called for by the supervisor.

It is important to provide opportunities for lower levels of management to discuss and examine the probable effects of new systems of operation and equipment on methods and modes of operation. Basic misgivings about company objectives, techniques of operation and administrative procedures need to be sounded out, otherwise industrial action may be taken in opposition to the change initiatives by a militant work-force.

Organisational units in which supervisors regularly consult subordinates and inform them prior to a change will be better prepared to develop ideas and plans for new improved procedures and systems of operation which overcome some of the unanticipated problems accompanying changes in methods and modes of operation. An important consideration is the measure of influence and support lower management has from the organisation. A supervisor who can represent the needs and interests of his work-force and influence his boss to accept modifications or extensions to his change plans positively affects work-group performance and satisfaction (Pelz, 1952; Meyer, 1972; Rowland and Scott, 1968).

The period of change is one in which people experience insecurity and uncertainty, and they therefore require to be informed of change developments and need to understand what contribution they can make to accomplishing change as smoothly as possible.

King (1974) found that managers who transmitted to their staff their own strong feelings about the efficacy of an innovation created a mutual expectancy of high performance and greatly stimulated producitivity.

Assessing the Responsiveness of Organisations to Change

An important element of organisational change is an ability to assess the capability of an organisation to adapt to the need for change.

Examining the impact of organisational changes in the past may serve to highlight, for instance, the difficulties of implementing certain practices and procedures necessary for securing improvements in performance efficiency due to inter-unit conflict and divisions. Serious malfunctions can occur in the use to which operating procedures, systems and controls are put by line units.

Malfunctions in the use to which control systems are put expose and undermine an organisation's ability to regulate its cash flow and to administer a policy of cost-effectiveness. The impact of previous structural changes on the differentiation and integration of unit operations may prove to be dysfunctional. Continual changes in an organisation's structure can create misalignment when they are out of step with the demands of ground-floor operations. If, in failing to define accurately the problems associated with the reasons for change, the organisation attempts to impose structural solutions to problems brought about by inadequate integration or unclear differentiation of roles, responsibilities and accountabilities between functions, then the essential element of organisational co-ordination and control suffers. Organisational changes in the past may reinforce the difficulty of removing certain obstacles to unit operations and inter-unit conflicts.

By examining the internal workings of the system management can then determine the restraints upon change initiatives and the steps which need to be taken in order to implement the new policies designed as a means of providing a co-ordinated and controlled response to environmental pressures and demands. By reviewing the role and responsibility of functions and individual departments management is able to establish the effectiveness of managerial/ supervisory procedures and practices for dealing with operational constraints. In identifying the commonality and difference of operational demands with those of service support departments, management is more able to recognise what impact conflict at organisational boundaries has on the co-ordination and control of change initiatives.

The Impact of Policy Changes on Organisational Performance

A primary step in assessing an organisation's adaptability and responsiveness to changing business demands is to establish the impact of present policies on operating capability and performance efficiency.

A major objective in a manufacturing company is the balancing of planned production requirements with efficient service support. In that plant performance is dependent upon effective resource management, both operations and engineering departments are concerned with ensuring a reliability and quality of service provision and resource deployment so that estimated production requirements can be met. In attempting to anticipate and respond to future market demands management seeks to shape and influence service support, operational procedures and working practices, and thus, effectively, the nature and level of resource support to operating plants who are concerned with fulfilling production requirements at economic cost.

However, each function measures its performance in different terms. The operations department attempts to maximise production, while engineering looks to minimising costs. Conflict ensues from these different methods and modes of working, based on separate performance objectives which are opposed to one another's efforts and interests. Operations' attempts to maximise production can sharply increase the costs of engineering maintenance when there is an increase in equipment failures brought about by neglect due to continuously pressing demands for production. Engineering, in its efforts to improve resource efficiency and the cost-effectiveness of the service provided, may attempt to introduce tighter control over resource deployment, and this restricts the flexibility necessary to deal with unanticipated breakdowns in operation which may consequently lead to significant production losses.

In such circumstances there may be conflicting demands and expectations about the role and contribution of a service support function in relation to the over-all demands of the business. A major organisational problem is the lack of common understanding and agreement about management policies on service support with regard to its cost-effectiveness and the balancing of its requirements with those of operations (to fulfil production programmes).

It is important to establish the impact of current management policies and practices on operating capability and efficiency in order to recognise which are the key organisational blocks which may significantly impede an organisation's progress in achieving its future plans and performance-improvement objectives. For instance, a major responsibility of production management is to establish how an optimum service support can be provided to mainstream operations so as to fulfil production requirements at minimum cost. Over all, the need is for a policy of service support which is consistent with general organisational objectives, while recognising that changing business needs necessitate redefining policies and plans and reappraising the role and contribution of service support functions in relation to operating demands and production requirements.

Stumbling-blocks to Organisational Change

One of the principal ways organisations respond and adapt to the pressures and pulls exerted by the external environment is by developing new policies and procedures, as (for instance) in coping and dealing with the legislation on health and safety following the Flixborough disaster. The growth of unionisation at supervisory level and the increasing demands for staff representation in the management process have at the same time led to more companies devising new structures of decision-taking in the form of staff consultative committees and works councils. Shell, British Petroleum, I.C.I., Scott-Bader and the Glacier Metal Company are examples of the major corporations which are currently (1980) engaged in various forms of management by participation. Shell U.K. embarked on a large-scale organisational development programme in 1966–9 which reviewed and revised its company philosophy, management–union relations and systems of operation with the introduction of collective bargaining and a socio-technical approach to plant operations (Hill, 1971).

More organisations have increasingly been seeking to adopt participative styles of management in order to reduce their problems of securing acceptance of decisions involving changes in methods and modes of operation (Thomason, 1971).

At the same time, greater efforts have been directed at improving cost-effectiveness, work programming and operational performance, and on tightening up on various procedures, rules and regulations which serve as controls intended to ensure that working practices comply with desired levels of performance efficiency. In such circumstances many organisations have fallen back more on centralisation of authority at the upper levels of the management hierarchy.

In an organisation's efforts to improve over-all levels of performance efficiency there are dangers to an organisation of a rigidly formalised system of operations when the external environment is unstable and uncertain. Evidence points to the fact that the highly structured nature of some organisations, with centralised policy-making, rigid hierarchical ranks, strict administrative routines and tightly drawn boundaries between departments, undermines the organisation's ability to respond to changing business demands. This may threaten its survival when new and unfamiliar economic problems arise which cannot be broken down and distributed between existing specialist roles (Burns and Stalker, 1961; Beer, 1974; Hedberg *et al.*, 1976; Norman, 1971; Lawrence and Lorsch, 1967).

Grinyer and Norburn (1975), in their study of twenty-one companies, found no evidence that concerns about objectives, clearly defined roles, or formal planning correlated positively with financial performance. It correlated positively instead with reliance on informal communication and with the diversity of valid and congruent information used to assess company performance. Miller and Mintzberg (1974) observed that companies operating successfully in turbulent markets had intensive internal communications, managed themselves participatively, utilised consultative committees, delegated discretion to individuals and units which had to cope with the environment, and devoted considerable effort to scanning the environment for change.

In such circumstances there is a need for less hierarchical systems of management, more frequent adjustment and redefinition of individual and departmental tasks with interaction and problem-solving communications cutting across normal hierarchical channels, taking more of a consultative form, by way of information and advice being given rather than orders and directives taken from above. This in effect contributes to a more flexible system of operation, and enables the organisation to be more specifically engaged in the process of adapting to external pressures, pulls and influences.

The range of specialist functions in organisations requires complex patterns of structural differentiation (i.e. division of labour), and this in turn creates a demand for structural integration (i.e. co-ordination and control) if the organisation as a whole is to adapt efficiently to the changing business environment.

A consequence of rigid hierarchical ranks and tightly drawn boundaries between departments are struggles for control and influence over policy-making and over decisions on matters of dispute.

An organisation's efforts to function effectively in a rapidly changing environment are seriously undermined by the inability of sectional interests to agree a common and consistent policy. If an organisation is unable to constructively resolve the differences of

terests, it will have considerable difficulty in achieving its
ls in a co-ordinated and controlled fashion. A major
..., therefore, of an organisation is the need for stability and
cohesion.

McMahon and Ivancevich (1976) found that for employees
generally, a crucial factor affecting them in their ability to fulfil their
task was the degree of agreement among higher-level managers in the
organisational hierarchy on the pattern of control within the
managerial authority system, rather than how much control existed
in the management system or the manner in which it was distributed.
The reason why agreement was so critical at this level was that
employees reacted favourably to a management system in which
there was a high degree of uniformity and consensus with respect to
control and consequently to decision-making among higher management. Such a system would appear to reduce the uncertainty,
ambiguity and frustration experienced by employees having to face
up to change. In other words, the system is marked with a degree of
stability and predictability.

Greater integration of the over-all system of operation may very
well mean less sub-system flexibility and greater vulnerability to
short-term planning. Since a failure in performance of one sub-
system will have an effect on the whole system, it is frequently
necessary in managing change to create new organisational structures
and procedures. The purpose of these is to plan broadly and well
ahead of the change, to decentralise control, and to provide for the
rapid communication of information about developing problems
from one unit to another (Neff and Mann, 1961).

Organisations call for decisive leadership and direction from its top
management which is consistent and relevant to the changing
demands of the social system, or rather the working environment
inside the organisation, in order for them to be able to deal effectively
with the necessary changes in methods and modes of operation.

The attempted enforcement of bureaucratic mechanisms of control
and of close punitive supervision raises internal tensions and hostility
towards higher productivity and cost-cutting, and lowers over-all
performance when it is inappropriate. In studies made of organisational change the very much improved levels of output and reduced
levels of absenteeism and turnover were found to be due to the
devolution of responsibility and authority to individuals and work
groups, enabling them to act on the problems and difficulties

constraining their ability to fulfil the organisation's task at the desired level of performance efficiency.

Steering groups and working parties involved in diagnosing organisational needs and planning management change initiatives do not readily form part of a well-integrated and coherent management body, receptive and responsive to changing business demands, when representatives from different specialist functions seek to advance or protect their own interest group's ambitions and designs at the expense of others. This is because inter-departmental committees tend to perpetuate old rivalries and to retain a traditional hierarchy of authority. Therefore, a new decision-making structure is required in which different functions and management levels possess overlapping rather than divided responsibilities for organisational performance objectives.

Management at all levels needs to be involved in the decision-making process at different stages in order to feel a sense of responsibility for the implementation of those decisions. Accountability by an individual for his actions cannot be assumed because his performance ought, theoretically, to contribute to the over-all task of the organisation. People respond to and support change initiatives more readily when there is a common task or purpose which they can see they are working towards, and which serves their joint interests and which can only be secured by mutual support.

However, if different functions and operating units pursue competing and/or conflicting performance objectives, working independently of one another, this seriously undermines an organisation's ability to respond effectively to changing business needs.

The Receptivity of Management to Organisational Change Needs

It is important in the first instance to assess the level of ownership of organisational problems and the commitment of key authority figures in the system to face up to and tackle the issues which restrain or impede current operating capability and performance efficiency. Hage and Dewar (1973) found that the values of key authority figures were significant in predicting support for and acceptance of change and innovation.

Early on the dissatisfactions that exist with the present system of operation, and the different perceptions of the problem areas detracting from performance efficiency at the different management/ supervisory levels, must be established. In discovering organisational needs and concerns higher management builds up a picture of what improvements other managers see as necessary and begins to recognise what change opportunities there are, and what commitment there is to want to resolve outstanding problem areas. Much more becomes known of the wishes for change and the commonality of concerns when the previously competing and conflicting demands of the different parties involved is established. In more accurately identifying operational concerns and problems higher management can more effectively realign the different understandings other managers may have had about matters which they were in dispute over. By achieving close collaboration in areas of joint concern and responsibility management may be able to obtain more willingness to confront differences and encourage individuals to take risks in disclosing matters of concern.

Receptivity and response from managers to change initiatives can be more readily obtained when agreement can be reached over the sort of performance improvements and initiatives that will promote more effective co-ordination and control of their own support functions with mainstream operations.

If higher management can identify the major problems and obstacles to organisational changes initiated by its managers in the past, it is more likely to understand and support its managers' attempts to deal with operational malfunctions. This is an important step for deriving greater commitment from managers to want to initiate improvements in the organisation's system of operation.

Gaining the motivation of key authority figures in the system to want to tackle things differently, thereby avoiding previous failures and unsuccessful approaches, is dependent on gaining their support for the reasons underlying change, and confidence in the outcome of the change attempts, in so far as this does not undermine their position in the organisation. For instance, unless different performance objectives pursued by separate functions are reconciled, then there will be little readiness or receptivity to want to risk altering current practices and procedures – which could undermine that function's capacity to realise its own performance objectives.

The Problems Constraining Management Change Initiatives

Now some of the major problems and constraints organisations have to come to terms with in realising performance improvements will be looked at. Plans designed for improving over-all levels of perform-ance efficiency necessitate alterations and perhaps sometimes funda-mental changes in modes of operation. Both working practices and organisational procedures are called into question. A prime responsi-bility of management is to ensure that changes are effectively co-ordinated and controlled in order that desired levels of performance improvement may be realised. Information systems are designed to provide management with the means of assessing how far perform-ance objectives are being met and what corrective action needs to be taken. A key stumbling-block to management change initiatives is the erosion and ineffectualness of control systems, which in practice undermine policy-making and decision-making. The impact of management change initiatives can in effect be frustrated or negated by historically developed working practices which defeat managerial controls and formal organisational procedures, rules and regulations governing working practices and performance standards. If in-dividuals, for instance, lack control over the material resources which are necessary to fulfil their task satisfactorily, they may well hide, neglect or distort the information needed by the management system for establishing unit performance and its relation to over-all perform-ance objectives and standards.

By separating policy-making from its implementation by middle management, an important control gap may arise. A strong case can be made for enabling each manager and supervisor to be responsible for control over unit operations and to be involved in direction-setting.

If people are held accountable for certain levels of performance which they cannot reasonably attain due to operating constraints, which involves fulfilling a specific level of production by a certain date dictated by production control, they may decide not to operate within the formal scheme or mode of operation in an attempt to overcome the obstacles which prevent them from fulfilling their tasks.

The use and abuse of organisational control systems by way of informal networks and actions enable people to retain the initiative, and thereby increase their own discretionary powers. In an effort to avoid sanctions being imposed from above for failure to achieve the performance criteria laid down by higher authority, temporary coalitions may be formed in order to evade or overcome the constraints imposed by the management control system.

Primary functions of management are to balance different unit objectives, to decide on priorities between competing and conflicting resource demands and claims of units, to relate their goals to the overall task, and to get these goals accepted by the organisation's members. Whether managerial control systems can ensure that modes of operation and resource utilisation match up to over-all performance objectives is very problematic when the programming and design of a task is divorced from the execution of it.

Authority, Responsibility and Accountability for Performance Improvement

In establishing and working towards some over-all performance-improvement objectives it is necessary for management bodies and operating departments to establish and agree what their own tasks, responsibilities and operating objectives are for the major activities and efforts they will be engaged in for the next year or two. Having identified the key tasks to be performed in terms of over-all performance improvement, management ·can then examine the different demands placed on the people in the system. At the same time, management needs to establish and define what each function's role and responsibilities ought to be in order for personnel to fulfil operating needs.

In the oil industry, as in other commercial companies, the escalating cost of raw materials created a need for wholesale energy-saving on the refining and manufacturing sides of the business. The role and responsibilities of the service support functions had to be re-examined and reappraised in the light of new fuel-saving policies and operating objectives aimed principally at energy conservation. With operating costs rising directly as a consequence of higher raw-material charges, restraints were enforced on plant expenditure. This prompted management to review the levels of accountability deemed necessary for effective cost control.

In an attempt to derive greater cost accountability from all levels of management and supervision cost-effectiveness became a more imortant measure of operating performance. Therefore, greater responsibility had to be placed on individuals in order for cost savings to be realised effectively. The cost-effectiveness of the service support effort was measured by the efficiency with which resources were deployed. A prime task and area of responsibility for managers was in ensuring effective utilisation of the technical skills and expertise of existing talent within support services. Staff departments were given greater support in enabling operating departments to save energy and improve plant utilisation by jointly devising specific operating guidelines, *not* by enforcing compliance with certain operating standards. Ultimately, powers *could be* dealt out in order to ensure that a policy of cost-effectiveness was implemented.

At the operational level, because of changing interpretations and understandings of functional roles and responsibilities among work groups, there may be a need to clarify present and future levels of responsibility, authority and accountability in key performance areas for certain major activities.

Improving Managerial Accountability for Systems of Operational Control

Also, the organisation has to consider the realism and validity of the management processes it adopts in order to translate new policies into operational plans and goals. By means of objective-setting, forward planning and monitoring control systems and procedures, organisations have a means of determining their current operating capability and performance efficiency.

In attempting to establish the progress of the organisation in working towards management plans and objectives the reality, quality and speed of information-processing or data retrieval has to be assessed in order to have an accurate picture of performance and possible deviations from desired levels of performance. One of the stumbling-blocks to this may be the ineffectiveness of monitoring systems and control procedures. In such cases it is important to assess the value of the systems put into operation and what degree of support or resistance there might be for their use in evaluating and reviewing performance efficiency.

There may well be problems faced in making a control system operate effectively because of the withholding, falsification or distortion of information fed into the system. This may be due to a defensive reaction to the controls implicit in new systems.

There may be certain abuses to which a system is put because of the conflict of interests between functions in owning up to and being held responsible for deficient levels of performance. Difficulties will therefore be experienced in obtaining commitment from individuals to systems and procedures which restrain or effectively control the actions and initiatives which are perceived as necessary in fulfilling operating needs.

One may need to re-examine and reappraise the ability of the system and the people within it to identify and resolve unacceptable deviations from normal system operations. While both engineering and operating functions in manufacturing organisations have the same desire to be cost-effective in relation to plant expenditure, in practice there is conflict and dispute over cost accountability and control. There is a need for managers to assume responsibility for cost-effectiveness right through the organisation, instead of wishing to duck out of cost-control problems.

Accountability will be accepted more readily when a manager is entrusted with the responsibility and authority to decide on expenditure proven necessary. If managers are more accountable for operating cost, they will have more incentive to introduce cost savings.

Support and Opposition to Management Change Initiatives

Once there exists a certain level of support and commitment from the management team to examine and reappraise key organisational problems and operational malfunctions, there is a need to test and validate their plans and thinking on the desired level of performance efficiency and operating capability in comparison with the needs of those lower down in the system who must carry them out. The translation of future plans and performance-improvement objectives into a workable change programme is dependent on the interpretation, understanding and recognition of how new policies and plans apply to operating needs. Management has to consider the degree of filtering, distortion and blurring of management plans and objectives in relation to current views of operating needs and the capability of the people system to fulfil them.

How management's plans and objectives are translated and reported down the line will determine the clarity of purpose with which its change initiatives are understood and responded to. Information needs to be fed back up the line, in order for management to establish how far its plans and objectives are consistent with and aligned to operational needs. At the same time, certain practical problems and operating constraints may not be recognised until management change initiatives become implemented. The response of the people in the system to new policies and procedures is not always predictable or consistent with that which managers intended.

The following provides an illustration of these points. In a large international oil refinery management, in response to the economic uncertainty in the then current business climate, was anxious to reduce operating costs. The chief contribution of the operations and engineering departments to this performance objective was considered to be one of making improvements in plant reliability.

In pursuing a policy of cost-effectiveness the engineering function began to challenge and resist makeshift repairs which led to premature equipment failures, and sought to re-establish a minimum standard of maintainance in order to reduce the frequency of equipment failures for which it was invariably blamed by operating departments. Plant expenditure is inevitably high in an oil refinery, and production managers, in an attempt to explain away some of its increased operational costs, laid responsibility on engineering for maintenance inefficiency in contributing to these additional costs.

The members of supervision in the engineering department considered that the need to tighten up on work standards was a veiled criticism of them in their ability to plan, organise and co-ordinate the work which had to be put in. At the same time, the cost constraints under which they now worked were believed to undermine plant reliability and to negate their primary role, which was to keep the plants running continuously by responding as promptly as possible to avoid production losses in spite of the additional costs which might need to be incurred.

Engineering management not only had to contend with the resistance and opposition of its own supervision to the policy of cost-effectiveness but had to answer the charges of operations about the declining standard of maintenance which accompanied it. In investigating these concerns management put operating units on the defensive, in terms of them having to justify their actions and thus defend their position.

Given that a situation like this can develop, there is obviously an element of misunderstanding and suspicion in any problem-solving effort designed to improve performance efficiency which can severely inhibit raising and dealing with thorny issues and key stumbling-blocks. Anxiety, fear of failure and resistance to change can effectively frustrate management's efforts to examine and reappraise the efficiency and effectiveness of current working practices and procedures.

In having to respond to management change initiatives, people have difficulties in coping, and resistance to new working practices and procedures builds up, because new methods of working, in the short run at least, create difficulties. When a new system of operation is introduced which has not been properly tried and tested under normal work pressures, errors and misjudgements arise. Changes are therefore baulked or unconvincingly entered into. This only adds to the likelihood of new systems and procedures being ineffectively applied.

If management evaluates too critically the efforts of individuals to work a new planning or control system, blame is not unnaturally cast in both directions. Under attack, an individual will become defensive and either distort, hide or neglect certain important aspects of the situation which might damn him in the eyes of his superior. He may justify his own actions by attributing system shortcomings to management's own lack of foresight and defend his own performance by detailing the operating constraints under which he works. Because management is unable to establish the real nature of the problems within the system of operation, it is unable to take the most effective course of action.

An important and essential aspect of this problem is the need for management to examine and appraise the capability of the people in the system to accept and develop change initiatives. There must be integration, liaison, collaboration and dovetailing between functions. The objectives and success criteria of each separate function must be compatible, not in conflict with one another. If one department is able to realise its own objective only at the expense of another's, then management is unlikely to get support and co-operation for implementing organisational change initiatives.

If the demands and expectations people have of change are in conflict, then again there will be an unwillingness to work together to improve situations and, if anything, efforts will be put into undermining the interests and standing of the other party in order to conserve their own.

Establishing Changes Needed in the Climate of Working

In order for performance improvement objectives and plans to be realised effectively the organisation has to provide the conditions of working under which the people in the system are able to respond effectively to operating needs.

An important measure of the ability of personnel to cope with and adapt to new change initiatives is the climate of working. For instance, to what extent is there a joint ownership of responsibilities, problems and tasks, as well as flexibility across functional boundaries to allow for co-ordination, liaison and communication in these matters.

To a large extent the climate of working influences the degree of support for and collaboration in change implementation. A responsive environment promotes the flexibility of working and quality of teamwork needed in organisational problem-solving efforts. It is also critical for achieving receptivity and commitment to group decision-making, which is essential for translating management change initiatives into performance-improvement plans and objectives.

In encouraging and supporting questioning by the organisation of the realism of its current operating efficiency for future needs, management endeavours to create a climate of awareness and understanding of the problems and frustrations faced by personnel in realising operational needs.

What is desirable is a climate of working which allows for the questioning of other departments' objectives – what their primary roles and responsibilities are and in whose chief interests. To the extent that a department engages in constructively examining and appraising its own support effectiveness to mainstream operations, there will be greater opportunities afforded for people to influence and respond to management change initiatives by more effectively realising operational needs.

The style of managing change is an important consideration. A more open style fosters collaboration, liaison and two-way communication in resolving organisational problems which act as stumbling-blocks to performance-improvement objectives and plans.

Establishing Changes Required in the System of Operation

There are often constraints, however, upon an individual's ability to influence and change operating conditions, and these frustrate initiative and reduce the sense of responsibility felt for performance improvements. By identifying dysfunctional elements in the system which retard future plans and objectives, people may be more able to respond and act on management change initiatives.

The problems and difficulties constraining people to respond and act on management change initiatives involves:

  (i) conflicting objectives among operating functions;
 (ii) inflexible procedures restricting actions and initiatives;
(iii) fragmented operations and teamwork leading to frequent breakdowns in progressing work;
 (iv) the hardening of functional boundaries and the creation of barriers restricting the necessary liaison and support required by departments; and
  (v) competing and conflicting pressures and demands for resources among operating departments.

By successfully tackling such organisational obstacles, an organisation may then enable people to release more productive energy towards future performance-improvement objectives and plans.

The Implementation of Management Change Initiatives

In attempting to translate future plans and objectives into reliable performance efficiency improvements management will have to come to recognise certain organisational stumbling-blocks. By validating its own data about performance with that lower down the system, management is able to identify more clearly the impact of certain constraints on the operating capability and performance efficiency of the organisation. If it can successfully establish a sufficient degree of interdependence of concerns and collaboration, then it may be able to get the organisation to tackle some of the malfunctions in the system which obstruct future plans and performance objectives.

By means of joint problem identification and resolution, different levels of management and supervision can more effectively understand how their respective concerns, problems and constraints commonly affect them. An examination of the causes and consequences of current working practices which contribute to certain operational malfunctions helps to establish greater awareness of the real nature of the problems facing the organisation and the support needed to resolve them. By clarifying the essential interdependence of one level's own problem-solving efforts with other levels of management, a greater sense of common purpose can be established.

Through the process of data-gathering and problem analysis, each level of management can recognise and understand more easily their joint responsibilities and accountabilities for dealing with a particular problem, and the full implications and possible advantages of changing working practices and procedures in their own province.

Having agreed on the key issues and concerns facing the organisation, joint collaborative efforts can be made to resolve certain outstanding organisational problems which will have to be tackled before certain management plans and goals can be realised. Management should then seek to identify the differences of views and opinions regarding the changes proposed in order to establish the extent and nature of these differences (what particular assumptions, beliefs and notions people have about current change attempts) based on their previous experiences of change initiatives, some of which were less successful than others. Where necessary energy will be put into taking corrective action in order to deal with organisational malfunctions only if there is a greater likelihood of success than was formerly the case.

What may concern individuals could be disruptive changes in organisational structures, roles and responsibilities which serve to confuse rather than clarify working relations. In such circumstances what individuals fear most, and wish to avoid, is the accompanying instability and uncertainty of change outcomes in terms of potentially disrupting accepted working practices and tried and tested systems and methods of operation.

Change brings about conflict and dispute and often creates a serious breach between sections of a department and between different levels of management. By establishing what changes individuals and functions are in support of, it may be found that previous change attempts floundered because of an absence of effective planning and implementation. The cause of this may be attributed to the lack of impetus and clarity of direction set from the top of the organisation.

An important consideration is the criteria of performance set for different departments – as to whether they are compatible or not with over-all organisational objectives and whether they are in conflict as a result or in opposition to one another's change initiatives. The validity and realism of the different measures of performance associated with management change efforts are critical in deriving support and commitment to organisational change programmes.

Such overriding considerations are important in enabling the people in the system to fulfil any change in their roles and responsibilities.

A fundamental requirement is that management comes to terms in this way with such needs and problems and resolves to tackle them by carefully planning and evaluating how certain essential changes in the organisation's system of working can be realised.

References

Beer, S. (1974) *Designing Freedom* (Toronto, C.B.C. Publications).

Beer, S. (1975) *Platform for Change* (New York, Wiley).

Burns, T. and Stalker, G. M. (1961) *The Management of Innovation* (London, Tavistock).

Grinyer, P. H. and Norburn, D. (1975) 'Planning for Existing Markets: Perceptions of Executives and Financial Information', *Journal of the Royal Statistical Society*, series A, vol. 138, pp. 70–97.

Hage, J. and Dewar, R. (1973) 'Elite Values versus Organizational Structure in Predicting Innovation', *Administrative Science Quarterly*, vol. 18, pp. 279–90.

Hedberg, B. L. T., Nystrom, P. C. and Starbuck, W. H. (1976) 'Camping on Seesaws: Prescriptions for a Self-designing Organization', *Administrative Science Quarterly*, vol. 21, no. 1, March.

Hill, P. (1971) *Toward a New Philosophy of Management* (London, Gower Press).

King, A. S. (1974) 'Expectation Effects in Organizational Change', *Administrative Science Quarterly*, vol. 19, pp. 221–30.

Lawrence, P. R. and Lorsch, J. W. (1967) *Organization and Environment: Managing Differentiation and Integration* (Cambridge, Mass., Harvard Graduate School of Business Administration).

McMahon, J. T. and Ivancevich, J. M. (1976) 'A Study of Control in a Manufacturing Organization', *Administrative Science Quarterly*, vol. 21, no. 1, March.

Meyer, H. H. (1972) 'The Effective Supervisor: Some Surprising Findings', in *The Failure of Success*, ed. A. J. Marrow (New York, Amacon).

Miller, D. and Mintzberg, H. (1974) 'Strategy Formulation in Context: Some Tentative Models', working paper, McGill University.

Neff, W. and Mann, W. (1961) *Managing Major Changes in Organizations* (Ann Arbor, University of Michigan Press).

Norman, R. (1971) 'Organizational Innovativeness: Product Variation and Reorientation', *Administrative Science Quarterly*, vol. 16, pp. 203–15.

Pelz, D. F. (1952) 'Influence: a Key to Effective Leadership in the First Line Supervisor', *Personnel*, vol. 29, November, pp. 209–17.

Rowland, K. M. and Scott, W. E. (1968) 'Psychological Attributes of Effective Leadership in a Formal Organisation', *Personnel Psychology*, vol. 21, pp. 365–77, Autumn.

Starbuck, W. H. (1975) 'Information Systems for Organizations of the Future', in *Information Systems and Organizational Structure*, ed. E. Grochla and N. Szyperski (New York, De Gruyer) pp. 217–29.

Starbuck, W. H. (1976) 'Organizations and their Environments', in *Handbook of Industrial and Organizational Psychology*, ed. D. Dunnette (Chicago, Rand McNally).

Starbuck, W. H. and Dutton, J. M. (1973) 'Designing Adaptive Organizations', *Journal of Business Policy*, vol. 3, pp. 21–8.

Thomason, G. F. (1971) 'Experiments in Participation', *Institute of Personnel Management*.

Thompson, J. D. (1967) *Organizations in Action* (New York, McGraw-Hill).

Toffler, A. (1970) *Future Shock* (London, Pan Books).

It's been so many days when your eyes met mine!

Author Index

Subject Index